To Jenny

Michael Foley

American political ideas
TRADITIONS AND USAGES

Manchester University Press

Manchester and New York

Distributed exclusively in the USA and Canada by St. Martin's Press

Published by Manchester University Press
Oxford Road, Manchester M13 9PL, England
and Room 400, 175 Fifth Avenue, New York, NY 10010, USA

Distributed exclusively in the USA and Canada
by St. Martin's Press, Inc., 175 Fifth Avenue, New York, NY 10010, USA

British Library cataloguing in publication data
Foley, Michael
    American political ideas. Traditions and usages
    1. United States. Politics
    I. Title
    320.973

Library of Congress cataloging in publication data
Foley, Michael, 1948–
    American political ideas / Michael Foley.
        p.   cm.
    Includes bibliographical references and index.
    ISBN 0-7190-3293-8 — ISBN 0-7190-3294-6 (pbk.)
    1. Political science— United States. 2. Ideology. I. Title.
JA84. U5F65   1991
320.5'0973—dc20   90-25493

ISBN 0 7190 3294 6 *paperback*

Reprinted in paperback 1993

Typeset by Koinonia Ltd, Manchester
Printed in Great Britain
by Biddles Ltd, Guildford and King's Lynn

Contents

Introduction

The United States is not generally noted for its political ideas. On the contrary, it has a reputation for doing without them. It is common for Americans to assert that they have no need for political ideas in the way that other countries and cultures depend upon, and are in turn afflicted by, systems of political thought and social explanation. This assertion is normally taken as read and accepted as a self-evident feature of American life. It can lead to concern and self-doubt on the part of Americans, 'who fear that they have no past, no patriarchial traditions or customs in the European sense, no feelings of rootedness and stability'.[1] On the other hand, it is much more common for the deficiency in political thinking to be celebrated as a positive good and as a verification that the United States is such a progressive society that it has left the need for ideologies behind. In other words, America's position as a new world is often based upon, and expressed through, the belief that in freeing itself from Europe, it also freed itself from those pathological European divisions that give rise to ideologies.

America's identity has accordingly been tightly wrapped up in the apparent dearth of its own political ideas. Its national pride has been based not merely on being different from every other nation, but in being wholly exceptional. The needlessness of political thought remains a popular virtue in a society believed to have emanated spontaneously from natural conditions: to have been 'born equal without ever having to become so' and, thereby, to have been born free from a reliance upon traditions of thought. America's lack of theoretical self-definition and ideological consciousness has become one of its central characteristics. America traditionally believes itself to be different but cannot explain how; and it thankfully cannot explain how because it is so different.

At no point was this American belief in its freedom from thought stronger or more revealingly expressed than during the 1950s. It was during this era that American scholars pronounced 'the end of ideology'. The post-war social consensus in the United States seemed final proof that America was the model of a successful society because it was a society which had overcome the need for ideologies. In the light of this perspective, the problems of industrialisation and modernisation had been effectively resolved. The only disputes that remained were those that could be negotiated to a satisfactory solution through the use of technical adjustments. The discipline and solidarity produced by the cold war helped to intensify the consensus still further. In doing so, it also helped to establish the idea of a society with neither the capacity nor the need for critical and analytical thought. During these years, America believed itself to be the 'good society' incarnate. It saw itself as the vanguard of western societies, showing how, under the right conditions, clashing political ideas could wither away to a residue of democratic competition between endlessly compatible interests.[2]

The languid serenity of such consensus politics was rudely shaken by the tumultuous events of the 1960s. War and civil dissent, drugs and crime, urban riots and political assassination, pornography and violence, provided the background to a widespread questioning of America's social and economic order. The era witnessed 'the sudden blossoming of an exotic literature of protest'. With it 'came fantastical missiles and turgid prophecies of woe and apocalypse'.[3] The drive for revelation, realism and critical evaluation produced a sceptical revision of the 1950s. Americans had become far more sensitised to the existence of structures of political thought. They became more aware of the linkages between political belief and social conditions. As a result, the 'end of ideology' became recognised for what it had always been: an ideology in its own right and a very effective and durable one at that.

Worldly wisdom and speculative ideas, however, came at a price. The social dislocation, moral discontent and the breakdown of governmental authority which accompanied America's new self-awareness prompted a desire to return to the lost anchorage of the 1950s. Radical critics may have felt they had stripped away 'the coercion which lay behind consensus, the brutalization behind homilies on freedom, and the imperial interests which sustained an advanced economy'.[4] Nevertheless, the disillusioning experience entailed in such fervent exposure led mainstream middle America to turn 'to the more openly disciplinary politics of the Nixon era'.[5] As the ardour for evaluative thought and political action cooled, America lapsed back into a scepticism about introverted speculation. As the 1960s became identified with disorder, instability, violence and governmental failure, so the era's propensity for critical and innovative ideas became widely discredited as divisive and counter-productive.

As a consequence of the 1960s, America's appetite for large-scale political action and for insurgent experiments in social thought declined during the 1970s. Even in the face of the most severe problems to confront an industrialised economy (e.g. inflation, stagnation, an energy shortage, unemployment, poverty, urban decay, crime, pollution), the emphasis was on caution and even fatalism. Americans were asked to reconcile themselves to the novelty of accepting that there were some problems which had no solution and that there were limits to economic advance and social progress. 'When a problem becomes too difficult, you lose interest,'[6] declared Irving Kristol. Americans had become much more knowledgeable about ideologies by the 1970s. And yet, during the same period of time it became clear that their relationship with ideologies remained highly ambiguous. The era could be characterised not so much by a belief that the end to ideology had been brought about, as by the emergence of an ability to transcend ideologies. Ideological schemes of thought were known about but were not thought to be really relevant to America's position. They were there in the background, but were not regarded as particularly salient.

The 1980s supposedly witnessed a resurgence of ideological politics in America. President Reagan's use of explicitly conservative convictions to challenge the established political order was widely described as being radical in content and revolutionary in nature. The claim that the Reagan programme was disruptive and confrontational is quite correct, but not for the reasons that are normally given. To say that Reaganism was challenging because it was extraordinarily ideological in content is misleading. Such assertions rest upon an assumption that American social stability is dependent upon an absence, or near absence, of social thought. As a result, any strident assault upon customary conditions necessarily carries with it connotations of a contrived and egregious attachment to a maverick world of critical ideas, alternative public philosophy, and even European flights of fancy.

While it is true that Reagan contested many of America's established social practices and governmental priorities, it is not true to suggest that this necessarily amounted to an ideological schism challenging the political traditions of the United States. Contrary to popular reputation, it is quite possible to be ideologically contentious in America and still remain genuinely American. It is quite possible to challenge political ideas and principles with other political ideas and principles without being regarded as subversively ideological or irredeemably divisive. In fact, it is the general norm. Reagan's radicalism, for example, was based not upon some set of principles separate from, and external to, America's conditions and experiences. Reagan's conservative crusade was not a denial of America's capacity to transcend conflicting ideologies, so much as a further reaffirmation of it.

The United States possesses a little understood ability to engage in deep conflicts over political ideas, while at the same time reducing the adversarial positions to legitimate derivatives of American history and development. This often gives American politics the impression of being non-ideological in nature. Europeans in particular fall prey to, and help to perpetuate, this notion. Because ideologies in the European tradition are closely associated with intransigent social dichotomies and even with outright polarisation, and because there is little evidence of such conditions in America, the conclusion often drawn by Europeans is that America has no ideologies, or that it has only one – which is the same as saying it has no ideological consciousness or ability to engage in idelogical debate. Americans themselves also tend to view the abstract phenomenon of ideologies in the same European light. For this reason, they have often convinced themselves that the European perspective of America is correct and that American politics simply does not have the social breadth or historical depth to sustain a politics of impassioned principles and vigorously argued ideas.

This is a delusion. In reality, America diverges sharply from its reputation as a land of conformist ideals servicing an amorphous social consensus. America may be hostile to the thought of ideologies. It may ostensibly regard social theory to be an uncomfortable and unnecessary pastime. America may simply not have the background or temperament for the totality of European-style ideologies. Nevertheless, the important point to note is that the United States does possess the means to engage in profound disputes over political ideas without succumbing to the intractability and entirety of European ideological conflicts. The United States is fortunate enough to have at its disposal a set of rich political currents set within its own historical and social development. These currents are intensely varied in content and application. They provide American politics with the raw material for its conduct, in that this storehouse of ideas, values and traditions serves to inform the language of political discourse and to provide the currency with which issues are identified and argued out in American society. Such a common core of indigenous principles can be used in varying permutations and with different degrees of emphasis to produce a quite startling diversity of political positions.

Far from possessing a political culture of grey conformity, therefore, the United States has in reality the bright colours of several political traditions, usually held together in a loose weave, but often coming apart and providing the occasion for a conflict of fundamental ideas and principles. The richness of these colours is normally obscured and unrecognised, but they are there latent and available all the time – as much so in the 'end of ideology' era of the 1950s as they were in the supposedly ideologically-inclined 1980s.

The purpose of this book is to identify and to examine those currents of American political thought that have been, and still are, instrumental in motivating and justifying political action. The intention is not to make American political ideas into something they have never been – namely, great systems of thought which are deployed logically and coherently in political argument. Neither is the intention to evaluate the rightness or wrongness of political ideas, still less to erect a social philosophy as both a normative guide and a comprehensive explanation of American political behaviour. Instead of a list of disembodied ideologies, which normally mark studies of this sort, the following analysis is concerned with ideas in their milieu of contemporary issues, social drives and political movements. The objective is to show what political thoughts move Americans, how they do so, what consequences flow from such movements, and the ways in which the origins, content and usage of these ideas give the nature of American politics its special character.

With these aims in mind, the book is organised into chapters, each one of which is devoted to an examination of a seminal idea, or set of ideas, together with those elements of America's development which have made these ideas into the means and ends of political attachments in United States. The analytical approach of each chapter will vary according to the properties and interpretive requirements of the theme in question. For example, on some occasions the emphasis will be placed upon an analysis of the ideas themselves, while on other occasions more weight may be given to the historical and political context of the ideas, in order to acquire an understanding of their meaning and significance. Having said this, the aim in all the chapters is to combine a study of the intrinsic properties of ideas with an examination of the historical and social circumstances that have transformed them into native political traditions. The concluding chapter describes and appraises the problematic character of a society possessing a series of potentially conflicting political traditions. It studies the different views of how the divisive character of America's political ideas and principles have been contained and how the normal coexistence of logically opposing values is occasionally interrupted by dramatic and violent outbursts of political antipathy when America seems literally to be pitted against itself.

Freedom

AS AMERICA'S FIRST PRINCIPLE

In June 1989, thousands of Chinese students amassed in Beijing to protest against the political repression of the Chinese Communist regime. In the midst of the insurgents' encampment in Tiananmen Square stood a makeshift Statue of Liberty which served to express the defiance of the protesters and also to symbolise the demands for greater political freedom in the face of a contemporary totalitarian state. This wooden replica of the Statue of Liberty, to which the huge protest movement affixed itself, clearly evoked the spirit of another place. Even in the late 1980s, and even in such a closed society as Communist China, the idealism and passion of libertarians devolved – as they had done so often before in history – upon the almost ancient inspiration of the United States. The Chinese dissenters showed that the old American model of freedom was still pertinent to those calling for emancipation and innovation.

The idea of liberty is still fused with this sense of place. Just as liberty is habitually connected to the United States, so America itself continues to make liberty seem an accessible condition, a concrete objective and, thereby, a timeless and universal object of emulation. Whatever else America is, or has been, it remains inextricably bound up with the ideals and intoxication of liberty. Its history is permeated by the calls to acquire and to defend freedom. Its culture is soaked in the meanings and values of liberty. The country possesses an astounding array of symbols, legends and insignia which ensure that America's equation with freedom remains constant and central. The American story is one of pilgrims fleeing from religious persecution, of dissenters fleeing from political oppression and of the impoverished fleeing from destitution. Americans are raised with the conviction that their society became American and rose to national consciousness during the revolutionary era when the 'sons of liberty' first risked dissent and defiance in order to defend their liberties. They then resorted to a declaration of independence, to a rebellion and to a long war of emancipation from the British Crown (1776-81) in an effort to secure those liberties for themselves and to make America free from outside control.

The nation is, therefore, celebrated for having been 'conceived in liberty' and dedicated to the proposition that freedom is a natural right which conditions and constrains all succeeding social arrangements. Patrick Henry's admonition to 'give me liberty or give me death' was the rallying call of the War of Independence, but it also became the battle-cry of all subsequent American wars. The pre-eminence of liberty to the formative processes of America is still visible in the symbols and mottoes of those states which acquired their independence in 1776. While the flag of Virginia portrays the destruction of tyranny, New York's flag is dedicated to the figures of liberty and justice. The flag of New Jersey also features the cap of liberty and has the motto, 'Liberty and Prosperity'. Pennsylvannia promotes 'Virtue, Liberty and Independence' and Massachusetts declares that 'With the sword she seeks peace, order and liberty'.

Such signs and symbols help to sustain the belief that America was 'born free'[1] and that American liberty was accordingly 'a matter of birthright and not of conquest'.[2] In Thomas Jefferson's words, 'the God who gave us life, gave us liberty at the same time',[3] by which he meant that the acquisition of independence was not simply a historical event, but a recognition that liberty was a condition natural to America and integral to its independent existence. Even when it was necessary for the Founding Fathers to form a stronger union and a necessarily more centralised framework of government, the effort was still successfully couched in terms of 'securing the blessings of freedom'.[4] The circumstances of America's emergence as a separate entity had made 'liberty an American speciality'[5] and set America on a course that would forever combine it with the prospects and promises of liberty and, thereupon, render America an exceptional society of universal and prophetic significance.

The potency of America's characterisation as liberty incarnate has remained peculiarly intact since the eighteenth century. The history of America is studded with libertarian experimentation. Thomas Paine's call in 1776 for America to 'receive the fugitive, and prepare in time an asylum for mankind'[6] seemed in many ways to have been answered during the nineteenth century. Integral to America's appeal was its vast profusion of empty lands awaiting cultivation and possession. This gave rise to a pastoral ideal in the United States whereby the landless would be converted into small yeoman farmers who in their turn would provide the virtuous backbone of the American republic. This imagery drew directly upon Roman and Greek parallels in which the simplicity, honesty and patriotism of the individual farmer were the recognised ideals of citizenship. On the gargantuan scale of the American interior, the agrarian ideal was made to look compelling and almost unavoidable. America was seen as a second Garden of Eden and the American as a second Adam.[7] The farmers who were moving into the wilderness and giving it a characteristically American identity were described by Thomas Jefferson as 'the chosen people of God'.[8] Jefferson was sure there was 'room enough for our descendants to the thousandth and thousandth generation'.[9] The millenial allusions seemed entirely appropriate to Jefferson because at a time when land was synonymous with wealth and virtue, America did appear to be prodigiously blessed with the agrarian instrument of emancipation. Its virgin lands conferred upon America the prospect of an actual 'state of nature' within which its inhabitants would have the unique historical opportunity to engage in a continuous act of individual and collective liberation.[10]

Although the spirit of earnest and altruistic emancipation was epitomised by the American farmer, it was not confined to him alone. The promise of land and the assurance of tolerance and opportunity encouraged the establishment of a profusion of religious communities. The absence of an established church, the separation of church and state and the recognition of religious tolerance as a basic civil right meant that the freedom of American conditions was translated into the content and manner of religious worship. America's origins had always been closely associated with the impulse towards religious freedom – the most notable example being that of New England's Puritan settlements in the seventeenth century. Even at that time, America had the reputation of being a refuge for Protestant dissenters who wished to turn their vision of original Christianity into reality by resorting to the American wilderness.[11] This dissenting tradition was an important influence in the creation of America's revolutionary ethos in the eighteenth century. It was also a characteristic of the developing republic which quickly became noted for its religious diversity and exotic sectarianism. Schism, fragmentation and physical flight became part of the American way to God.

The Shakers, for example, were founded by Mother Ann Lee who, in 1774, had emigrated along with her first followers from Manchester to Albany, New York. By the middle of the nineteenth century, the Shakers had six thousand members in eighteen villages. Their faith was based upon the belief that Ann Lee was the embodiment of the Second Coming of Christ. Ann herself had been persecuted and jailed in England for blasphemy. Her fundamentalist positions on pacifism, devotion and purity brought her into conflict with the Church of England which she denounced for encouraging the sinful state of marriage, declaring it to be a covenant of death and an agreement with hell. After receiving a vision from Christ, Ann Lee and her disciples were inspired to establish a new church and community in America. The Shakers' devotion centred upon dances and, ultimately, upon hypnotic trances and violent bodily agitations. Shaker society was based upon celibate commune-like settlements geared to minimal possessions and craft skills and to complete sexual equality.

Perhaps the most distinctive product of America's religious freedom has been the Mormon Church of Jesus Christ of the Latter Day Saints. The Mormons believe that America is the new promised land and that their New Jerusalem will be the centre of Christ's rule after Armageddon and the Second Coming. Their chief article of faith is that a year after the crucifixion, Christ appeared and preached in America to a lost tribe of Jews, whose prophet, Mormon, and his son engraved the records of their people on golden plates and buried them on a hillside in New York. They were found in 1823 by Joseph Smith, who in a series of visitations by Saint Peter, Saint John, Saint James and God translated the plates and established the Mormon Church. In a trial by ordeal, the Mormons, under their second leader,

Brigham Young, suffered gross hardship in their trek across the continent to found the new Zion in Salt Lake Valley. By the end of the century, the Mormons had achieved their objective of 'making the desert bloom' and of establishing a unique social and economic organisation based upon the church. Today, it is one of the richest churches in America with much of its wealth employed to safeguard its heritage in enormous bomb-proof and air-conditioned caverns that are designed to preserve the Mormons throughout Armageddon for the Second Coming of Christ.

American liberty could also mean the freedom to experiment directly in secular living.[12] While it is true that religious communities had extensive social repercussions, nineteenth-century America witnessed the rise of a profusion of planned societies modelled specifically on human needs and motivations. Robert Owen's New Harmony in Indiana, the Perfectionists of Oneida in New York, the Inspirationists of Amana in Iowa, the Fourierists of Phalanx in New Jersey, the Union Colonists of Greeley in Colorado were all dedicated in one form or another to the strategy of employing American space to fulfil the ideal in communitarian living and to show that the Jeffersonian promise of freedom could be lived out in a variety of conditions. The community of Phalanx, New Jersey, for instance, was based upon Charles Fourier's 'science' of human nature and relationships. He believed that the natural passions which motivated individuals could be identified and categorised. Fourier's ideal community, or 'phalanx', would contain working groups in which the various passions of the members would be held in productive equilibrium. Although the Fourierist communities in New Jersey and Wisconsin were eventually abandoned, they typified the spirit of social reconstruction and secular utopianism for which America justly became renowned.

As the United States developed into a more industrialised society, the American tradition of freedom was increasingly recast in terms of personal acquisition, technological efficiency, material prosperity and social progress. Wealth was no longer reducible to land. Liberty was no longer synonymous with land ownership. By the end of the nineteenth century, wealth and liberty were more associated with individual opportunity, freedom of contract and capital accumulation in an increasingly enclosed industrialised world. This was a world where the old rural frontier was being replaced by new 'frontiers' in the form of scientific invention, social mobility, profit maximisation and concentration of ownership. Liberty in this new abundance was emancipating the inner resources of the continent, so the new wealth was vindicated in terms of what it could provide to ever larger numbers of people. It provided an American benefi-cence in which individuals were offered not only the prospect of an escape from impoverishment and destitution (i.e. the basic compo-nent of any sort of liberty), but also the chance to improve their own position.

> Americans never picked up the European concept of social station – which meant that you were born into your position in the world. For most Europeans of the 18th and 19th centuries, success meant main-taining your place in the fixed order. In Europe, but not in America, it meant that a person was entitled to respect and dignity in his place, wherever it was. In France, a shoemaker's son could become a shoemaker and inherit not only his father's business but his father's standing in the community. In the United States, the indentured immigrant who worked his way up to a prosperous shoemaking shop had met the standard of success. But to meet the same standard his son had to push on to something, or somewhere else.[13]

These increased opportunities for personal affluence and social improvement which industrialised advance brought in its wake enriched the old American message and heightened the appeal of America as a place of freedom.

Nowhere was America's equation with the concept and practi-calities of freedom given greater expression than in the exodus of peoples prepared to detach themselves from their indigenous socie-ties and migrate to the United States.[14] The volume of humanity prepared to change worlds, from old to new, was of epic proportions. Between 1820 and 1920, over 35 million immigrants entered the United States. It was not unusual during these years for the proportion of foreign-born in the American population to reach as high as one-eighth. They came for many reasons, but the over-whelming motivation was that of economic security. It is a testa-ment to the pull of America that such large numbers of people were prepared to submit themselves to the risks of cholera, dysentery, malnutrition, fire and shipwreck during the steerage, in order to reach America. In the midst of the notoriously insanitary conditions of the Atlantic crossing, the immigrants sang their songs of America. For example,

> To the West, to the West, to the land of the free,
> Where the mighty Missouri rolls down to the sea;
> Where a man is a man even though he must toil
> And the poorest may gather the fruits of the soil.[15]

We can now only imagine the excitement and anticipation of the immigrants as they sailed past the soaring edifice of the Statue of Liberty and absorbed the idealism of its inscription:

> Give me your tired, your poor,
> Your huddled masses yearning to breathe free
> The wretched refuse of your teeming shore.
> Send these, the homeless, tempest tost to me,
> I lift my lamp beside the golden door![16]

The verses and the voyages became part of the legend. They came to characterise the imagery of American freedom as a universal panacea equally attractive and applicable to all the peoples of the world.

This social evangelism was to become an active creed in the twentieth century when American liberty received further vindication by the United States's emergence as the world's richest and most powerful nation. American freedom was now no longer to be a passive model, but an active force to emancipate peoples within their own borders. Instead of the world coming to the United States, America now took its military and moral standing to the world. It measured the world according to its own criterion of freedom. It fought two world wars in the name of freedom.[17] America became the leader of the 'free world' and in 1961 an American president pledged that America would 'pay any price, bear any burden, meet any hardship, support any friend, oppose any foe to assure the survival and success of liberty'.[18] From the Puritans seeking the freedom of worship and the right of sectarian privacy from the old world in the seventeenth century, America had massively broadened its territory, its power and its conception of freedom. The twentieth-century apotheosis of America coincided with an apotheosis of American liberty, in which freedom had come to be recognised as a fundamental value in its own right – a value to be defined and cultivated in an increasingly threatening world by reference to American conditions, priorities and traditions.

In the industrialised world, no other nation has had this exceptional relationship with the hopes and promises of liberty. No other society has been so strongly dependent for its sense of identity upon the quest for freedom. America always has been, and still is, in the words of Clinton Rossiter, a nation obsessed with liberty.

> Liberty over authority, freedom over responsibility, rights over duties – these are our historic preferences. From the days of Williams and Wise to those of Eisenhower and Kennedy, Americans have talked about practically nothing else but liberty. Not the good man, but the free man has been the measure of all things in this 'sweet land of liberty'; not national glory but individual liberty has been the object of political authority and the test of its worth.[19]

Max Lerner agrees and believes that freedom is 'the first image the American invokes when he counts the blessings of his state'.

> He has gazed so long into the pool of freedom that he has fallen half in love with his own reflection in it. He may be at the base of the income pyramid or a segregated Negro in the South, yet whatever his place in the social system, he sets store by freedom; it gives him a yardstick to measure his deprivation and a hope that he can remedy it.[20]

It is not just that America is seen as having relatively more freedom within its borders than that of other societies. It 's the belief that America possesses the peculiar quality of being the defining characteristic of liberty. According to this view, the state of American nature confers upon liberty the conditions of its own existence; it marks the outer limits of its potential. It is only in America that liberty has been maximised to the fullest extent possible within the constraints of social arrangements. America's religious freedoms, political tolerance, civil liberties and constitutional rights evoke a culture dedicated to the notion that governmental powers are voluntarily and provisionally granted by free individuals who retain their sovereignty. This level of autonomy is epitomised by America's celebrated liberty of conscience which acknowledges the independence of the individual's mind freely to form conclusions from its environment. Thomas Jefferson described this ultimate liberty as the rights of 'Thinking, speaking, forming and giving opinions, and perhaps all those which can be fully exercised by the individual without the aid of exterior assistance – or, in other words, rights of personal competency.'[21]

The extent to which such statements are sanctified in American society bears witness to America's libertarian core of values. But it is more than this, for an integral part of America's ethos of liberty is the belief that it really does exist; that the statements of intent have actually been realised. The commonplace conviction is that America is free; that America makes people free and keeps them free – even that it can make other people free by making them more American in outlook.

It is liberty in this broadest sense that has served to characterise America. In comparison to the old world of Europe, Americans have always been swift to point out with pride that 'America was new in nature, new in people, new in experience, new in history. Nothing had prepared the old world for what now confronted it, fearfully, alluringly, implacably.'[22] But there were many in the old world who were only too willing to concur with this vision of America and to add their weight to the notion of America being the embodiment of liberty. Goethe, for example, praised the fact that the Americans were not riven by useless memories and that there were no crumbling castles in America to keep alive the dissensions of feudalism. Hegel also celebrated America. He saw it as 'the land of the future ... and of desire for all those who are weary of the historical lumber-room of Old Europe'.[23] In this respect, America does appear to be a wholly exceptional society in that by freeing itself from the old world, it emancipated itself from all preconceived structures and impositions; so much so that America is often reputed to be the first entirely new nation, free from the past, free from historical processes and, therefore, free from the intractable restrictions upon liberty found everywhere else.

It is precisely because the idea of liberty is so central to American culture that there is so much interest in its origins. The status of American liberty as idiosyncratic, and therefore authentic, has always been dependent upon its own historical roots. America's conception of itself as liberated enough to be uniquely free of the rest of the world is necessarily linked to the conception of its formative processes. The past has had to allow for America's protean state, in order for its reputedly special liberty to be substantiated as a plausible proposition. The need for America's past to support its present conception of liberty has been answered in two main ways: first, by reference to America's *experience* of liberty, and second, by America's *ideas* on liberty.

The first view of the origins and development of freedom in the new world is governed by the belief that America drew to it people of exceptional durability and independence who, when given the opportunity to work for themselves and to worship according to their own principles, generated communities which were spontaneously free from the dynastic, class and feudal divisions of the old world. When the people were combined with the natural conditions of an American wilderness which appeared to give a *tabula rasa* for the displaced of the world, then the impulse to view the subsequent settlements as natural havens of autonomy can be overwhelming. The early American churches can be presented as typifying one aspect of this indigenous predisposition towards liberty. Although the bulk of the colonial settlers owed nominal allegiance to the Church of England, they tended largely towards a radical Protestantism which was aided and abetted by the geographical isolation of the new world. Before the Revolution, there was no episcopal hierarchy in the colonies. The resultant lack of authority encouraged even Anglican congregations towards independence and, ultimately, towards sectarian fragmentation in which the divine truth could be followed freely by separate communities.

Another aspect of the American mould being apparently cast by the interaction of American conditions with the inner properties of human nature is provided by the notoriously hardy Scotch-Irish settlers. Finding land too expensive in the East, they took matters into their own hands and moved into the Appalachian mountains which, in the eighteenth century, formed the western limit of the known new world. These settlers were implacably hostile to Catholicism, to Anglicanism and to taxation. They pushed into lands which, although nominally belonging to the established colonial governments, they effectively claimed as their own property by force of possession. Once there in the seclusion of mountain country, the settlers celebrated self-sufficiency and fundamentalist Protestantism and were allowed to develop freely into the distinctive Appalachian culture which is still evident today.

These forms of direct, and almost tangible, religious and social emancipation were also discernible in the pattern of political arrangements. The space and distance of the new world had direct consequences for government. In the colonies, there was no central structure or standard of administration. This permitted an immense variety of governmental priorities to develop. The position of the royal governors, for example, became increasingly precarious throughout the eighteenth century as the colonists grew adept at using the remoteness of London to their own advantage. When a colonial legislature had its enactments vetoed by the government, the enactments were 'frequently put into effect pending the obtaining of the assent of the Crown authority in England, and if the governor was sustained, sometimes the legislation was re-enacted, perhaps in a slightly altered form, and put into effect pending another appeal to the Crown.'[24] All this would take an inordinate length of time and contribute to the *de facto* decline in the governors' position well before the American Revolution.

According to this sort of environmental perspective, the construction of the American order was determined by its physical and social components, which were drawn exclusively from the distinctively free conditions of the American experience. In other words, free and spontaneous conditions produced a free and spontaneous society. It was something that many believed could actually be observed. Robert Louis Stevenson was one who was prompted to make the following observation by the sight of a transcontinental railroad in the 1870s.

> When I think how the railroad has been pushed through this unwatered wilderness and haunt of savage tribes, and will now bear an immigrant for some £12 from the Atlantic to the Golden Gates (in San Francisco)...! How in these uncouth places, pigtailed Chinese pirates worked side by side with border ruffians and broken men from Europe, talking together in a mixed dialect ... it seems to me as if this railway were the one typical achievement of the age in which we live, as if it brought together in one plot all the ends of the world and all the degrees of social rank.[25]

In this context, the railroad can be seen as a metaphor of American society. The railroad's liberating force was itself both a visible expression and a direct product of the liberated social energies which had allowed the railroad to be constructed so quickly and efficiently.

Despite America's avowedly ahistorical sentiments, this sort of cultural history has always been important to the society's self-identity. The belief that the American environment has been an active force directing American society along predetermined and unprecedented paths is a widespread American conviction. In examining the state of democracy in the 1840s Alexis de Tocqueville, for example, drew particular attention to its New England roots. The region's original lack of hierarchical rank had spontaneously produced 'a democracy more perfect than any which antiquity had dreamed of'.[26] In New England, de Tocqueville found the 'germ and gradual development of that township independence which [was] the life and mainspring of American liberty'.[27] That germ had already been formed by the mix of people and place as early as 1650. The uniqueness of popular sovereignty found in the New England townships was, to de Tocqueville, an emanation from 'not only an ancient but a primitive state'[28] of social existence in the new world.

The grandest declaration of American faith in freedom being a legacy of free American conditions came in Frederick Jackson Turner's celebrated thesis on the American frontier. His basic assumption was that America's continually advancing frontier marked a line of recurrent American primitivism where 'unrestraint was triumphant'.[29] On this dividing line between settlement and the wilderness, social development was successively reborn in the light of the frontier's rampant opportunity, its impulsive energies, its social simplicity and its antipathy towards controlled direction. More than anywhere else, in Turner's view, immigrants at the frontier were 'Americanized, liberated, and fused into a mixed race'. Because each frontier 'furnish[ed] a new field of opportunity' and 'a gate of escape from the bondage of the past',[30] Turner believed that it was the frontier's geographical and social environment which had released the forces most responsible for the American character.

Despite the fact that Turner's thesis has been heavily contested, its message undoubtedly touched a chord of cultural sentiment in the United States. The notion of a self-generated national character, embodying an American proprietorship over America itself was compulsively attractive. Its appeal is still evident today in the works of historians like Daniel J. Boorstin. In *The Genius of American Politics*, for example, Boorstin responds to the American desire to be as free of external influences as it is of the past by referring to the notion of 'givenness': '"Givenness" is the belief that values in America are in some way or other automatically defined: given by certain facts of geography or history peculiar to us.'[31] To Boorstin, an essential part of such 'givenness' is the belief in the continuity and homogeneity of American history – 'it is the quality of our experience which makes us see our national past as an uninterrupted continuum of similar events, so that our past merges indistinguishably into our present'.[32]

The alternative way of explaining the origins, and thereby, the nature, of American liberty is through the influence of ideas. This approach to American freedom throws into doubt not just its claim to social autonomy, but also its claim to be the cradle of liberty. For example, it can be argued that the early American affection for the classics led to a cultural dependence on the principles and virtues of antiquity. These interpretations plot the influence of Greek and Roman authors like Plato, Aristotle, Sophocles, Thucydides, Plutarch, Cicero, Tacitus, Seneca, Ovid, Cato, Justinian, Lucretius and Polybius upon the development of colonial ideas on law, forms of government, political stability, republicanism, tyranny and liberty. It is claimed that these ideas became so ingrained in colonial political life that they were a major source of the Americans' ideology of dissent against Britain, and later became the inspiration behind the new constitutions of the independent republics in the 1780s.[33]

Another interpretation gives emphasis to the more immediate contemporary context of the British constitution, within which the initial American struggle took place, and in reference to which much of the subsequent American speculation concerning the roots of government and the meaning of liberty has been made. Since the 'colonists of every political shade were dedicated wholeheartedly to the English constitutional tradition ... and could count no greater blessing ... than their inheritance of the English form of government',[34] it could be said that the newly-independent Americans could not help but be moulded by hallowed English precedents. It is claimed that the Americans were guided by the desire to reinstate the ideal of the English balanced state through the strength of their own Whig allegiances and their zeal for the liberties of England's Glorious Revolution of 1688.[35]

An important variation of this perspective holds that while American conceptions of liberty were strongly influenced by Britain's political culture, that influence was drawn far more from what was called the 'Commonwealthman' tradition. This term refers to those early eighteenth-century dissenters and radicals who sought to revive the spirit of an ancient English liberty which had been so effectively exploited by the Commonwealth's republican apologists in the seventeenth century (e.g. James Harrington, John Milton, Andrew Marvel). These writers saw authentic English liberty as existing in the freehold tenure of Saxon times before the imposition of the Norman 'yoke'.[36] Over the centuries, this original state of indigenous freedom had been progressively reinstated, but the process had not been completed. The struggle continued. The Glorious Revolution (1688) of the Whigs was not the culmination of the process. On the contrary, the 'Commonwealthmen' concluded that liberty was as fragile as ever and constantly in danger of being eroded away. It was this 'Commonwealthman' tradition which, it is claimed, appealed to the non-conformist American dissenters and which permeated their conception of liberty and republicanism. Instead of the founding of America being dominated by the constitutional arrangements, legal rights and property consciousness of the Whig tradition, it has been argued that it was much more the product of an English-cum-classical republican ethos which stressed civic virtue, moral fervour and the ideal of community.[37]

Another perpective places the roots of American liberty firmly in the intellectual ferment of the eighteenth century Enlightenment. This era witnessed the rise of the modern concept of nature being a single entity directed by its own permanent and objective principles of operation. The belief that the rational order of nature's laws were accessible to human intelligence became the inspiration behind the Enlightenment's emancipation of reason. Building upon John Locke's arguments in the seventeenth century for natural rights as representing the central condition behind the original formation of any civil government, the Enlightenment thinkers proceeded on the assumption that nature was no longer simply a philosophical device to reason into the source and meaning of social arrangements, but a material force to be elicited and channelled into positive use.

Since humanity was part of the natural order, it was believed that the mechanics of social nature could be discovered, and political organisations could be constructed that would provide the best fit for mankind's inner properties. Many American scholars have been particularly susceptible to the idea that clinical reasoning and a conscious synthesis of empirically derived knowledge on government and politics explain the origins of America's constitutional freedom. Accordingly, America can be seen as having been 'conceived by a mental act, in the spirit of liberty'[38] by which emancipated reason became the handmaiden of colonial liberation. According to this view, freedom in America became a practical science.[39] The creation of the American polity was 'history's first great political experiment and massive effort at political engineering'.[40] From this standpoint, it is possible to construe American liberty as so much the product of Enlightenment principles that America can be characterised as the 'Enlightenment in practice'.[41] In the opinion of Henry Steele Commager,

> the Old World imagined, invented and formulated the Enlightenment, the New World – certainly the Anglo-American part of if – realized it and fulfilled it ... It was Americans who not only embraced the body of Enlightenment principles, but wrote them into law, crystallized them into institutions and put them to work. That as much as the winning of independence and the creation of the nation, *was* the American Revolution.[42]

Far from American liberty being merely a derivative of European experience – or even for that matter of American experience – the Enlightenment's conceptions of America's past can depress the role of historical continuity, cultural autonomy and traditional habit practically to the point of oblivion.

Apart from underlining the importance of liberty in America's origins, these two accounts of America's attachment to freedom illustrate the problematic properties inherent in the meanings and usages of freedom. The American presumption of creating a new nation through the conscious design of liberated reason in the cause of freedom, is matched by the equally American contention that its society represents a liberation *from* reason by emanating directly from its peculiar and unrepeatable circumstances and not by virtue of any ideologies of freedom. The two perspectives raise the question as to which one better embraces the spirit and content of liberty. There is no ready answer to this question for two basic reasons.

Firstly, neither account necessarily explains the link between the United States and its faith in liberty. It can be claimed that those intellectual influences (e.g. common law, natural rights, Enlightenment ideas) coming from outside America amounted to an American conformity to European ideas and tradition, and as such represented a cultural intrusion into the new world, thereby rendering it no longer so new or so free. Likewise, it can be argued that for a society to develop of its own volition and notionally free from external influences made it in effect the slave of its own instincts and impulses – even of its own myopic intolerance.

The second reason for the difficulties raised in using American history to validate American freedom is that liberty itself is a term notoriously immune to hard definition. It possesses a profusion of meanings and the conditions of its existence are plagued with the most severe conceptual and practical problems. Accordingly, Americans have not been noted for giving detailed specifications of what they mean by liberty. Although freedom has traditionally been the focus of American history, it is rarely subjected to close analysis.[43] More often than not liberty is treated as a self-evident fact and the point of departure for any social examination. This has tended to make the study of liberty a circular process in which the substance of liberty is lost through its status as a presupposition of American life. And yet the American story is just as redolent in the problems of liberty as it is in the professed successes of liberty. As such, the American experience can be as valuable in revealing the inner complexities of liberty as it has been in burnishing its exterior varnish. Indeed it might be said that because America has an avowed ideology of liberty and because its national identity is so closely bound up with the passion of liberty, the country is better qualified than any other to know the difficulties posed by an attachment to freedom. Any immigrant intoxicated with the ideal of freedom being fulfilled by the dramatic act of an ocean crossing acquires liberty in one sense by being able to turn his back on the old world. In another sense, however, that liberty is only a very provisional form of freedom. In the very act of emancipation from Europe, the immigrant is immediately faced with the need to live in liberty and, thereby, with the liberty of other people.

This is the difference between enjoying a liberating experience and acquiring the experience of freedom. Liberation may be a precondition of freedom but, as Hannah Arendt has explained, it is not the same as a sustainable condition of liberty which is far more elusive and dependent upon social arrangements.[44] Liberty has to be organised into social forms. The anarchic freedom of being liberated from Europe would not have lasted longer than the dock gates. Once in America, 'liberty' had to be transformed from an abstract ideal into a set of material practicalities. Each immigrant would have to come to the realisation that liberty needs to be placed in a social context of reciprocal obligations and restraints before it could acquire meaning and actual content. But in being accommodated to social arrangements, the pure water of idealised liberty would necessarily be muddied with qualifications, provisos and ambiguities.

It is possible to argue that America itself had had to undergo the same process of reconciliation to the practicalities of history. After tossing off the authority of the British Empire and indulging in an excess of republican emancipation, the new states had to come together in 1787 to establish a framework of national order by which American freedom might be controlled and preserved. By that time, a number of contemporary leaders had come to realise that the 'vigor of government was essential to the security of liberty'.[45] The subsequent convention at Philadelphia accordingly provided a constitution for the United States which, in the words of its chief architect, was intended to combine 'the requisite stability and energy in government with the inviolable attention due to liberty'.[46]

Liberty is directly concerned with the reduction of coercive constraints and impediments and with the consequent increase in opportunity for choice and voluntary action. But liberty is also, ultimately, dependent upon order and control. This is because one person's liberty will very often not be conducive to another person's liberty. It becomes necessary to talk of liberties rather than simply of liberty. There are, for example, political, economic, legal, religious, moral, social and personal liber*ties*. Many liberties of urban dwellers may conflict with those of farmers. The liberties of an ethnic minority may clash with the liberties of the mainstream majority. Some liberties may even be incompatible with one another. In the American context, the property rights of slave-owners confronted the basic liberties of the enslaved; the principle of freedom of contract enunciated by industrialists such as Andrew Carnegie was not compatible with the liberties of association amongst workers; the freedom of religious worship has clashed with those who have wished to protect their freedom from religion; and the free press intrudes constantly upon the rights of individual privacy. No other country has had more experience than the United States with the clash of such liberties. Correspondingly, no other country has had more experience of the way that such conflicts can not only generate intolerance and prejudice, but also lead to governments paradoxically having to resort to coercion, and even oppression, to maintain what it regards as the proper framework of ordered liberty.

It may even be claimed that, far from being an asylum of freedom, the United States has often been a black museum of illiberalism. The experience of America has included the bondage of indentured servitude, the exclusion of women from the full rights of citizenship and the enslavement of blacks in the eighteenth century; the genocidal clearance of Indian tribes from their lands, the industrial exploitation of child labour, the degradation of immigrant ghettoes and the carnage of the Civil War in the nineteenth century; the intolerant nativism of the Ku-Klux-Klan, the anti-communist witch hunt of the McCarthy era, the forcible internment of Japanese American citizens during World War II and the continuing presence of ethnic and racial discrimination in the twentieth century. America has often had to devote as much of its energies to living down its illiberal reputations as it has to living up to its reputation for liberty. It is within this 'evident chasm between its proclaimed values and its actual practice'[47] that exists a darker side to American liberty.

American freedom which can on occasions look like a form of benevolent anarchy can on other occasions turn into an earnest political morality brooking no opposition and regarding anything other than conformity to be tantamount to disloyality and even heresy. American liberty in this light can be simultaneously open and closed. It allows newcomers to pass freely into the American mainstream, but at the same time demands an orthodoxy from them that restricts their freedom to a set of social expectations that essentially reduces American liberty to a fixed form. In one dimension, therefore, freedom can be a genuine allegiance to a prodigious social diversity and political licence. In another dimension, liberty can be the expression of a social unanimity, that defines liberty in terms of its own principles and prejudices, and which evokes John Winthrop's puritan conception of liberty as the freedom to submit to an absolute moral authority.

This is not the occasion to assess the merits or demerits of such indictments of American liberty. Many of the problems confronting American liberty will enter into the subject matter of other chapters. What is important to note at this stage is that America's experience with the opportunities for liberty is matched by its experience with the opportunites for its abuse. And yet in spite of the problematic nature of liberty and America's evident blemishes in the field of freedom, the United States remains dogmatically libertarian in its public philosophy, in its forms of social inspiration and in the posture it strikes towards the rest of the world. America still believes that its problems are the problems of liberty. The enquiries made, the solutions proposed and the energies directed towards its social and political problems are always couched in terms of liberty. In the conduct of its affairs, America's intentions and objectives remain resolutely dedicated to the preservation and enlargement of freedom.

In examining the ideas that move Americans, liberty clearly ranks as the peerless quality of American inspiration. It continues to be the ideal by which America characterises itself and projects itself to the outside world. Americans have in the past been mobilised into war by calls for freedom. President Woodrow Wilson took the United States into World War I 'for the ultimate peace of the world and for the liberation of its peoples'.[48] President Franklin D. Roosevelt justified joining the allied cause in World War II by casting the commitment as a crusade to bring the 'four freedoms' of the new world (i.e. the freedom from want, and from fear, the freedom of religion and of speech) into an old world afflicted by fear and oppression. From the Civil War onwards, it is true to say that 'the legendry of America as the land of freedom has served as a dynamic weapon of political warfare on the side of every American cause'.[49]

Even in recent times and even against a social background of formidable corporate power and bureaucratic hierarchy, the nation can still be aroused by its leaders, invoking the continuity of America's present role with its libertarian origins. President Jimmy Carter, for example, clearly sought to mobilise America into facing up to its social and economic problems by way of a re-dedication of public faith in the meaning of America: 'Ours was the first society openly to define itself in terms of both spirituality and human liberty. It is that unique self-definition which has given us an exceptional appeal.'[50] President Ronald Reagan used much the same strategy to launch his national emancipation from government spending and regulation, and to reinvigorate America's posture towards the world along the lines of righteous self-assertion in the cause of liberty. President Reagan called his fellow Americans 'One people under God, dedicated to the dream of freedom that He has placed in the human heart, called upon now to pass that dream on to a waiting and hopeful world.'[51] It was these dreams of freedom, connected as they were to the tangible entity of America, which the Chinese students tried to emulate in Tiananmen Square. Their failure was marked by the destruction of their 'Statue of Liberty'. But the fact that they erected it at all bears witness to the remarkable way in which America still evokes the spirit of freedom and still offers the prospect that the universal ideal and basic impulse of liberty can be translated into a tangible and endurable form.

Individualism
AND THE AMERICAN
ETHOS OF CLASSLESSNESS

The United States is a large and highly heterogeneous society. The potential for conflict is great because America's ethos of freedom allows the free play of liberties to wander into confrontation with one another. Yet this potential for clashing liberties is never fulfilled, for the very libertarian ethos which gives rise to the possibility of disorder also provides the vehicle for stability. America is known for liberty, but it is also known for a social consensus of moderation and assimilation dedicated to the abstract value of freedom. America is characterised by a social deference towards a single, generalised and capacious tradition. American politics is centred around what this tradition consists of and how political positions can best draw legitimacy to themselves through their claim to approximate to the authentic American norm.

In the general effort to narrow the core value of American liberty into a definite and tangible condition, there can be little doubt that the chief characteristic is one of individual liberty. American liberty is traditionally a property that acquires its meaning through the agency of individuals, rather than that of classes, social orders, or nationality. In American eyes, it is a matter of simple logic that a society dedicated to liberty should have as its hallmark the freedom of the most fundamental constituent unit of that society (i.e. the individual citizen). America is believed by Americans to be free because its liberty is the liberty of human possibilities being released and maximised in a society in which individuals are given, 'the opportunity and encouraged to develop and to use their powers, to live their own lives and to participate in the renewal and development of the culture and in the development, reform and functioning of the social structure.'[1] Individualism and liberty are, therefore, synonymous with one another in American conditions. Liberty is only comprehensible in terms of the actions and thoughts of self-governing individuals, while individuality is meaningless without the attribute of freedom by which a person can be emancipated into the fullness of his or her potential.

There are many reasons why American liberty should be so closely linked to the individual as to make individualism a value in its own right. America's Protestant tradition, for example, encouraged its followers to see themselves as responsible for their own souls. The emphasis was not placed on an episcopal hierarchy, or on a central guiding organisation of church authority and common law, or on the required mediation of priests and sacraments to secure salvation. Instead, the Protestant impulse was towards the individual's direct relationship with God, and consequently on the need for the individual to be answerable for his actions and thoughts, not only in this world, but in the next as well.[2] In American conditions, this devolution of responsibility for salvation down to the individual level inevitably spawned a profusion of congregational churches and breakaway sects that allowed individuals to follow their own courses to God.

The very fluidity of these early social conditions also promoted the onset of an economic individualism. Apart from the low density of population and the easy availability of land which permitted the widespread ownership of property, American society was noted for the absence of established orders and of any rigid scheme of social stratification. In answer to his celebrated question, 'What is an American?,' the French observer, Hector St John de Crevecoeur, referred to the fact that there were

> no aristocratic families, no courts, no kings, no bishops, no ecclesiastical dominion, no invisible power giving to a few a very visible one; ... We are a people of cultivators, scattered over an immense territory ... united by the silken bands of mild government, all respecting the laws, without dreading their power, because they are equitable. We are all animated with the spirit of an industry which is unfettered and unrestrained, because each person works for himself.'[3]

The lack of princes and autocracy, however, did not denote the presence of a uniform mass culture; quite the contrary. At the end of the eighteenth century, 80 per cent of white men were self-employed as entrepreneurs, professionals, farmers, merchants and craftsmen. 'Because property, especially land, was distributed relatively equally, ... [it] was a liberating force' and made the United States 'a truly revolutionary society.'[4] In America, 'there was no established system of feudal ranks, no historical memory of an aristocratic order of society which could provide a model for a new social hierarchy'.[5] While some Americans worried about the missing integrative properties of a society without a harmony of social orders, most Americans were content to indulge in their own personal independence and to maximise their opportunities for individual advance in what promised to be a throughly open-ended society.

The social composition and outlook of these early Americans appeared to constitute a tangible fulfilment of John Locke's philosophy of rights and contracts. Locke has often been called 'America's philosopher' because his theory of civil society and government seemed not only to conform to American conditions, but to explain and rationalise them so well that it served to deepen and reinforce them into a guiding creed. Locke had been the main theorist of the English Whigs' Glorious Revolution in 1688. His theory of political revolution proceeded on the basis that each person was the possessor of certain immutable and non-transferable rights, which were neither derived from, nor secured by, the state. They pre-existed any form of government. Since each person was an individual creation oi God's universe and, therefore, a unit of intrinsic moral worth, Locke reasoned that God-given natural rights were an organic part of each person's individuality. The individual, therefore, exercised his own liberty through his own being and on his own authority – not on behalf of others or through an inter-mediary agency.[6] It was this central proposition of the individual ownership of rights which led, ultimately, to the modern ethos of individualism in which a man is seen literally as being his own person.

The composite natural rights of life, liberty and property were not objectives to be fulfilled, so much as a birthright from man's natural condition and one that invoked inviolable limits on the operation of any subsequent state. Locke's position was that while men were born free in a stateless condition, there was sufficient unpredictability and enough inconvenience for men to form civil societies, and thereupon states, to promote peace, safety and the public good. In doing so, men would inevitably suffer some restriction in their individual discretion but they would not, and could not, forfeit their basic natural rights. Any assertion that they had done so was both implausible and irrational because, to Locke, the whole objective of governing arrangements was always to protect and preserve men's natural liberties. Far from being an end in itself or a device to ensure order and peace at any price, Locke's state was formed by the consent and contract of free men expressly to serve their interests and to promote their welfare. If a state were to fail in the obligations entrusted to it, then the citizenry would have a right of revolution to reformulate the structure of government, in order to make it a better medium for the exercise and enjoyment of individual liberties.

Locke's philosophy established the individual as the seat of moral worth. The individual and his liberties were in existence prior to the formation of the state and remained ethically superior to any subsequent civil organisation. Accordingly, the authority and legitimacy of a state were made dependent upon the protection it afforded to individual liberties. Locke's fundamental theory of the state and of the citizen's relationship to it had always held the interest of America's Whig gentry in the eighteenth century. But, as the crisis with Britain deepened, Americans became far more susceptible to Locke's categories of natural rights and liberties, and much more receptive to his theory of revolution. In the end, the American revolutionaries broke out of the clawing technicalities of their legal and constitutional dispute with Britain and resorted to the lucid and uncluttered dictates of natural law and of individual liberties lying outside the complexity of imperial jurisdiction and common law.

The Americans aspired to a new puritanism in which the original ideas and arguments of the Whig ascendancy in Britain were deployed against the legatees and successors of the Glorious Revolution. Lockian natural rights were coming home to roost and being turned on to the mother country. In 1776 the colonists declared their independence in the following terms:

We hold these truths to be self-evident, that all men are created equal, that they are endowed by their Creator with certain unalienable Rights, that among these are Life, Liberty and the pursuit of Happiness. That to secure these rights, Governments are instituted among Men, deriving their just powers from the consent of the governed. That whenever any Form of Government becomes destructive of these ends, it is the Right of the People to alter or to abolish it, and to institute new Government, laying its foundation on such principles and organizing its powers in such form, as to them shall seem most likely to effect their Safety and Happiness.

It is not necessary to enter into the debate over the extent to which the Declaration's author, Thomas Jefferson, imitated Locke's prose. What is important are the ideas conveyed and the occasion upon which they were proclaimed. The ideas are those of radical individual liberty, and the occasion was the birth of an independent America. The net result was that the foundation of America's separate existence, the expression of its new identity and the purpose of its independence were all conveyed in the guise of individual liberties.

At its very inception, America was soaked in the pungent ideals and vocabulary of natural rights and personal freedoms. During the eighteenth century, the 'great common denominator of American social thinking was the ideal of social freedom – freedom to rise, that is – individualism, and social fluidity'.[7] America's attachment to the principle of individual liberty culminated in the Declaration of Independence.

There could be no clearer statement of the right of revolution or of the principle that government is the servant, not the master, of the people and that it serves at their pleasure. Fully as clear is the emphasis upon the individual human being as the basic unit of society and government, and the assumption that the foremost consideration is the basic right of each human being to live in freedom.[8]

These sentiments became America's guiding ideals and are as prevalent today as they were in the eighteenth century. The significance of the American Revolution, therefore, might be said to lie 'less in battles and martial triumphs than in the creative effort ... of building constitutions and declaring systems of rights'.[9] The emphasis on natural individual rights was later reaffirmed in the preamble of the United States Constitution[10] and in the subsequent attachment of the Bill of Rights which stands tòday as the chief monument to American individualism. The Bill of Rights, which includes the personal rights of free speech, free assembly, the free exercise of religion and the free access to a fair trial, represents the clearest statement of the American belief that freedom preserved by the state must always be qualified by guarantees of freedom *from* the state.

Whether or not it is appropriate to attribute American sentiments on rights and freedoms to Locke, and whether it is right to describe Locke as 'the advance ideologist of the American Revolution'[11] are matters which remain open to question. What is certain is that America's sustained celebration of Locke and its conscious allusions to Locke serve to underline the new world's attachment to individualism as both a social fact and a normative value. As a consequence of this outlook, America 'has been awash with every variety of philosophical belief about individualism'.[12] The impulse towards the self has been present in the life of 'the frontier farmer with his anarchic individualism'[13] and in the outlook of America's transcendentalist writers (e.g. Ralph Waldo Emerson, Nathaniel Hawthorne and Henry David Thoreau) who immersed themselves in their own self-consciousness confident in the belief that 'a single man contains within himself, through his intuition, the whole of experience'.[14]

The emphasis upon the individual has also been prominent in such utopian schemes as the 'Modern Times' community founded by Joseph Warren. He propounded a doctrine of individual sovereignty in which he claimed that 'peace, harmony, ease, security and happiness' would be 'found only in individuality'.[15] Even in everyday life, the sense of personal autonomy amongst American citizens has been a conspicuous feature of American society. This social ease has not simply been an aspect of the frontier, which Frederick Jackson Turner characterised as having a 'dominant individualism, ... withal that buoyancy and exuberance which comes from freedom'.[16] It has been commonplace throughout the United States. 'Since becoming a real American,' declared Paul Bunyan in a famous expletive, 'I can look any man straight in the eye and tell him to go to hell!'[17]

Americans have always had this reputation, especially in European eyes, for lacking a due sense of social deference and with it a lack of social integration and community spirit. Alexis de Tocqueville in particular drew attention to this American trait of individualism. It was de Tocqueville in fact who first coined the term and he did so specifically with reference to the conditions he found in America – 'individualism is a novel expression, to which a novel idea has given birth'.[18] De Tocqueville, however, used the term disparagingly. Because 'private interest directs the greater part of human actions in the United States',[19] de Tocqueville believed that America was in jeopardy of falling into the vices of individualism in which individual persons

> owe nothing to any man, they expect nothing from any man; they acquire the habit of always considering themselves as standing alone, and they are apt to imagine that their whole destiny is in their own hands ... Individualism ... disposes each member of the community to sever himself from the mass of his fellow-creatures; ... so that, after he has thus formed a little circle of his own, he willingly leaves society at large to itself.[20]

There is little reason to suppose that Americans believed either that they were susceptible to such vices, or, more significantly, that such individualistic tendencies were indeed vices at all. The cultivation of the individual has remained the leitmotif of the American way. So extensive has been the emphasis on individualism that it has had a profound effect on America's social organisation and on the content of its social values.

In no other single instance has this predisposition towards the centrality of the individual been more evident, more conclusive or more far-reaching than in the era of rapid industrialisation and rampant *laissez-faire*, which occurred at the end of the nineteenth century and the beginning of the twentieth centuries. This was the era of Social Darwinism when America's various constructions of individualism were subsumed within a single and all-embracing code of total self-assertion. The individualism of withdrawal and private self-enhancement was superseded by an active and rugged individualism and of competition and struggle against others. Individual liberty was at one and the same time elevated to a position of emphatic and dogmatic personal licence – irrespective of the consequences produced by the exercise of that liberty – and relegated to the status of being a necessary adjunct to the newly declared

Darwinian dynamics of social and cultural advancement.

In the light of this attachment to Darwinian principles, individual freedom was processed into a component of acquiescence to what was conceived as a law of nature that subjected man to an unavoidable conflict for existence in the cause of human progress. This liberty was no longer simply an expression of a natural right regarded as an end in itself, or an affirmation of individual sovereignty over society, or a pathway to moral self-development. It was more an exaggerated and unconstrained extension of individual negativist freedom (i.e. freedom from previously imposed restrictions), inflated into dogma by the pervasive sanction of evolutionary necessity, in which individual aggression and competitiveness would act as the unwitting agents of social development and human achievement.[21]

Darwin's biological categories of 'struggle for existence', 'adaptation to the environment', 'survival value' and 'progressive evolution' were especially appealing to a society undergoing the convulsive effect of accelerated industrialisation. A new aristocracy of 'steel barons, coal lords, dukes of wheat and beef, of mines and railways'[22] had suddenly emerged. They had not only developed the economic resources of the country, but had amassed such gargantuan fortunes by the most rapacious means that they were an elite in urgent need of social legitimacy. These *nouveau riche* outsiders (e.g. Andrew Carnegie) who had often come from the lower ranks of American society appeared in one respect to have acted out, on a large scale, the old American ethic of individual achievement and social mobility. In other respects, however, their business interests had been unscrupulous and amoral in character. It was these men who were peculiarly susceptible to Darwinian analogies by which the atavistic and predatory nature of their economic behaviour could find validation in an overwhelming biological scheme of self-interest and the maximisation of competitive advantage.[23] This natural order had its own empirically derived ethic of necessary selfishness in which the individual ownership of accumulated capital was both the means and the mark of social improvement.

The British social theorist, Herbert Spencer, was the first to provide a comprehensive rationalisation of the era's virtual anarchy of hyper-production. It was Spencer who first popularised the phrase, 'the survival of the fittest'. He linked it directly to the dynamics of an advancing civilisation. With each individual 'having freedom to use his powers up to the bounds fixed by the like freedom of others', then, according to Spencer, 'there is maintained the vital principle of social progress; inasmuch as, under such conditions, the individuals of most worth will prosper and multiply more than those with less worth.'[24] The apparent means of evolution were equated with the benefits of progress. From being *a possible* contribution to progress, the social equivalent of the Darwinian struggle was transformed into *the only* pathway to progress. All progress was a derivative of evolutionary techniques and, therefore, attributable to the compulsive medium of self-seeking materialism through which society measured its dynamic energies and secured its advances. Upon reading Spencer, Andrew Carnegie said: 'Light came as in a flood and all was clear ... Not only had I got rid of theology and the supernatural but I had found the truth of evolution. "All is well, and since all grows better" became my motto, my true source of comfort.'[25] Carnegie felt vindicated. His working priorities could now be affirmed as ethical principles.

Herbert Spencer's chief disciple in America was William Graham Sumner. Sumner not only elucidated some of Spencer's more obscure theorising, but also sought to incorporate the new economic licentiousness specifically into the American tradition of individual liberty. According to Sumner, if society is left to its own forces, those with the greatest capability will survive and prosper. In the struggle for existence, societies should recognise and even seek to advance those individuals who have demonstrated their fitness to survive. Fitness, to Sumner, was determined by the universal standard of the possession of material property. 'Let it be understood that we cannot go outside of this alternative: liberty, in equality, survival of the fittest; not – liberty, equality, survival of the unfittest. The former carries society forward and favors all its best members; the latter carries society downwards and favors all its worst members.'[26] Sumner was prompted to make the following conclusion: 'If we do not like the survival of the fittest, we have only one possible alternative, and that is the survival of the unfittest. The former is the law of civilisation; the latter is the law of anti-civilisation.'[27] The natural right of individual liberty, to Sumner, was nothing but a fiction because nature offered only the experience of constant struggle. Rights were not an inheritance. They were contingent upon what society saw fit to provide at any one time. Such rights had to be in accordance with the overriding principle of social utility whereby private property was rightfully possessed by those who were self-evidently fit to own it by the mere fact of having it. Individual liberty, therefore, came to mean 'merely such liberty as was consistent with the ... maintenance of the property right ... Other kinds of liberty were precluded if they conflicted with the ruling standard.'[28]

The assertions of theorists like Spencer and Sumner enjoyed widespread popularity.[29] It was not merely that their ideas suited the interests and pretensions of the new industrial warlords, or that they lent legitimacy to the rising commercial classes in general. It was that the principles associated with Social Darwinism appeared to explain both the sudden onset of industrial power and technological innovation, and the rapid emergence of a new, and apparently natural (i.e. naturally selected), elite. It is true that the relationship of 'fitness' to 'survival' always risked becoming a tautology (i.e. those who survived the competitive struggle were those who were fit to do so, whilst those who were the fittest revealed their fitness through nothing other than the competitive struggle) and that 'progress' and the 'triumphant industrialist' tended to be defined and validated in terms of each other. Nevertheless the tenets of this creed proved to be remarkably convincing to an American where the budget of the federal government could be dwarfed by the assets of a single trust and where Horatio Alger's stories of meteoric 'rags-to-riches' success were the staple diet of the reading masses.

By the end of the nineteenth century, the subordination of personal freedom to the dictates of economic liberty had penetrated the upper reaches of government. Ultimately, the ideas of a biologically-based natural order within society were established in the constitution itself. The Supreme Court gradually redefined constitutional liberty in the light of allowing individuals to find their own natural level of economic success or failure. In the crucial precedent of *Lochner* v. *New York* (1905),[30] for example, the normal powers which a state possessed to protect the health and welfare of its citizens were swept aside because they were seen as having compromised the rising principles of economic liberty. Using the Fourteenth Amendment which prevented states from depriving life, liberty or property without due process of law, the Court injected the due process clause with the substance of Spencerian sociology and rendered legislation conditional upon its precepts. According to New York, the law was a health measure, but to the Supreme Court it was an unreasonable and arbitrary interference with the contractual liberties of the employers and the employees to arrive at the best possible terms of agreement between one another. The prevention of lung disease was, in the Court's view, simply a pretext for engaging in economic regulation which was an abuse of the state's powers. The Court concluded that, 'the freedom of master and employee to contract with each other in relation to their employment ... cannot be prohibited or interfered with, without violating the federal Constitution'.[31] In his celebrated dissent, Mr Justice Holmes declared that 'the Fourteenth Amendment does not enact Mr Herbert Spencer's Social Statics.'[32] In so far as the majority of the Court was concerned, he was quite wrong. The Court's tradition of higher law had been used to accommodate the high doctrines of Darwinian dynamics.

In the end, the encouragement of individuals to satisfy their reputedly instinctive quest for self-promotion over other individuals, and the derogation of the concept of society as a self-conscious and self-determining community into an agglomeration of individual appetites, was severely challenged. In particular, it became increasingly evident that the economic freedom by which an employer and employee entered freely into contracts as co-equal negotiating partners was a fiction. The choice open to workers was very often either that of poorly paid work in bad and even dangerous conditions, or that of penury and starvation.

Upton Sinclair's *The Jungle* is perhaps one of the best descriptions of the reality of Darwinian individualism during this time. *The Jungle* describes the bestial conditions that were prevalent in the Chicago stockyards and slaughterhouses at the turn of the century. Sinclair recognised the productive energy of the industry, but he also pointed out the corruption that attended it. The packers not only evaded what little regulation existed, but in their ceaseless quest for gain were prepared to deceive the public into consuming poisoned meat.

'It was hard to think of anything new in a place where so many sharp wits had been at work for so long.'[33] But it was the working conditions in the slaughterhouses that Sinclair reserved for special condemnation.

> There were the beef-luggers, who carried two-hundred-pound quarters into the refrigerator cars – a fearful kind of work, that began at four o'clock in the morning, and that wore out the most powerful men in a few years ⋯ There were the wool-pluckers, whose hands went to pieces even sooner than the hands of the pickle men; for the pelts of the sheep had to be painted with acid to loosen the wool, and then the pluckers had to pull out this wool with their bare hands, till the acid had eaten their fingers off ... Worst of any, however, were the fertilizer-men ... These people could not be shown to the visitor, for the odour of a fertilizer-man would scare any ordinary visitor at a hundred yards.[34]

As the dogmas of economic freedom were producing conditions in which it was difficult to detect what individual opportunities were open to the men of the slaughterhouses and of the hundreds of mechanised industries like them, so those self-same dogmas were used to justify and to ennoble the vast wealth of a small number of proprietors. If the poverty was chronic, affluence was proportionally lavish. The bloated self-hood of those who came to be known as 'robber barons' was reflected in their conspicuous consumption of everything from Roman bronzes, Merovingian jewels, Italian tapestries and medieval armour to custom-built baronial palaces complete with coachmen and footmen in their master's personal livery. It became clear that the millionaires and monopolists of America's great leap forward had opened up an enormous gap in society. They believed their liberties to be independent of society. Some believed that the social consequences of their behaviour were utterly irrevelant. J. P. Morgan, for example, was known for his silence, his Cuban cigars and his contempt for the public. 'I owe the public nothing,' was his famous retort.[35] This sort of unchained individualism ultimately became a self-consuming individualism in which its beneficiaries were seen to be flouting their own tenets of Social Darwinism (i.e. by bequeathing wealth to their heirs who had done nothing to prove their fitness for the rewards of the competitive struggle) and to be actively reducing the stock of individual liberty to an ever-diminishing cadre of the super-rich.

The abuses and excesses of this age of individualism generated a series of reform movements and prompted serious revisions of American public philosophy. The pragmatist school of theorists, for example, stressed the importance of knowledge as an instrumental value to be used experimentally, in order to ameliorate social problems in a spirit of openness and a lack of finality that refused to see man as part of any closed or predetermined natural order. Radical utopian writers like Henry George and Edmund Bellamy forced their readers to evaluate critically the state of contemporary society. The Social Gospel movement encouraged the revival of Christian social ethics. Social theorists, like Herbert Croly, who were heavily influenced by Hegelian historicism and idealism, sought to regenerate a sense of social unity by redefining popular sovereignty in terms of a collective directional will formed from the historical and moral fact of an underlying and all-inclusive American community.[36]

Lastly, and perhaps most significantly to the present discussion, the onset of the social sciences at the end of the nineteenth century began to perceive the person as social in essence. While traditional American individualism had conceived of society as an atomised collection of mutually independent agents, contemporary social science proceeded on the basis that men and women are primarily social creatures who are shaped not only by an outside physical environment, but by an interior environment of social values, beliefs and practices. It was social psychology, in particular, which attempted to reconstitute the Darwinian category of an organism from a competitive individual to a society of integrated, interdependent and co-operative components. According to this science, neither the individual nor society pre-existed the other. They both presupposed each other so that the community was as natural a feature of life as was the individual. It was this organic community of individuals which represented the base unit of human evolution and the medium through which mankind could progress to a higher plane of development and fulfilment.[37]

One of the chief consequences of this altered perspective of evolution was the belief that man had been able to mould society by conscious invention and regulation from within. Evolution in this form, therefore, was an active assertion of collective will, rather than merely a fatalistic experience of blind purposeless forces acting upon society. The emphasis laid upon the creative consciousness in evolutionary progress by such influential figures as Lester Ward made a marked impression upon progressive thought and is widely regarded as having been a major source of inspiration behind the experimental activism of the New Deal.[38]

From these various sources, the harsh orthodoxy of Social Darwinism was softened by a succession of structural and substantive reforms which in the present day has culminated in a vast infrastructure of government controls and industrial regulations, and a social welfare system providing a wide range of benefits, entitlements and protections. And yet, just because the Carnegies and Rockefellers have disappeared, and the United States now has a welfare state dedicated to enlarging the spheres of personal freedom, this does not mean that the central problem of American individualism has been resolved.

American society has still not yet found a way of reconciling its traditional individualism with the conditions of a large, modern and heavily-populated country. The overblown tycoons of the Gilded Age – who were at once both the heroes and the villains of American individualism – were not eliminated by progressive income tax in the name of improved individual opportunities for others. They simply sold up and allowed their assets to be concentrated still further into publicly owned corporations. The problem of concentrated wealth and power was not so much resolved by the demise of America's merchant princes, as extended and prolonged into the present day. The pattern of corporate capitalism has been one of take-over and merger so that now America's top 500 corporations control three-quarters of the country's industrial assets.[39]

The centralisation present in the economy has been matched in society and government. Increasingly in the twentieth century, America has generated a more uniform national culture of mass media, closed frontiers, standardised products, suburban sprawl and white-collar jobs. In politics, the trend in the configuration of the federal government has been one of increased concentration at the centre. From being a junior partner in the federal system, accounting for only 31 per cent of public expenditure (i.e. 2 per cent of the Gross National Product) in 1902, the federal government now has a budget of over 1,000 billion dollars, employs over 5 million people and accounts for nearly 60 per cent of public expenditure and over 20 per cent of the GNP. Moreover, the nature of American politics reflects the centralist character of society and government with marked nationalisation of issues, candidates, symbols and electoral coalitions.

Given the massive centralisation of American society, the evident presence of enormous hierarchies of wealth, power and status and the decline of social mobility in an economic structure where over 90 per cent of the workers are salaried or wage earners, it might be thought that the position of the individual and of American individualism in general may well have deteriorated to a point of irrelevance. It is true that plenty of evidence exists to show that American society has many of the privileges, barriers and divisions that have traditionally characterised the class-stratified societies of Europe.[40] Nevertheless, it is equally true that Americans resist class categories and persist with an extraordinarily resilient attachment to a belief system of classlessness, mobility and individualism. Even in an increasingly mass society of multinational corporate structures, the normative model remains that of the independent proprietor and the self-made man.[41]

The archetypal American heroes are still the rail splitter, the sodbuster, the Indian fighter, the backwoodsman, the mountain man and, most of all, the cowboy. The cowboy represents the quintessential self-image of American manhood: a loner with integrity and courage on the frontiers of both settlement and human subsistence. The cowboy fable dramatises the American as an individual pitted against the natural grandeur of the West and dependent upon his own faculties to conquer hardship and evil. Modern Americans like to re-enact the western epic by repairing to woodland cabins and hunting lodges. American politicians make traditional references to the ethos of the cowboy and to the muscular chivalry of the frontier. When Senator Barry Goldwater ran for President in 1964, he used to attack government spending by explicit references to the making of the West. His campaign used to feature the life story of the Goldwater family in which he would relate how his relatives had ventured across the western deserts, had suffered every possible privation, had been attacked by Indians and had finally established the Goldwater settlement in Arizona. Goldwater would then wonder, amidst laughter and applause, how it had been possible for his forefathers to have done such things without the support of federal aid! Goldwater did not win in 1964. He was 'out-cowboyed' by the tall Texan figure of Lyndon Baines Johnson who rode horses, wore cowboy hats and was still running his own ranch.[42]

Goldwater and Johnson were by no means exceptional. Presidents Truman and Eisenhower used to speak in coded cowboy phrases like 'facing your man down', 'square shooting' and 'the even break'. But the most deliberate and recent personification of the cowboy figure has been that of Ronald Reagan. President Reagan deliberately set out to legitimise his programme of 'getting government off the backs of the people' by identifying it with the code of western virtue and justice. He openly invoked the rugged self-reliance associated with the call of the wild and referred to such figures as Daniel Boone, Kit Carson and 'Wild Bill' Hickok, as examples of heroic individual integrity to be emulated in modern American life. Although Reagan himself was no cowboy, he had contributed to the prevailing Hollywood construction of the epic western figure arid, as such, was able to present himself as an authentic advocate of the nostalgic appeal of the American cowboy legend.[43]

That an American President should seek to exploit the mythology of the American cowboy is entirely consistent not just with a culture which values individualism but with a political office that has become the embodiment of that individualism. The Presidency has always been held up as the plausible objective of any American child. Over the last generation, however, the office has become personalised in style and content to such an extent that the state of the American nation has become synonymous with the state of the Presidency, which in turn is seen as being tantamount to the condition of the President himself.

In the same way that Presidents have to promote their individuality through the mass media in order to generate the public support and political resources required for leadership, so the American citizenry is encouraged to see its own individualist values portrayed, and even realised, in the pioneering solitude of the modern era's 'super-individualists' in the White House. American Presidents are now the best-known figures in the United States. The

Presidency is analysed on the basis that the office's power is highly dependent upon the personality, skills and abilities of the individual incumbent.[44] Furthermore, Presidential elections are increasingly run as personality contests with candidates continually having to remind themselves that they are appealing to a nation of individuals, and that even in the most important exercise in public choice and policy consideration, the voters are invited to use their personal evaluation of the candidates' individual qualities in arriving at their decisions. In this way, Presidential elections have become vast festivals of American individualism, in which complex issues are transmuted into debates over personal competence and individual leadership qualities, and into charges and counter-charges over the personal usurpation of power and over the promises of social salvation by means of personal intervention.[45]

For American heroes to be heroic they have to be heroically individual. They have to have pitted themselves against the mass, or the state, or just against the odds. And they have to embody the virtues of negative liberty, by which the removal of restrictions leads ineluctably to a maximisation of freedom. The onset of an industrialised mass society has not proved to be a barrier to this conception of individual autonomy. The conditions of such independence have simply been transferred to large organisations so that individual freedom is possible either by escaping from the imprisoning structures of modern life or more conceivably in a corporate world, by working out one's liberty within it and through it – in effect by exchanging the geographical mobility of traditional America for the social mobility of modern America.

The exemplification of this heroic role model in the 1980s was Lee Iacocca, a second-generation Italian American, who had not only fought his way up to the top of one corporation (Ford) but, after being fired, had risen to the top of one of its competitors (Chrysler). Furthermore, he went on to save Chrysler from bankruptcy and closure through the sheer force of his personal determination to succeed. His memoirs, *Iacocca*, headed the best-seller lists for five weeks in 1985 and sold 1·5 million copies, making it the most popular biography in United States' publishing history. He became a cult figure because he had single-handedly turned a giant corporation around and had, therefore, defied industrial fate and shown that a huge complex organisation was susceptible to individual leadership and personal will-power. Iacocca's philosophy was simple but profoundly American.

> People say to me: 'You're a roaring success. How did you do it?' I go back to what my parents taught me. Apply yourself. Get all the education you can, but then, by God, *do* something! Don't just stand there, make something happen. It isn't easy, but if you keep your nose to the grindstone and work at it, it's amazing how in a free society you can become as great as you want to be.[46]

Given Iacocca's gift for promoting the ideal of American individualism through his own person, it was quite natural that he should be considered as a possible Presidential candidate for the future.

Critics of American society complain that its attachment to an individualistic set of values drawn from a time when the country was dominated by small businesses and self-employed artisans is an anomaly in the second half of the twentieth century. It is said that the anomaly is a sign of a reclusive self-absorption in an increasingly narcissistic society,[47] which has not only lost faith in the collective character of political purpose, but also lost contact with its own history in the sense of 'belonging to a succession of generations originating in the past and stretching into the future'.[48] The American emphasis upon an individualistic consciousness is also said to be a dangerous delusion at a time when the conditions of modern America require imaginative planning and the mobilisation of resources into genuinely collaborative efforts to respond to ever more extensive problems. In the face of a need for central authority and direction, American politics is notorious for its individualised election campaigns, its rising volume of volatile independent voters, its increased incidence of split-ticket voting, its dislocated administrative apparatus and for a welfare state condemned to struggle for 'social equity from a credo of homogenized individualism and pulverized government'.[49] And yet, the one aspect of American individualism which the critics cannot refute is the fact of its remarkable existence. Despite criticisms that it is anachronistic, unsustainable and counter-productive, American individualism survives and prospers.[50] Survey research shows again and again that the old dogmas of individual autonomy are still present in American society. Three-quarters of Americans, for example, still agree that everyone should try to reach a position higher than that achieved by their parents. The same proportion believe there is something wrong with a person who is not willing to work hard, in order to gain this sort of success.[51] This link between individual freedom and social mobility is made even more explicit when the question of personal autonomy is linked to government. For instance, in a poll that asked respondents which of the following statements came closest to their position – (i) that the government is responsible for the well-being of citizens and has an obligation to take care of people when they are in trouble, or (ii) that people are responsible for their own well-being and have an obligation to take care of themselves when they are in trouble – nearly 60 per cent of the respondents chose the latter.[52] This pattern of attitudes is consistently repeated with a clear preponderance of Americans finding that they agree more with the proposition that 'each person should be let alone to get ahead', than they do with the proposition that 'government should see to it that every person has a job and good standard of living'.[53]

It is sufficient for the purposes of this chapter to record that such sentiments persist with the strength that they do. The question of why they endure in American society; of why freedom is seen as being reducible to, and expressed through, the individual; and what consequences and applications such an outlook has in a wider social context is examined in the next chapter.

Capitalism

AND AMERICA'S
PROPERTIED FREEDOMS

In his book entitled *American Conservatism in the Age of Enterprise 1865-19*, Robert McCloskey posed the great question of the *laissez-faire* era of industrialisation and brutal Social Darwinism. Why had the United States been so receptive to the dogmas of economic individualism that it was prepared to relinquish the moral dimension of America's traditional precepts? 'How was it that the ideals of democracy could be so cavalierly used? And why was it, above all, that so little counterargument was directed' to the notion that liberty was nothing other than 'the freedom to engage in economic enterprise' and that progress was only 'the accumulation of capital and the proliferation of industrial inventions'?[1]

McCloskey's answers were essentially the same as those which have echoed down the years to the present day – namely that America was peculiarly susceptible to the fervour of economic individualism because it drew upon several roots in the American condition. The work ethic of ascetic Protestantism; the Calvinistic belief in wealth as an outward sign of God's grace and of an individual's inner wealth; the plenitude of resources in an underpopulated area; the need for the country to develop as quickly as possible by all available means; and the natural resonance of classical economics in a land whose birth had coincided with the breakdown of the mercantilist order and whose formative years had been marked by the emancipation of old structures of authority – all contributed to America's special affinity with individualised ambition and material achievement.[2] But the most potent factor in the process was the systematisation of these separate historical impulses and these several economic conditions into a comprehensive order of explanation and justification. 'Capitalism' grew up with the United States and served to rationalise not only the organisation of its society, but to secure its identity as a nation. Just as the United States tended to exemplify the postulates of capitalism, so capitalism tended to define the dynamics and value of America's social order. As a result,

> Capitalism is much more than a descriptive term for most Americans. It is an ideology, because those Americans who subscribe to capitalism make value-based assumptions about the nature of man and the desirability of certain procedures and their expected results. Such a network of assumptions about man, about ways to reach particular goals, and about the desirability of those goals converts capitalism from a descriptive term to a prescriptive and justifying ideology.[3]

It is an enveloping ideology which in the United States even extends to encapsulating American experience and to providing a *raison d'être* to the American way of life.

In the abstract, capitalism refers to a form of production financed and controlled by individuals who have accumulated wealth over and above their immediate needs and who are prepared to forgo the benefits of this wealth in the expectation of receiving a greater accumulation of wealth in the future. It is assumed that privately-owned capital will be directed to those schemes which can be expected to make the maximum return on the investment. Invested capital is conjoined to privately-owned land and labour – also in search of the greatest gain possible – with the result that goods and services, profits and wages are maximised and efficiently allocated by way of the price mechanism of competitive markets. It is this reliance upon the market which makes capitalism into a system. The supposition is that underlying private economic activity is a naturally harmonious and self-regulating interaction between the factors of production expressed and secured through the market. According to capitalist theory, as long as those market forces (i.e. supply, demand, competition and price) are not subverted or misdirected by restrictive practices, economic privileges or outside interference, then and only then will they reach equilibrium and, thereby, realise their full benefit to society in allowing for the maximisation of production at the minimum cost to consumers. Through the free movement of productive resources, capitalism is thought to release the full potential of a society's inner wealth and to reduce prior structures of authority and organisation to the level of historical anachronisms.

Capitalism both relies upon and validates the free play of individual self-interest, for it is only through this agency that the market can function as the unsurpassed register of social information which capitalists believe it to be. According to F. A. Hayek, for example, it is the complexity of modern conditions which makes the competitive market the only method by which co-ordination can be achieved.

> Because all the details of the changes constantly affecting the conditions of demand and supply of the different commodities can never be fully known, or quickly enough be collected and disseminated, by any one centre, what is required is some apparatus of registration which automatically records all the relevant effects of individual actions, and whose indications are at the same time the resultant of, and the guide for, all the individual decisions ... This is precisely what the price system does under competition ... The more complicated the whole, the more dependent we become on that division of knowledge between individuals whose separate efforts are co-ordinated by the impersonal mechanism for transmitting the relevant information known by us as the price system.[4]

Individual self-interest, however, does not merely make for an effective repository of market information. It is also thought, paradoxically, to ensure the greatest material benefit to society as a whole. With every individual 'continually exerting himself to find out the most advantageous employment for whatever capital he can command, it is his own advantage ... and not that of society which he has in view'.[5] Nevertheless, 'by pursuing his own interest, he frequently promotes that of the society more effectually than when he really intends to promote it'. Adam Smith's celebrated 'invisible hand'[6] which promotes a social end from myopic self-concerns ennobles economic individualism from merely an empirical motivation into a normative principle and an ethical arrangement.

Some defenders of capitalism would go even further and claim that because economic progress leads to the 'freedom and equality of the individual in a free and equal society',[7] individuals have a moral responsibilty to serve themselves in a calculated and uninhibited manner. As Peter Drucker points out, 'the capitalist creed was the first and only creed which valued the profit motive positively as the means by which the ideal free and equal society would be automatically realised'.[8] According to the system's apologists, capitalism is so geared towards the functional objective of sheer production that it is inherently libertarian in nature. It not only frees people from want but, in order to acquire such liberating abundance, it requires a liberation of economic and social arrangements.

> To put a positive social value upon the profit motive requires the freeing of individual economic activity from all restrictions. Capitalism has therefore to endow the economic sphere with independence and autonomy, which means that economic activities must not be subjected to non-economic considerations, but must rank higher.[9]

Despite the evident inequality implicit in the concentrations of capital needed to generate production, there nevertheless remains a strong egalitarian, anti-feudal, anti-authoritarian streak within the capitalist framework. Capitalism is purported to encourage and to reward individuals on the basis of their diligence, intelligence, talents, judgements and entrepreneurial skills – irrespective of rank, background or manners. In such a system, the society moves inexorably forward, not only in the material sense of goods and services, but also in the moral sense. Capitalism is thought to release human potential to the full by having each individual rely on his own resources and capabilities for his place in society and for his own sense of achievement, contribution and self-esteem. Capitalism in this classical perspective can be seen as not merely a device for material production but the very touchstone of individual liberty itself.

Turning from the abstract to the material characteristics of America's development, it is clear that there has been a close relationship between the United States and the principles, and even the ideals, of capitalism. To many observers, America has acted out and fulfilled to the greatest extent possible the true potential of capitalism. It has done so intuitively by exploiting its own peculiar position, its own wealth of resources and its own disposition towards individual achievement and self-advancement. The rudimentary government of what was initially an agrarian republic allowed an incipient capitalism to grow and permitted its beneficiaries (i.e. entrepreneurs and merchants) to maximise property rights and to maintain a government of limited powers.

By the end of the nineteenth century, America had become 'the capitalist fatherland' and 'the home of the world's most confident and energetic business community'.[10] The United States had undergone a 'great leap forward'. By the turn of the century, the United States had outstripped Britain in coal and pig iron production and had surpassed Germany in iron ore production. In 1900, America was producing as much steel as Britain and Germany combined. The extraordinary advances made by the United States have been widely attributed to the zealous indiscipline of capitalist energies. Indeed, the period of American history from 1875 to 1910 has often been cast as the world's litmus test of capitalism when, at a time and in a place of unprecented industrial freedom, America's development was regarded as both a living embodiment of capitalist principles and a conclusive vindication of those principles. This was the period of reputedly unrestrained capitalism because nothing compelled American capitalists to be anything other than unrestrained. America's subsequent economic development allowed it to become an established international power, to fight two world wars and finally to emerge in 1945 as a global colossus exerting vast economic and military influence. By the middle of the century, America had come to see itself as 'the classical country of classical economics'.[11] As the United States reached a position of unprecedented affluence and of international ascendancy, 'God and free enterprise' were recognised as the 'undoubtedly twin pillars of the edifice' of America. Accordingly, 'Americans saw capitalism as everlasting like its God'.[12]

Capitalism in the United States is far more than a set of economic arrangements. It denotes an entire way of life. It is thought to provide a characterisation of American history; to represent the quintessence of America's social nature, and to explain the causes and meanings of America's success and power. In the words of George C. Lodge, it is a 'pervasive, quasi-religious entity which ... has remained unassailably the primary source of legitimacy for our institutions, whether economic, political or social'.[13] Capitalism on this scale is not merely a means to liberty, but the mark and measure of a society's very conception of liberty. As such, capitalism has become a portmanteau term that can assimmilate American principles and conditions in such a way as to make them not merely compatible with, but synonymous with free enterprise. If Calvin Coolidge was right in saying that the 'business of America is business',[14] then it can also be said that the business of business in America has been that of individualism, equality of opportunity, competition, economic progress, limited government, private property, social mobility and personal rights.[15]

The spectacular nature of America's development helped capitalism to be conceived as a comprehensive economic and social system. By the same token, the capitalist system has permitted the United States itself to be seen as a system with a unified basis, a predetermined history and a set of exclusive social dynamics that have precluded even the possibility of alternative courses of economic or political development. The customary manner by which capitalism has been systematically insinuated into American history is through the claim that Locke's conception of property rights became firmly established in American attitudes at the outset of the new world's journey into independence. Locke incorporated individual property rights within his scheme of natural law. Man had a natural right to what he had produced from the land and resources through the mixture of his own labour. Just as a man's body belonged to him, so the result of the work performed by it also belonged to him. The value of his labour, therefore, entitled him to the property produced by it. The individual ownership of property amounted to a basic right to enjoy it and to exclude others from its possession.

It is true that Locke laid down certain provisos and qualifications to this central right which, it has been argued, did not clarify the position so much as generate a series of insoluble problems concerning the individual's relationship with the rest of society.[16] It has also been claimed that Locke's concern for property has been misconstrued in that he did not confine property to external possessions. According to this view, by emphasising that 'man has a property in his own person',[17] Locke wished to underline the proposition that each individual had the proprietorship of universal natural rights in his own possession. Despite the different interpretative constructions and irrespective of Locke's own true position, the fact remains that Locke's philosophy became identified with the rights of personal property and with the ethos of possessive individualism.[18]

What is also certain is that eighteenth-century Americans were very much drawn to Locke. 'Most Americans ... absorbed Locke's work as a kind of political gospel.'[19] His 'ideas formed an important element in the system of thought that exerted so much influence upon the Founding Fathers'.[20] The noteworthy point is that Locke's ideas were a system. They came as a package embracing such powerful themes as liberty, contract, consent, natural rights, revolution, limited government, dispersed authority and private property. To many in the eighteenth century and in the formative years of the American republic, it was property which was the central component of Locke's system and upon which all the other parts were dependent. Through Locke, individual liberty and property ownership came to have the same root. The ideal of individual liberty was defined and secured by the practical attribute of private property. It was because property was seen as being indistinguishable from freedom that James Madison was prepared to acknowledge that government was 'instituted no less for protection of the property than of the persons of individuals'.[21]

To America's burgeoning class of merchants and entrepreneurs as well as its mass of small farmers and self-employed artisans, Locke's philosophy was influential because it conformed to the outlook and opportunities of early America. But it is seen as being more than just a set of supportive ideas, concomitant with an expanding social order. Because Locke's political philosophy was so persuasively rational, so intellectually accessible and so practically relevant to the era of the Founding Fathers, it is widely thought to have been instrumental in setting the United Sates on a course of historical development which led inevitably to *laissez-faire* capitalism, to decentralised government and to a disjunction between economic power and political authority. It is for this reason that 'Lockianism' in America is a byword not for capitalism, but specifically for American capitalism.

The work which has done most to fix Lockian capitalism within the American tradition to the extent of making one seem the fruition of the other is *The Liberal Tradition in America* by Louis Hartz. In this seminal work , Hartz asserts that American history and society can only be understood in terms of a deep and impregnable consensus, which has confined both American conflict and vision to very narrow boundaries. Because America lacked a feudal past, then according to Hartz it possessed a unique social chemistry in that it had neither a real reactionary tradition, nor a true revolutionary tradition. Instead, America was filled by individuals devoted to toleration and freedom within a context of abundant land and opportunities. Class antagonisms and political polarities failed to develop because social conditions had spontaneously produced 'an absolute and irrational attachment'[22] to Lockian ideas. To Hartz, 'the historic ethos of American life, its bourgeois hungers [and] its classlessness'[23] is the living embodiment of Locke and, as such, the entire range of the nation's social relationship is inevitably pervaded by Lockian principles. The result is a consensus centred upon Locke's propertied liberalism – 'for a society which begins with Locke, and ... stays with Locke ... has within it, as it were, a self-completing mechanism which ensures the universality of the liberal idea'.[24]

Hartz subordinates all social tensions to the underlying American unity of bourgeois competition and reverence towards property and capitalist enterprise. 'The magic alchemy of American life ... transform[ed] passive peasants into dynamic liberal farmers, ... proletarians into incipient entrepreneurs.'[25] All aspects of American history and society served only to confirm, to Hartz, the extent of America's extraordinary moral unanimity. The constitutional restraints of the Founding Fathers, for example, had only been able to survive in such dynamic surroundings because of the 'compulsive impact of a single creed'.[26] The unanimity of Lockian liberalism marked the existence of a society with only one estate – thereby ensuring that no one sector would feel permanently frustrated, or discriminated against by the Constitution's checks and balances. America's 'reality of atomistic social freedom'[27] and the 'compulsive power of Locke made ... "success" and "failure" ... the only valid ways of thought'.[28] Hartz portrays America as locked tight within an overwhelming uniformity which Americans cannot transcend and from which they cannot escape. They are trapped by Locke's central value of property aspiration and, accordingly, cannot help but be permanently engaged in the 'relentless running of the Lockian race'.[29]

Since all social conflict is reduced to mere differences of emphasis or technique, Hartz not only precludes the existence of fundamental social dichotomies, but dismisses the possibility of them ever occurring. Major political failures in America have been due to attempts to introduce European ideologies into the United States. Alexander Hamilton's eighteenth-century elitism, the aristocratic pretensions of the early nineteenth-century American Whigs, the feudal reaction of the *ante-bellum* south and the collective programmes of industrial radicalism were automatically doomed as they were simply incompatible with the liberal mainstream of American society. They were hopeless attempts to break the American consensus into artificial fragments and to attach European labels and analysis to the parts. American conditions – especially the lack of an anti-industrial right wing and the absence of a class-conscious peasantry or proletariat – have produced, in Hartz's view, a wholly invincible consensus that excludes any basis for fundamental conflict and, therefore, for any ideological divisiveness.

Hartz has been called the American Marx, not just because he provides a systematic conception of society that depends primarily upon economic forces and relationships, but because he introduces a deterministic quality to the analysis, which endeavours to establish the United States as a society wholly dependent upon its own iron laws of materialistic development. To Hartz, the United States is set upon its own pathway of history which essentially is a combination of economic advance on the one hand, and social and philosophical immobility on the other. Hartz's laws produce an America sustained in a static and timeless world of capitalist harmonies, self-regulating balances and consensus politics. In this way, Hartz is the prince of American exceptionalism. 'In a brilliant analysis of the relationship between social structure and ideology',[30] Hartz provides a coherent social and economic framework that transforms a basic American wish to be seen as different to the rest of the world into a systematic exceptionalism, rendering the United States immune to European categories of analysis and to European lines of development.

For these reasons, it would perhaps be more accurate to see Hartz as America's antidote to Marxism. Instead of class antagonisms and social contradictions, Hartz portrays America's social consensus as being ubiquitous and permanent. The faith in possessive and competitive individualism is so deep that, in America, capitalist principles are seen simply as being self-evident axioms. America's instinctive allegiance to capitalism may well have led to the 'atrophy of the philosophic impulse'[31] but, to Hartz, it ensures the maintenance of American capitalism against all challenges. Furthermore, it is predetermined to prevail for, in Hartz's view, America possesses the unique characteristics which allow capitalism to sustain itself indefinitely.

While it is true that Hartz's thesis can be criticised on several fronts, what is significant about it is the durability of its appeal. It successfully encapsulates America's historical development in terms which can comprehensively accommodate all of the supposed and actual origins of American capitalism into one inevitable social order. Under these terms, everything from the Protestant work ethic to constitutionally limited government, and from American independence to Social Darwinism – together with the pantheon of American principles (e.g. liberty, individualism, democracy, rights, property, competition, equality) – can all be made to seem integral to one another. This is because they can all be embraced by and expressed through capitalism; they can all be assimilated as instrumental in the creation of a singular society uniquely characterised by the capitalist impulse.

Capitalism in this Hartzian guise becomes both the culmination of American conditions and the collective embodiment of American values. Hartz essentially systematises the various strands of American society through the agency of capitalism, which in its turn is changed into a systematic embodiment of the American experience. The actuality of this fusion may be open to question and may even be circular in nature, but this does not detract from the approving reception it has had in the United States, where capitalism has come to be synonymous with the American way, to be an evocation of the American past and to be the essence of American exceptionalism.

Nothing exemplifies more that American public spirit, which prides itself on being exceptional by being exceptionally capitalistic, than the long-running debate on why America has no socialism.[32] This controversy, which has generated an enormous literature, proceeds upon the central premise that the United States has no tradition of socialist politics. It does not even possess a mass-based working-class political party. According to basic Marxist theory, an industrialised society like the United States should, by the universal laws of historical materialism, develop the sort of class antagonisms that would inevitably produce a progressive drive towards socialism. Socialism in this sense is a reaction to, and a development of, advanced capitalism.

Even without the dogmas of Marxist theory, developed capitalist societies have generally been drawn towards an increased consciousness of the disparities of wealth and have generated an impulse, amongst concentrations of industrial workers in particular, to press for greater social equality and, accordingly, for the public ownership and control of major sectors of the economy. The accelerated advance of American capitalism, together with the rapacity of American industrialists, led even Marx himself to believe that the United States might be the first country to undergo a socialist revolution. In 1881, Marx commented that in the United States 'the capitalist economy and the corresponding enslavement of the working class [had] developed more rapidly and shamelessly than in any other country'.[33] And yet apart from some localised and temporary penetrations, the American socialist party and associated groups have continually failed to disturb the edifice of American capitalism.

The reasons offered for what seems like an aberration of world history are legion. They can be divided into two main groups. First are the socio-economic causes; second are the political–constitutional causes.

The socio-economic factors include the frontier, which acted both as a safety valve for propertyless workers and as a continuous drain on the working population of the Eastern cities, with the result that the labour supply remained limited and industrial wages were kept high. The relative affluence and mobility of the American worker compared with his European counterpart was thought to have made him far less receptive to radical politics and far more interested in moving up the ladder of social status in the Horatio Alger tradition.[34] Even amongst those workers who were not so taken with the individualist promises of success, who favoured greater solidarity with one another, found that any collective consciousness stopped at racial, ethnic and religious barriers. The American labour force was notoriously splintered by such animosities, which were marked by divided neighbourhoods and segregated settlements. Divisions were perpetuated at the work-place by Protestant and Catholic discrimination, by factories split into ethnic and racial enclaves and by sternly-defended barriers dividing the skilled from the unskilled workers. As the Irish communities, for example, solidified in their areas with their own customs, schools and churches, so the Jewish communities, for example, did likewise. Neither grouping would be receptive to the idea of joining hands against an abstract economic system in a campaign that might jeopardise their jobs and their opportunities for advancement in a society with little or no provision for social welfare or economic security.[35]

The general belief is that at the very time when a working-class consciousness might have developed in the United States (i.e. 1880-1920), the socialist movement was stillborn because American society offered a mass culture of individual progress and consumption. It also provided a permanent and identifiable black underclass that defused the dissatisfaction of the poor whites and dissuaded them from any egalitarian radicalism that would risk eroding the racial barrier.

The political–constitutional factors lay emphasis on the the United States' traditional attachment to popular sovereignty and to individual rights and liberties. In particular, the extension of the male franchise in the early nineteenth century is thought to have eliminated a major source of social dissent. In European countries it was precisely the lack of political participation through a limited franchise that helped to harden class lines and to give focus to broader-based social and industrial complaints. Because the American worker had already been enfranchised before the onset of full industrialisation and, therefore, prior to the possible emergence of a proletariat, it meant that American workers were denied the stimulus which may have drawn them together and prompted the formation of mass-based, autonomous organisations to serve their collective interests.[36]

Once weakened in this way, it is thought that industrial labour was maintained in its fragmented form by a variety of political and constitutional circumstances. These included an established two-party system that militated against the emergence of a third component; the Populist movement's exacerbation of sectional antipathies between the agrarian West and the industrial North which prompted a generation of northern workers to vote for the Republican party; the divisive effects of interest-group politics and of a governmental structure dedicated to checks and balances; the Constitution's values of limited government, civil liberties and individual rights which were thoroughly analogous to the capitalist dogmas in society at large; the disaggregative effects of the federal structure which meant that 'there was, in effect, no national pattern of law, legitimisation or repression to confirm a socialist critique';[37] and not least the explicit antagonism shown towards left-wing sympathisers and radical groups in the impulsive 'red scares' of the 1920s and 1950s when socialists were openly subjected to intimidation, persecution and social ostracism.[38]

All of these ascribed causes and the differing emphasis given to each of them have generated a considerable volume of scholarly debate.[39] This is not the occasion to appraise the relative merits of the varying arguments. What is important to note is the extraordinary attention given to this theme in American history and the conspicuous satisfaction in what seems to be the incontrovertible condition of 'no socialism'. Most Americans take some pride in the belief that their society has distinguished itself as the bulwark of freedom. According to this general belief, the fact that there is no socialism in the United States is conclusive proof that America is different from other industrialised states. The freedom preserved is defined as freedom *from* socialism and its supposed leviathan of authoritarian state controls and central intervention, of property expropriation, and of redistributed wealth to those with no moral right to it. America's preference for capitalism over socialism serves to exemplify the American antipathy towards the state, which is deep enough to be sustained even when the state purports to embody the collective interests and purposes of the American public.

America's celebration of capitalism as a counterweight to socialism and as a rebuttal of Marxism has undoubtedly contributed towards the civic integration of the United States. Nevertheless, the instinctive identity of Americans as non-socialists raises a number of problematic points that strike at the very heart of American capitalism and of the public's attachment to it. Some of these points relate to general analytical difficulties over socialism. For example, since socialistic attitudes in history have not correlated with any one set of objective economic preconditions, then the 'failure' of American socialism should not perhaps be seen as a deviant case of social development. The affluence and mobility of American workers, therefore, might just as well have led them to socialism as to capitalism.[40] Furthermore, since the motivation to Marxist socialism is recognised to be as much a consequence of feudalism as it is of capitalism, then America's lack of an *ancien régime* may well be more responsible than capitalism for its lack of socialism. This would hardly rank as a refutation of Marxism – it might even be a vindication of it.

But the main point raised by the controversy over American socialism is that it always tends to overlook the possibility of socialist elements and objectives already present in American society. To put it bluntly, it may well be that the main reason for the lack of full socialism in the United States is not that America is fully capitalist, but that it is only partly capitalist, and that the United States possesses several socialist characteristics which make it comparable to other western democratic countries. Any objective examination of the United States reveals a mixed economy and a public sector accounting for 40 per cent of the country's Gross National Product. After the watershed of the Great Depression and President Franklin Roosevelt's reaction to it in the form of the New Deal programme, the United States developed into a positive state with a massive permanent infrastructure of controls, regulations, subsidies, contracts, benefits, entitlements, insurance facilities and loans. Keynesian economics – which assumed that markets were not naturally self-regulating and that they required government intervention to manage the level of demand within the economy – had once been thought to be dangerously subversive. By the end of World War II, the United States had formally accepted

Keynesianism. In the Employment Act of 1946, the federal government was obliged to take all the necessary steps 'to promote maximum employment, production and purchasing power' in the economy. By 1971, even a conservative Republican President felt able to declare that 'I am now a Keynesian in economics', shortly before imposing a sweeping programme of wage, price and rent controls on the American economy.[41]

The growth of, and the acknowledged need for, government expenditures and even deficit financing has led America to an enhanced realisation of the past and especially of the historic role of the state in the rise and development of early American capitalism. Contrary to common reputation, the formative period of American capitalism was not an idyll of pure competition and unbridled enterprise amongst the self-employed. Early entrepreneurs very often acquired their wealth by extracting privileges and subsidies from the governments of the day. Government supported and financed such entrepreneurs through land grants, 'internal improvements' (i.e. roads, canals), tariffs and military and naval protection. It is now accepted that the development towards the regulation of business by government was instigated as much by industry as by social reformers. In order to prevent ruinous competition and to stabilise prices and markets, and even to offset the prospect of more radical measures especially at the state level, business supported federal regulation through such agencies as the Interstate Commerce Commission, the Federal Trade Commission and the Federal Reserve Board.[42]

This partnership between government and business has grown in scale to the point where the two elements are now virtually inseparable from one another. On the other hand, federal regulations have ramified into a profusion of areas (e.g. securities, credit, advertising, the environment, occupational safety, car design, nuclear hazards, drug testing) to such an extent that by the late 1970s, it was estimated that compliance with federal regulations was costing industry over $65 billion per annum.[43] On the other hand, business has direct access to government, possesses a virtual veto on governmental proposals wholly adverse to business interests, and benefits from the government's position of being the largest purchaser of goods and services in the country.[44]

Defence expenditures, for example, amount to $28 million per hour every day. They help to support over 20,000 prime contractors and more than 150,000 subcontractors in the American economy.[45] Even non-defence expenditures on industry are high. When Lee Iacocca of the Chrysler Corporation had to approach the federal government for a $1•5 billion loan guarantee, he initially had to battle with his own capitalist scruples: 'Here I was, a free enterpriser, coming hat in hand and asking for Government involvement when I was against Government involvement and regulation.' Iacocca was quickly educated, and once in Washington he soon learned that loan guarantees were 'as American as apple pie'.[46]

Given the penetration of the state into American society, together with the extent of its welfare and social security arrangements, it has become a plausible proposition to see a form of socialism in the citadel of capitalism. It can be claimed, for instance, that the United States not only has a social democratic tradition similar to that which supports the Labour Party in Britain, but it has a social democratic movement which has been organised within the Democratic Party since the Great Depression.[47] The tradition and the movement have fostered schemes of economic regulation and industrial supervision together with supportive programmes of pensions, unemployment insurance and health care that are comparable to anything produced by Europe's more conspicuous social democratic forces.

Such has been the rate of progressive government intervention and of increased economic and social integration in the United States that George C. Lodge detected in the 1970s that the old ethos of Lockian individualism was breaking down in favour of a greater communitarian spirit. Lodge perceived that the expanded scale of government and industry was inducing a collective outlook in which the rights to membership of this steadily integrating community (i.e. income maintenance, health provision) were superseding traditional property rights in social importance. Moreover, not only was government 'bigger in proportion ... than in those countries we call socialist', but it would inevitably expand 'to embrace the concept of the state as planner'.[48] Lodge's optimism lent weight to an older proposition – namely, the idea that Americanism is after all a kind of substitute socialism[49] and that American capitalism is a socialist form of capitalism because it is based upon a social informality and mobility that is tantamount to an equality greater than that found in the class-bound societies of Europe.[50]

And yet, in spite of the apparent integration of Keynesian economic management, and despite a general consensus on the need for welfare provisions, and a widespread concern that capitalism was in decline as a result of its own economic and ethical contradictions,[51] the late 1970s witnessed a fundamentalist revival in traditional capitalist philosophy. A diverse set of critics and ideas that became known as the 'new right' challenged the notion of a historical progression towards greater state planning and increased social regulation. Economists and social theorists, like Milton Friedman and F. A. Hayek, believed that the modern afflictions of state intervention, bureaucracy, public expenditure, social instability and governmental failure could only be cured by recourse to those axioms of human nature and social advance that were embodied in the free market. The emancipation of the market mechanism was advocated as a fundamentalist panacea that would spontaneously generate economic growth and social benefits whilst respecting individual freedom of action and promoting social stability. The 'new right' sought to confirm to the American public that the state's activities amounted to nothing more than a morass of restrictive and divisive practices. True improvement would only be secured by man being true to himself and to his self-interest. He needed to recognise that real progress came, not from rational and conscious design, but from the unintentional and incidental side-effects of a system geared directly to the forceful reality of human instinct and voluntary behaviour.[52]

In the face of the American economy's evident failures and uncertainties in the 1970s (high inflation, high unemployment, high interest rates and low growth), the new right's accusation – that America's problems were attributable to its deviations from authentic capitalism – revealed the popular appeal of old capitalist dogmas relating to market-place competition, wealth and progress. Just when the United States was arguably in the greatest need of central assistance to revitalise old industries, of central investment in technological innovation and industrial infrastructure, and of central decisions over national priorities,[53] the country elected Ronald Reagan. His public rhetoric was filled with references to market economics, deregulation, reduced taxation, lower social expenditures, balanced budgets, the work ethic, individual incentives and rewards and a 'supply-side' economic boom. Reagan made it clear in his inaugural address that it was 'time to check and reverse the growth of government'.[54] He proposed to get government off the backs of the people with the firm expectation that the entrepreneurial energies within American society would be released to the mutual benefit of all.

The record of 'Reaganomics' in the 1980s was a thoroughly mixed one. For example, it generated a profusion of new jobs; but it also produced towering deficits that transformed the United States into a debtor nation for the first time since 1917. It would be difficult to prove or to disprove the existence of a capitalist renaissance, for the mixture of Reagan's record reflects a deeper paradox that lies at the heart of American capitalism. On the one hand, the 1980s revealed just those sorts of developments that evoked the imagery of an unbridled enterprise culture – namely that of deregulated industries, venture capitalists, tax incentives for the rich, union-busting, decreased benefits for the poor, a growing concentration of corporate power, 'workfare' instead of 'welfare', and a thriving 'black economy'.[55] To many, the style of the period was symbolised by the new 'robber barons' like T. Boone Pickles, the predatory corporate raider, and Ivan Boesky, the notorious financier, whose insider trading practices produced huge fortunes and led Boesky to conclude that 'greed is alright, greed is healthy'.[56]

On the other hand, the 1980s was also characterised by the rise of corporate expenditures on environmental protection and on social enhancement, by the improved quality control and reliability of products, by the growth of company liability for its own goods and services, and by better safety conditions for workers. Development in the 1980s also led to the increased imposition of equal opportunity laws with respect to women and ethnic minorities, to wider share ownership, to a growth in the small business sector, and to the onset of companies like Avis which in 1988 was taken over by its own employees in a 'capitalist form of socialism' and within one year became the most profitable car hire firm in the United States.[57]

It is this diversity in industrial organisation and practice which makes generalisations about American capitalism very difficult. Whether the record of the American economy in the 1980s was due to Reaganomics or even to capitalism, therefore, is open to question. It can be claimed that capitalism has been tried and that it has failed to fulfil its promises. It can also be claimed that it has yet to be properly invoked. But such disputes rapidly become esoteric debates because there are no objective criteria by which it is possible to define the constitution of capitalism. Should it, for example, be seen as a fixed order to which a society could conform if it possessed the political will to do so? Or should it be regarded as an endlessly evolving system of organisation dependent upon assimilating technological and social changes? But then, is the former a mystical chimera, and is the latter merely an empty vessel into which anything can be poured? Should terms like 'welfare capitalism' or 'state capitalism' be regarded as representing authentic derivatives of capitalism, or subversive departures from capitalism, or merely as superficial deviations from capitalism with the ultimate purpose of maintaining the established substructure of ownership and control of profits?

Although there are no final answers to these questions, this does not detract from their significance. And nowhere is this significance greater than in the United States where the debate on the identity of capitalism is at its most intense. This is not only because the variation in the size and nature of free enterprise is greater than anywhere else, but because free enterprise is culturally more important to Americans than to anyone else. As a result, 'the United States is ... one of the few places left in the world where 'capitalism' is generally thought to be an OK word'.[58] No other people are more dependent upon the meaning and value of capitalism for the conception of themselves, their history and their purpose in the world.

As Ronald Reagan's rhetoric demonstrated so dramatically in the 1980s, the appeal to free enterprise was compulsively popular. This was because Reagan was an artist in political communication, and a conservative who knew precisely how to link the capitalist ideal of America's past with the continued availability of those capitalist techniques and principles, by which the country might return to the era of America's youthful rise to ascendancy. It was also because free enterprise was seen as America's own distinctive characteristic and thereby as a system incorporating and embodying such American ideals as liberty, individualism, emancipation, democracy and even equality.

Ten years earlier, President Nixon had tentatively suggested that Americans ought to be proud that their system had produced 'more freedom and more abundance, more widely shared than any system in the history of the world'.[59] In Reagan's free-enterprise culture, there was no hesitation in making the link between capitalist prosperity and freedom a direct and necessary connection.

> If we look to the answer as to why for so many years we achieved so much, prospered as no other people on earth, it was because here in this land we unleashed the energy and individual genius of man to a greater extent than had ever been done before. Freedom and the dignity of the individual have been more available and assured here than in any other place on earth.[60]

Reagan openly recognised the interdependence of capitalist liberties with the wider dimension of political freedom and social advance – 'freedom and incentives unleash the drive and entrepreneurial genius that are the core of human progress'.[61]

Reagan in effect took Hartz and popularised him to the American public as a factual truth and as a normative principle. He used a heroic, and perhaps even mythical, form of nostalgic capitalism and presented it to the American people as their history and, thereby, as a standard to which they could aspire. Capitalism, in Reagan's hands, was a highly suggestive instrument of public consciousness. It was not merely 'a rallying call to take advantage of the genius of our economic system'.[62] It was a medium through which Americans' varied attachments to the past and their several political traditions might be satisfactorily recognised, reconciled and assimilated within a single emotive form. Reagan's abstraction of capitalism into an amorphous, but irresistible, expression of America's historical experience and of its contemporary opportunities was highly effective in its appeal to general American values. Because Reagan's images were 'too high or too deep for ordinary political criticism',[63] he was rewarded with extraordinary warmth and affection. Reagan showed that by impulsive appeals to past visions and old faiths, capitalism could still mobilise Americans into the belief that in an increasingly interdependent world, they still held the key to their own salvation through the autonomy of their economic energies, rather than through any co-operative organisation or governmental direction.

Democracy
AND THE SPECTRE
OF MASS GOVERNMENT

The United States celebrates itself as the one nation truly dedicated to the principles and practices of democracy. Democracy is accepted as a central article in the American faith, and one that is thoroughly compatible with such other articles as liberty, individualism, property and equality. The United States prides itself as being the country of the heroic common man whose sense of rank and history has been so eroded by his displacement to the new world that he is left free from traditional sources of authority. Accordingly, American democracy is often portrayed as a corollary to this type of open-ended freedom which threw large numbers of people into circumstances of literal self-government. Democracy in America, therefore, is commonly conceived to be the natural outgrowth of America's own peculiarly informal and egalitarian conditions in a society much given to the belief that its institutional arrangements are the inevitable and self-evident consequences of its own extraordinary historical and geographical conditions. Against this backdrop, democracy in America has become something of a truism and one that is necessarily derived from the Founding Fathers and their Constitution, which in the succeeding years came to be known as the 'bulwark of American democracy'.[1]

And yet, in the same way that democracy itself is in reality a highly complex phenomenon, so America's association with it is far from being as simple and straightforward as it is so often reputed to be. On the contrary, it is afflicted by all manner of qualifications, tensions and contradictions. In fact it can be said that the United States probably exemplifies, rather than clarifies, the problematic ambiguities endemic in the nature of liberal democracy.

To the extent that it is true to say that American political arrangements and attitudes are derived from the Founding Fathers and their federal Constitution, then it is equally true to say that those gentleman scholars, lawyers and merchants of the eighteenth century bequeathed a distinctive ambivalence over democracy to later generations of Americans. Whilst it would be quite wrong to ascribe a uniform outlook to so varied a group of men, it is true to say that amongst them was a strong element of distrust and even disquiet over the prospect of America developing into a democracy. The Founders' misgivings over democracy were based on the traditional belief that democracy was a social order separate from, and different to, aristocracy and monarchy. Democracy was a component of society and, like the other two components, it was dangerous to allow any one social order to become dominant.

According to classical theory, 'simple governments' were invariably oppressive governments. A preponderance of monarchy would lead to despotism, a preponderance of aristocracy would produce oligarchy and a preponderance of democracy would run into violent anarchy. In order to prevent pure constitutional forms from degenerating into tyranny, classical theorists like Plato, Aristotle and Polybius advocated the incorporation and mixture of the different social orders into government. This arrangement would maximise the virtues of each, while minimising their respective vices. It was Polybius in particular who pushed mixed government to the point where it became a deliberate institutional device to achieve a balance between the three classes of society. In effect, the three social units were to be directly translated into government through separate class-based institutions which would share in the process of government and at the same time promote a genuine mixture of class interests in government.[2]

These Greek- and Roman-based theories were revived by Machiavelli in the early sixteenth century, and from then on they increasingly became the currency of reform and dissent in the political and constitutional turbulence of the seventeenth and eighteenth centuries. The term 'mixed government' suffered from a host of different interpretations supporting a variety of positions and lending legitimacy to a diverse set of social and political developments. It was complicated by the emergence of the 'separation of powers' doctrine which was similar with respect to its emphasis upon the dynamics of interaction, but different in that it depended upon separate institutions geared to abstract governmental functions, instead of on explicitly class-based institutions providing a mixture of social orders. These two doctrines became closely bound up with one another so that the notion of separate governmental functions came to have class connotations, while mixed government's ancient rationale of balance came to characterise the underlying theme of separated institutions.[3]

By the eighteenth century, balance had become the touchstone of constitutional propriety and authority even though it was by no means certain what balanced government consisted of or how it might be achieved and mantained. In only very general terms was the composition of constitutional balance understood and agreed upon. What was sufficiently certain to become dogma was that in one form or another the British constitution's pastiche of powers, branches, institutions and traditions had developed into a stable equilibrium which accounted not only for Britain's national and commercial success, but for the preservation of her subjects' liberties. Writers such as William Blackstone, William Paley, Jean de Lolme, Henry St John Bolingbroke and especially Charles Louis Montesquieu, duly recognised and celebrated the principle of balance in the British constitution. They implied that if the liberties of other peoples were to be made comparable to those of Britain, a balanced constitution similar to that of Britain's would be needed.[4]

The American colonists were part of this British culture and believed their own freedoms to be derived from the British constitution's genius for balance and stability. John Adams, for example, described the British constitution as 'the most perfect combination of human powers in society which finite wisdom has yet contrived and reduced to practice for the preservation of liberty'.[5] This was no empty flattery but representative of a common and genuine conviction. Such was their belief in balanced government that the concept became a key instrument in the colonists' opposition to Britain in the revolutionary crisis. It is clear from the Declaration of Independence that the Americans were challenging Britain on the basis of balanced government by claiming that George III and the

King's party in Parliament had disrupted the equilibrium of the British constitution and, in doing so, had undermined the traditional liberties of the colonists.

Even during the period after independence when the new states were experiencing their initial euphoria over popular sovereignty, legislative supremacy and contractual consent, they were nevertheless unable or unwilling to extricate themselves from the sanctions and prescriptions of balanced government. Confronted with the propect of constructing new frameworks of government, Americans were aware of the need to reconcile the avowed simplicity of their new republicanism with the ambiguity and complexity of balanced government. Their concern for the heritage of equilibrium was reflected in their acute consciousness of the absence of the additional social orders (i.e. aristocracy and monarchy) required to construct a balanced government.[6]

The new state constitutions reflected that tension. They incorporated the radical principles of universal manhood suffrage, majority rule, natural rights, government by consent and a rigid separation of powers which was made thoroughly compatible with the central feature of a dominant legislature. However, the constitutions were also notable for their retention of many of the structural features associated with colonial government. Not the least of these was the principle of bicameralism. In the end, most states followed the dictates of antiquity or the sanctions of the British constitution and established upper chambers, the membership of which usually required some form of additional property qualification.[7] Even if these chambers did not compromise the principle of legislative supremacy, they certainly qualified the principle of majority rule. Furthermore, they facilitated the reintroduction of the old balanced government framework of internal checks and balances. Thomas Jefferson, for example, declared the need for Virginia to have a second chamber made independent in some way from the people. It is true that in two states, Pennsylvania and Virginia, the democratic principle of a single chamber was adhered to, but even here the chief American advocate of unicameralism, Benjamin Franklin, hoped for and trusted in the emergence of a natural aristocracy of public-spirited and virtuous men who would check the factionalism and self-interest of the assembly.

It is clear that the old norm of balanced government still exerted a very strong influence in the reputedly radical period following the War of Independence. Moreover, this influence was to become even stronger, so that by 1787 when the constitutional convention met at Philadelphia, the Founding Fathers regarded the enhancement of constitutional checks and balances as one of their highest priorities. Although the new constitution continued to emphasise the separation of powers as the structural basis to government, the principle's rationale was modified into a system of contending powers more closely related to the old self-regulatory format of mixed government. If Americans in their newly independent states saw 'themselves creating mixed republics, with the democratic element, the lower assemblies playing a very dominant role',[8] then the Founding Fathers' constitution 'was a retreat from the democratic efforts of the states'.[9]

The Founding Fathers were no democrats in the modern sense of the word. After their experiences of the state governments of the 1780s when several assemblies had felt the insurgency of hosts of ill-educated small property owners, many of the founders believed individual liberty to be at bay in the ominous shadow of the restive masses. 'The people it seemed, were as capable of despotism as any prince; public liberty was after all no guarantee of private liberty.'[10] Indeed, in conditions of insurgent democracy, republican liberties were likely to be abused and usurped. Gouvernor Morris warned that the mob had begun to think and reason. 'Poor reptiles! ... They bask in the sun and ere noon they will bite, depend upon it.'[11] Even the sober-minded James Madison had no doubt that pure democracies 'have ever been spectacles of turbulence and contention; have ever been found incompatible with personal security or the rights of property; and have in general been as short in their lives as they have been violent in their deaths'.[12]

And yet, the formal origin and basis of political authority in the new states was clearly founded upon those principles of social contract and popular consent formally expressed in the Declaration of Independence. James Madison summed up the problems confronting the Founders in the following way: 'To secure the public good and the private rights against the danger of a (majority) faction, and at the same time to preserve the spirit and the form of popular government, is then the great object to which our inquiries are directed.'[13] The many Founders who were classicists knew that the new republic would need the restraining hand of an aristocratic elite and the virtue and public spiritedness of America's patrician families. They also knew that there was no chance of formally investing such a social order to perform that stabilising function in an ostensibly egalitarian world. But the many Founders who were also men of the Enlightenment knew that individual liberty was not only the logical precondition and objective of rational government, but was also a universal natural right and, therefore, an iron law of human existence theoretically immune to the mere will and opinions of others. Practice might be made to conform to theory through the judicious application of 'political science' by which the systematic empirical knowledge of government and political forces might be deployed to enable government both 'to control the governed; and in the next place oblige it to control itself'.[14] James Madison relied on what he termed 'auxiliary measures' to keep government in its place by a combination of structural fragmentation, institutional dynamics and formal limitations.

Finally, the Founders were politically adept enough to realise the need for democracy to be acknowledged to the wider public, whilst at the same time confining its effect to the tenets of their own republicanism. Gordon Wood argues convincingly that the Founders and their supporters 'had to work within the egalitarian and populist currents flowing from the revolution'.[15] Accordingly, they employed the language of democracy and rooted all the offices and institutions of the state in 'the people'. Nevertheless, their objective was to limit the potential for democratic indiscipline through sober republicanism. This was to be secured by balanced institutions all ostensibly derived from the people, but whose effect would be to disaggregate democracy, to direct the state's power to that of self-limitation, and to permit the emergence of a natural aristocracy in the guise of democratic leadership.

The more democratically inclined Anti-Federalists were swift to point out the Constitution's equivocations on democracy. Not only was the new government a standing denial of the principle of direct democracy, it also raised doubts over its allegiance even to representative democracy.[16] It did so because it had a relatively small

House of Representatives, and a Senate and Presidency only indirectly elected by the people. It had a second chamber which smacked of aristocracy because its requirements were higher than those for the House of Representatives and because its membership was based upon state sovereignty rather than on population. The Constitution was also noted for having a powerful single executive with full veto powers and institutional independence. Lastly, whatever abbreviated democratic credentials the federal Constitution may have possessed, its status as a central national framework of government and as the 'supreme law of the land' would inevitably amount to a preventative cap upon the activities of local democracy.[17]

If the conditions and status of American democracy were thought to have been left unresolved at the end of the eighteenth century, it was reputedly clarified in favour of mass participation and vigorous democratic rule in the nineteenth century. The stiff republican objections to democracy appeared to have been swept away in a flood of democratisation which brought a steadily increasing rate of enfranchisement, not only because of a general increase in property ownership, but because property qualifications to voting were steadily phased out. By the 1830s most property qualifications to voting had been abolished and, therefore, most white men were able to vote in local, state and national elections.

The 'Jacksonian Revolution' of the 1830s witnessed the full force of such participation. Andrew Jackson, a westerner and certainly no Virginian patrician, won the Presidency and established the 'spoils system' by which a President's supporters were rewarded with offices, thereby rendering the federal government more responsive to changing patterns of public support. Jackson also encouraged the development of the 'long list' which transformed large numbers of state and local offices into elective positions. These changes, together with the popular election of members of the Electoral College, the onset of party conventions and the development of national campaign organisations, appeared to set American politics on a course of democratic progression.[18]

It was during the 1830s that Alexis de Tocqueville toured the United States and wrote his classic description of democracy in America. He was left in no doubt that America had achieved a state of democracy which should provide both a model and a cautionary

tale to other countries. To de Tocqueville, the principle of popular
sovereignty had acquired 'all the practical development which the
imagination could conceive'.[19] In some countries,

> the ruling force is divided, ... But nothing of the kind is to be seen in the
> United States; there society governs itself ... Sometimes the laws are made
> by the people in a body ... and sometimes its representatives chosen by
> universal suffrage, transact business in its name, and almost under its
> immediate control.[20]

Such was the extent of American democracy that de Tocqueville
believed it might constitute a danger, not just of majoritarian
tyranny, but of a mass conformity of opinion. He feared that because
no alternative locus of authority existed in such a democracy,
nothing would be capable of resisting the absolutism and orthodoxy
of democratic opinion.

Charles Dickens was another writer to visit the United States
during the same period. He deplored the vulgarity of democratic life
in America – 'the intrusion of the most pitiful, mean, malicious,
creeping, crawling, sneaking party spirit into all transactions of life
– even with the appointments of physicians to pauper madhouses'.[21]
Dickens had hoped to experience the benefits of an ideal republic
freed from rigid class rule, but America disappointed him. 'The
nation is a body without a head, and the arms and legs are occupied
in quarrelling with the trunk and each other, and exchanging
bruises at random.'[22] Whether the evaluations are those of de
Tocqueville or of Dickens, the stimulus to both of them clearly
seemed to be the fact of democracy's existence in America. The
subtle connotations of mixed government and balanced social
estates that were present at the end of the eighteenth century had
been eroded away by the uninhibited drive towards democracy.[23]

By the 1860s, even the glaring anomaly of slavery and racial
oppression had been satisfactorily resolved by a civil war and a set
of constitutional amendments. Thereafter, the war between the
states became commemorated as both a victory for the American
nation and for American democracy. The two were inseparable from
one another. The Civil War secured the integrity of the United States
and ensured, in Abraham Lincoln's words, that 'government of the
people, by the people, for the people, shall not perish from the
earth'.[24] This climatic reaffirmation of democracy allowed it to

become fixed as a guiding motive of American history and as a central objective of American development.

Ever more democracy always appeared to follow each and every advance in democratic government. Whether it was the Seventeenth Amendment establishing the direct election of senators; or the Progressives' reforms of the initiative, referendum and recall together with the increasing provision of primary elections; or the extension of the suffrage to women through the Nineteenth Amendment – America seemed set on a course of exponential democratic growth. After two world wars and a prolonged cold war in which the United States identified itself as the cradle and citadel of democracy with a mission to make the world 'safe for democracy',[25] America has emerged today with the conviction that it is the supreme democracy.

Democracy not only dominates the language and concepts relating to the nature, origins and purposes of political authority in America, it dominates the visible appearances and tangible arrangements of government. As a consequence, elections in the United states are ubiquitous. There are over 900,000 elective offices in 80,000 units of government. American citizens may be called upon to vote in a profusion of elections at any one time. Moreover,they may also be expected to state their preferences in a number of state and local referenda. Many of these will be 'citizen petitions' put to the voters after having attracted the required number of signatures. In 1988, for example, Arkansas and Michigan approved bans on state-financed abortions, while Californians agreed both to a surcharge on cigarettes to pay for health care and to a 20 per cent reduction in insurance premiums. American voters have so many choices to make that in many constituencies voting machines are provided to facilitate the registration of their many decisions. In some areas of California, the number of elections and propositions is so large, and the queues of voters so long that it has become necessary to impose a time limit of ten minutes for citizens occupying the voting booths!

From these developments, it would appear that the early equivocations over democracy have been abandoned in favour of an uninhibited popular sovereignty in which the supreme and absolute power to govern rests with the people. American democracy has come to be known as a 'bottom-up' democracy – i.e. one built up in authority from a popular base so that government is nothing other than an extension of the people and its authority is drawn from a source which never relinquishes its prerogative of self-rule. In America, the problems of government are seen as the problems of democracy and the traditional solution to such problems has been that of more democracy.

> Most citizens assume that the American political system is consistent with the democratic creed. Indeed, the common view seems to be that our system is not only democratic but perhaps the most perfect expression of democracy that exists anywhere ... To reject the creed is to reject one's society and one's chances of full acceptance in it – in short, to be an outcast ... To reject the democratic creed is in effect to refuse to be an American.[26]

And yet in spite of the evident vigour and inventiveness of American democracy and in spite of the continual allusions to popular sovereignty, America is plagued with self-doubts concerning its democracy. Ironically, it is the United States' chief virtue which is so often described as its chief vice. Americans possess a deep disquiet over their democracy because they feel that it suffers from all manner of flaws, afflictions and even outright failures. To begin with, there is enormous confusion over the composition of American democracy – i.e. not only what American democracy consists of but what it should consist of to be both authentically American and authentically democratic. This leads to a number of differing perspectives as to the type of democracy that is actually present in the United States. American democracy is variously characterised as a liberal democracy, a constitutional democracy, a federal democracy, a national democracy, a representative democracy, a participatory democracy, a popular democracy, a majoritarian democracy and a pluralist democracy. Sometimes the separate properties of these constructions will be compatible with one another. But very often they are not, and at that point conflicts can arise, for example, between the rights of local democracy and the authority of national democracy, or between the force of the majority and the democratic privileges of the minority. Since there are no universally accepted criteria of democracy, there are no ready solutions to these problems. Such conflicts may be the price of an active democracy, but they also detract from the identity and operational integrity of its processes.

Another major problem of American democracy is the belief that it suffers from excess. Critics complain that there is altogether too much democracy. Just as the modern drive towards the democratisation of America's political parties has led to them becoming weaker organisations and less able to act as major intermediaries between citizen and government,[27] so America's constitutional fragmentation leads to a profusion of elective offices with differing tenures, functions, constituencies and objectives. This produces a form of democratic overkill. Instead of the government being constituted and informed by the single beam of a popular mandate in a unified election, it takes on the character of a kaleidoscope, full of colourful activity but possessing very little in the way of coherence and direction.[28]

America's traditional concern for minorities within its democracy is widely thought to have produced a system whose disaggregated structure not only recognises and affords governmental access to minorities, but actively promotes their proliferation in order to prevent the formation of a majority faction that might lead to oppressive and, thereby, undemocratic government.[29] This 'open door' policy to groups in the United States is thought to generate an excessive minority consciousness which leads interests to regard themselves, and to behave, as beleaguered minorities requiring special protection and particularised benefits. The 'silent' or vacuous majority becomes exploited by coercive minorities. This in turn can produce a vicious circle in which more and more groups press for greater and greater sectional benefits from governments that increasingly seek to appease such minorities in order to stay in office. The price of such appeasement, however, is a declining ability on the part of government to make priorities, to manage the economy and to prevent its own fragmentation. According to Samuel Huntington, it was the very vigour of this type of democracy, particularly in the 1960s, that produced a 'democratic distemper' involving the expansion of governmental activity on the one hand and the reduction of governmental authority on the other. By the end of the 1970s, this had led to the paradoxical situation of Americans 'progressively demanding and receiving more benefits from their government and yet having less confidence in their government than they had a decade earlier'.[30]

It is claimed that America is confronted with a legitimacy crisis over democracy itself. It is a crisis in which the democratic credentials of high participation and easy access to government have been seen as being thoroughly self-nullifying in nature. This has produced a condition in which too much democracy has become tantamount to too little. The content of American political debate reflects the strains and contradictions of this position.

It is common to hear anxious American analysts bemoaning the fact that their political system was designed for deadlock and inaction. They point out that the Constitution's checks and balances have a 'formidable grip on government'.[31] These devices have not only 'enfeebled policy'[32] and produced 'an almost total paralysis of political decision-making',[33] but have generated 'an accumulation of unresolved problems and a build-up of public frustration so great that ... millions of Americans now feel that they have lost control of the government'.[34] It has been asserted that in a 'structure that almost guarantees stalemate', it is 'no longer feasible to "form of government" '[35] in the United States. Even a recent President complained that the American people were 'losing ... faith not only in government itself, but in the ability as citizens to serve as the ultimate rulers and shapers of our democracy.'[36]

It is on these grounds that critics and reformers press for the establishment of party government as a way of unlocking and releasing the frustrated majority. In the terminology of Jane Mansbridge, these critics complain that the United States has too much capacity for 'adversary democracy' – featuring the representation of conflicting interests and the breakdown of policy into compartments of group concessions. By the same token, this adversary form of democracy allows too little attention to be directed to the potential for a 'unitary democracy' – featuring a recognition of common or national interests and the making of policy by a consensus, or at least by a large majority.[37] But other commentators do not even discern the presence of such a broad majority, or at least not a frustrated one – perhaps only a dispersed and a tolerant one. Accordingly, they object to the proposal of devices that might unnecessarily encourage the mobilisation of a majority faction which would inevitably endanger the liberties of democratic government.

If it is true that there is a 'democratic creed' in the United States, then it is also true that it can be seen in different ways and used with different motives. It can be differently understood, serve differing objectives, assume different forms and incorporate differing assumptions. For example, it can be claimed that there is not enough democracy in respect to elections and participation, and that if only there were more, then it would lead to the resolution of America's problems. On the other hand, it can be claimed that there is altogether too much electoral democracy in terms of the responsiveness of separate and cross-cutting institutions and procedures, and that this leads to a *de facto* diminution of political democracy by the people and for the people. It is a testament to the centrality of democracy as a self-evident value in American life that so much political argument revolves around how it might be not so much acquired, as refined and completed.

Democracy has remained an object of compulsive attachment on the part of Americans. It has withstood extensive criticism and remains immune to the many calls for radical change. Democracy has retained its central position in America because it has, for the most part, incorporated the acceptable ways and means of public action with the substantive purposes and traditional principles of American society. Studies of democracy often break the subject into these two categories of procedural means and social ends. Democracy can be characterised by reference to the ways in which political decisions can be made attributable to popular choice, or at least to popular participation in the political process. But democracy can also be regarded as a form of government that acts in the interests of the people, or rather the greater number of them.

For example, the nineteenth-century city bosses in one sense represented the absolute corruption of the democratic process by their gerrymandering, ballot-rigging, bribery and fraud. In another sense, however, the bosses provided a rudimentary form of social welfare and public assistance (e.g. food, jobs, schools) that very often represented the only institutional response to the interests of the thousands of newly-arrived immigrants in the slums of eastern cities. Even though a city like New York may have had its formal procedures of democracy utterly subverted by a boss like William Marcy Tweed, it was in the words of one historian 'a working democracy'.[38]

Notwithstanding the experience of the city bosses – or the subsequent public administration movement which sought to reduce the corruption of democracy by reducing the amount of democracy in government – American democracy has always been part of the western tradition. As such, it approximates to that conception of democracy which emphasises the role of popular choice, elections and representative institutions. This type of democracy is often taken to be self-defining and open-ended in that, logically speaking, it can be anything its citizens want it to be and it will go in any direction the processes of public consultation and consent lead it. While there may be an implicit assumption that the general welfare and the national interest will, and should be, maximised through the required procedural arrangements, there are no conscious or formal devices by which to ensure that such ends are achieved. It is the structure and autonomy of the processes themselves which are valued as objectives because they are the collective means to political solutions. The prima-facie view of American democracy is strongly suggestive of precisely this construction of democracy. It is demonstrably and conspicuously activated by a participant political culture of mass political parties, competitive elections, responsive institutions and decisions reached by negotiation and compromise. And yet for a democracy so apparently given over to the freedom of its means, it is peculiarly guided towards certain pre-set directions.

It is no doubt true that, despite appearances to the contrary, no form of democracy is entirely value-free. But with American democracy the disjunction between the openness of its forms and the confinement of its ends is probably greater than in any other democracy. American democracy is open-ended in name only. In reality, it is substantive and end oriented. Its critics argue that it is not only predisposed to certain ends, but that the ends themselves are not particularly democratic in content.[39] It is often claimed, for example, that the United States may have a political democracy, but it does not have a social democracy when the variation in living standards are taken into account. The insinuation is that America's political democracy is quite ephemeral and subsidiary to the vested interests and inequalities of socio-economic forces. This is perhaps too harsh a judgement in a society with institutions and processes sufficiently accessible for major reform to be undertaken, should the political will be present. It is not enough to dismiss the timidity of American democracy as the result of a populace deliberately divided against itself and then mercilessly checked and balanced into immobilisation by institutional trickery. The reasons are more fundamental and they go back to the Founding Fathers' traditional anxieties over governmental power. It will be recalled that

> the founding fathers were never infected by the continental republican belief that a republic, being a people's thing, could be magnified only to the public advantage. They inherited from their British Whig forbears the belief that all state power is mischievous if not severely limited and held in check.[40]

The Founding Fathers proceeded on the assumption that the condition of republican liberty had already been achieved. A wider political community and a stronger political framework were required to ensure its continuation. In defending individual liberties and private property *through* government, it was also essential to defend them *from* government – and especially from democratic government which the Founders believed to be the most likely corruption of republicanism and the one social order most likely to enlarge government to the maximum possible extent. Individual liberty was both the social presupposition and the political objective of the Founding Fathers.

In so far as it was needed, government was there to provide the practical arrangements for preserving the largely negative nature of republican liberties. This conception of the government's role was never abandoned during America's democratic development. It may occasionally have been obscured and even temporarily subdued, but it was never eliminated. And so, despite the appearance of a continuous intensification of American democracy, it has been a democracy informed and conditioned by a fundamental apprehension of government and a fear of the uses to which government can be put. The 'quintessentially American' attitude to democracy is that 'all authority stems from the people and that, therefore, all government is an object of suspicion'.[41] In other words, the American tradition tends to see democracy wholly in terms of the protection of individual rights against collective action ... Democracy begins with the autonomous individual and as we move away from him so democracy progressively degenerates.'[42] As a result, American democracy is today a peculiar hybrid possessing both a vigorous tradition of popular sovereignty and a distinctively anti-statist political culture.

Americans have been quite prepared to base their government upon democratic principles, but their intellectual attachment to the pre-eminence of democratic authority has always been less than complete. They have perhaps been more keenly aware of the problems of democracy to the liberty of the individual than those in the European radical tradition, who used to see democracy as a panacea to existing intolerable conditions. In America, the social potential for unrestrained democracy was perhaps too real and too threatening for the comfort of libertarian artisans, proprietors and small farmers. As a result, the American political tradition has tended to embrace a thorough commitment to the principles and structures of democratic government, while at the same time accommodating this to a genuine resistance to majoritarian rule and to central power in the name of 'the people'.

The force of democracy in America, therefore, can often be seen as more of a negative technique, by which the populace can prevent the misuse of power by politicians and interests. Rather than rationalising the exercise of popular power for community purposes in a positive and coherent way, American democracy can be characterised more by its defensiveness. In spite of the United States' historical attachment to the ethos of 'popular sovereignty',[43] nothing seems to mobilise large numbers of Americans more effectively than opposition to power or a crusade against the state. American equivocations over political developments and American objections to policy, therefore, tend ultimately to be reduced to the question not of 'who rules', but of how much rule there should be. American conditions have produced a democracy which elsewhere has traditionally been a state-building device, but which in America has been supported by a political culture that 'tends to deny that which national sovereignty grants: the existence of a state'.[44] As a consequence, 'while there is an American state, there is no acceptable tradition of one ... for in the tradition of the state lies a tradition alien to the American experience.'[45] There is, in the words of Ralph

Gabriel, 'no Hegelian concept of the state in American thinking'.[46] The state may be necessary but it is still not acceptable – however democratic it may be – for liberty remains to most Americans a condition which is inversely proportional to the physical scale of governmental activity.

The viability and popular acceptability of American democracy rests upon a general approval of the limited functions it performs. It is not enough simply to say that most, if not all, Americans are Hartzian clones who think and act in the same way and, therefore, who consent to a democracy which always moves roughly in the same direction and consistently produces similar results. The practices and ideals of democracy after all have often clashed in American history with the practices and ideals of capitalism. However, it is true to say that American politics have generally been conducted within identifiable parameters which have mostly been congruent with the traditions of limited government and the associated cult of individualised liberties and personalised rights. No doubt it is true that democratic politics in America have been compatible with capitalism, or rather with the traditional conception of competitive capitalism, but this is a long way from saying that American democracy is simply reducible to capitalist motives and purposes.

American democracy is distinctive because it rests upon a social basis that supports the processes and structures of democracy as concomitants of a free society. It is, for example, a rarity in the United States for democracy to be described as the 'unhampered expression and prompt enforcement of public opinion'.[47] By the same token, it is commonplace for American democracy to be defined as a means of widening individual opportunities and redressing individual grievances, through the due process of law and the preservation of such liberties as free speech, free assembly and a free press. The rich potential for massive diversity which exists in the open processes of American democracy is never fulfilled because American attitudes ensure that it will be a democracy directed to the common defence of a set of generally accepted social conditions. It is this social and ideological base which conditions American democracy and translates it into political processes and institutional devices which will be consistent with it.

This base is also the reason why Americans are so extraordinarily tolerant of the Supreme Court's defence of republican liberties, very often in the face of intense local majorities – and why they are so supportive of the modern Presidency's powers and its capacity to transcend lines of constitutional jurisdiction in the service of the national interest. Elsewhere, such entities as the Supreme Court would be dismissed as undemocratic and such activities as those performed by modern Presidents would be severely questioned on grounds of authority and accountability. In the United States of all places, they attract relatively little controversy because in the United States popular sovereignty is not seen as being necessarily defined or expressed in terms of direct popular self-rule or of simple majoritarian power.

Pluralism

AND THE AMERICAN
CONCEPTION OF MARKET POLITICS

In examining the ideas which move Americans, it is evident that the concept of democracy poses several serious problems. It is true that surveys of American opinion will almost invariably reveal a level of 90 per cent support for the proposition that democracy is the best form of government, that public officials should be elected by a majority vote, that minorities should be free to contest majority decisions and that every citizen should have equal opportunity to influence government policy. And yet it is also true that huge numbers of Americans do not vote, do not participate in the political process and have less than liberal attitudes when democratic principles of tolerance come to be applied to concrete political situations. Moreover, the general conception of American politics seems to be less related to democratic structures, mass opinion and public choice, and more associated with interest-group bargaining and with competitions between different sets of leaders for the public's acquiescence in policy.

To be more specific, if democracy is one of America's chief motivating ideals, then it is true to say that, in terms of voting, democracy no longer appears to motivate Americans in the way it used to in the past. In the second half of the nineteenth century, it was common for over 75 per cent of the electorate to turn out to vote in Presidential elections. In the 1970s and 1980s, the figure has normally been in the region of 55 per cent. Because '45% [of the electorate] are more or less habitual non-voters', Walter Dean Burnham is prompted to 'assert that the shift toward voting abstention since 1960 is by far the largest mass movement of our time'.[1] In a classic study of political participation in America, Sidney Verba and Norman Nie concluded that one-fifth of the American population (22 per cent) is completely inactive and that 40 per cent either do not participate in politics at all, or limit their participation to voting.[2]

Democratic attitudes of tolerance and of minority rights also serve to throw America's democratic credentials into doubt. According to several surveys, four out of five people would limit voting to tax-payers, half would limit voting to those who were properly informed of the issues, and a majority would not allow a public speech for a communist.[3] Well over half (58 per cent) of the general electorate believe that 'the main trouble with democracy is that most people don't know what's best for them'; a majority believe that 'it will always be necessary to have a few strong, able people actually running everything'; and one in four agrees that 'the majority has the right to abolish minorities if it wants to' and 'that there are times when it almost seems better for people to take the law into their own hands rather than wait for the machinery of government to act'.[4] Even though there are signs that certain expressions of intolerance have declined in incidence over recent years (e.g. over racial segregation, women's rights and anti-semitism), the public's com-mitment to protect the rights of dissent and of democratic opposition remain open to question.[5]

Given the lack of political activity amongst the public at large and the public's innermost ambivalence towards some of the integral arrangements and processes of democracy – and given the evident weakness of America's political parties as effective intermediaries between the citizenry and the government, and the increasingly distant, anonymous and unaccountable nature of much of gov-ernmental activity – then it follows that American democracy has been regularly subjected to waves of critical enquiry. This sort of criticism has amounted to an empirical challenge to democracy in the United States and even, by extension, to the feasibility of democracy in general. The response has been similarly empirical in character. It has produced a revised conception of democracy in the United States based upon actual American conditions and experi-ences, and serving the functional objective of maximising the democratic consequences of the political process without dwelling unduly upon the merits of the formal procedures. This reformulation of democracy in the image of American circumstances is called pluralism or pluralist democracy. It integrates what appears to move most Americans most of the time in politics with a construction of democratic activity and objectives that has become part of the American mainstream.

Pluralism is a broad and notoriously diffuse term, but in this particular context, it is used to refer to a conception of politics and government which views society as a collection of distinct, yet interrelated and interacting parts. The constituent units amount to an amalgam of interests. Interests may compete and conflict with one another. They may, on the other hand, simply transcend one another. But together, they have a cultural identity and share an agreed form of social conduct through which they achieve a state of co-existence. To the pluralist, these social units do not add up to an integrated and corporate whole. Neither do they accumulate to form a stratified social and political hierarchy. The value of such units lies in their provision of social and political diversity which prevents any aggregation of interests developing into a permanent form of class dominion. The pluralist conception of society, therefore, sees a vast profusion of group interests represented and embodied by political groups, none of which has the power to prevail over the rest. Because they are obliged to accommodate one another by extensive negotiations, it ensures that no one centre of sovereign power can emerge.[6]

There is plenty of prima-facie evidence to support the proposition that American society is pluralist in nature. American politics, for example, is replete with group activity of every sort. Groups gravitate towards government in the firm belief that they have the right to exert whatever force they can command in order to further the interests of those whom they represent. Political groups take advantage of the large numbers of access points in the American checks and balances system. Operating as groups and pursuing group interests, they can penetrate deep into government without having to aggregate themselves into a broader party organisation, in order to stand a chance of participating in political decision-making. Some groups like the Farm Bureau Federation have acquired such penetration into government that they have become a *de facto* part of it. Government now relies on groups like this for information, consultation and for the prior clearance of policies.

It is in the United States Congress, however, and especially in Congress's legendary committee system that American group politics can be seen at its greatest intensity. The division of Congress into two chambers, its further division into different processes (e.g. investigative authority, appropriation, budgeting) and its division yet again into a honeycomb of over 300 specialised committees and sub-committees provide the perfect environment to encourage and to receive pluralist politics. Group representatives, including over 15,000 professional lobbyists, fill the corridors of Congress, each maximising the technical merits and political significance of their respective positions in the law-making process. Every species of group and every type of group behaviour is on show. Business groups, consumer groups, trade associations, labour unions, professional associations, environmentalists, racial, ethnic and religious groups, reform lobbies and conservative committees generate a never-ending supply of friction and a never-ending need to compromise. It is a working maxim in Washington that everyone has a group and, as such, no interest remains unserved. There is even a Virgin Islands Gift Shop Owners' Association.

With the advent of 'political action committees', groups can now assume many of the roles once performed by political parties. 'Political action committees' provide candidates not only with electoral funds, but also with campaign management and media resources.[7] Such is the profusion of groups and the ferocity of the politics between them that even government departments and agencies must lobby for their programmes and budgets to the extent that they become indistinguishable from the other group interests. The presence of group politics in Washington, therefore, is endemic. Its prevalence once prompted even President Jimmy Carter to give a televised address to the American nation on this very topic. In it, he claimed that

> You see a Congress twisted and pulled in every direction by hundreds of well-financed and powerful special interests. You see every extreme position defended to the last vote, almost to the last breath by one unyielding group or another. You often see a balanced and a fair approach that demands sacrifice, a little sacrifice from everyone, abandoned like an orphan without support and without friends.[8]

Ostensibly at least, there does exist a good deal of evidence which suggests that the structure and style of American politics conforms to the pluralists' description of an interplay of groups. Observing Congressional committees in action can even lend a tangible quality to the impression. To this extent, pluralism can convey a sense of the prominence of political groups in American public life. From an early stage, Americans are encouraged to see themselves, and to act, as one of a group or set of groups.[9] Even as early as the 1830s, de Tocqueville observed that 'Americans of all ages, all conditions and all dispositions constantly form associations'.[10] The political system with its cellular compartments of power acknowledges, receives and gives access to minorities as minorities. Citizens are everywhere encouraged not merely to categorise themselves as one of a group or a composite of several groups, but to support the interests of such groups with uninhibited civic enthusiasm. This is reflected by the fact that in Presidential election campaigns, it is common practice for contenders and candidates to set up separate campaign committees to target and to negotiate the support of such groups as businessmen, farmers, labour unions, blacks, Hispanics, women and senior citizens.

In this repect, pluralism can provide a general characterisation of American politics and government. It recognises the heterogeneity of American society with its multiplicity of social, ethnic and religious cleavages. It combines the evident profusion of political groups and a citizenry actively engaged in associational life with the clear evidence of a decentralised political system requiring extensive inter-group consultation and negotiation to reach any agreement over policy. As a result, 'decisions are made by endless bargaining; perhaps in no other national political system in the world is bargaining so basic a component of the political process'.[11]

Pluralism is not confined, however, to being merely a descriptive summary of American politics. It also ranks as a comprehensive system of cause and effect which serves to account for all the relationships and processes between society and government. Pluralism, therefore, does not simply propound the existence of interest groups engaged in political decision-making. It assumes the property of a general law of political existence by presupposing that all the constituent elements of political activity are ultimately reducible to the base units of group interests, group motivations and group demands. Bargaining is not just a distinguishing characteristic. It represents an elemental feature of political accommodation and, as such, is *always* present in policy making because all interests are thought to exert a force through the mere iact of their physical presence in the process.

According to Robert Dahl, 'a central guiding thread of American constitutional development has been the evolution of a political system in which all the active and legitimate groups in the population can make themselves heard at some crucial stage in the process of decision'.[12] The end product of such a mechanistic conception of politics is the belief that whatever emerges from the process is, by definition, an expression of an equilibrium acquired through the autonomous dynamics of group interests and group power. Instead of being simply a form of political accommodation, therefore, pluralism in this classical form is tantamount to a sovereign self-regulatory system of political benefit, in the same way that a capitalist market supposedly leads to an automatic equilibrium of economic benefit between parties based upon their market advantages and disadvantages.

The preconditions and corollaries of this conception are many and varied. The pluralist position on power, for example, is that it is dispersed in accordance with the diversification of interest groups and their different political resources. There may be inequalities between such resources but they do not accumulate into one permanent, self-perpetuating inequality between any given sectors of society. Economic power does not necessarily translate into either social or political power. There is no self-conscious and cohesive elite at the commanding heights of society. Instead, the inequalities are dispersed throughout American society. While it is true that some groups will have better opportunities, resources and organisational skills with which to compete for political commodities, it is just as true that other less advantaged groups will have alternative sources of political force (e.g. voting strength, publicity, the withdrawal of labour or political support) that they can deploy against their notional superiors. The result is claimed to be an open competition for government which is fairer than other systems of rule and which constitutes a highly responsive form of government, where power is never still, but always at the mercy of ceaseless bargaining and of constantly-changing coalitions of attentive minorities.

Such a view of the nature and origins of political life exerts substantial pressure on the integrity of democratic terms like majority rule, popular consent, the public interest and an electoral mandate. Majority rule becomes a misnomer for rule by minorities, while popular consent is converted into either a nonsensical myth or a basic agreement on the rules of engagement for group conflict. The public interest loses much of its meaning because in an environment of competitive group interests it becomes difficult to conceive of a set of overriding interests that would attract the support of the entire public.[13] As for an electoral mandate, the pluralist vision sees politics as a permanent election in which interests are continually vying with one another in order to maximise their resources in the political market-place.

It is the notion of the state itself, however, which is the heaviest casualty. The pluralist emphasis upon group interests as the engine-room of politics tends to transform the government's role into one of being merely a broker between conflicting group demands. In the pluralist framework, government institutions become the medium through which group interests negotiate and arrive at accommodations with one another. The government is the arena within which the market-place is situated. As such, the government embodies the 'rules of the game'. It regulates the market place, in order that it should retain and even extend its efficiency in the exchange of power and influence. As a result, the state is not only fragmented in terms of its structure and sovereignty, but it possesses no authority independent of the groups that inhabit its interior. The state becomes little more than the political system: a neutral balance of social demands. The only legitimate source of sovereignty remains with the people, but in the pluralist vision, the people can never translate that sovereignty into government because they are con-genitally fragmented into so many minorities that even a unified majority, acting on behalf of the people, would be impossible to form. As a result, sovereignty which rests – however notionally – with 'the people' is never conclusively mobilised or channelled into direct or positive representational authority at the governmental level.

The pluralist view of American politics continues to arouse fierce controversy in the United States. The principal objections to it come in two main forms.

First, are those critics who simply do not like the pluralists' construction of democracy. They believe that pluralists are guilty of redefining democracy to fit the contemporary conditions experienced by pluralist analysis. They also believe that pluralists impose an artificial continuity on the development of American democracy, by seeking to establish present-day conditions as the culmination of an evolutionary process oriented towards group politics.[14]

It is true that in Federalist Paper Number 10, James Madison did make a number of allusions to groups and to their potential for conflict as an instrument in the management of political power. Madison was prepared to acknowledge that 'the latent causes of faction' were 'sown in the nature of man' and that mankind had a 'propensity ... to fall into mutual animosities'.[15] 'The regulation of these various and interfering interests forms the principal task of modern legislation and involves the spirit of party and faction in the necessary and ordinary operations of government.'[16] Madison's solutions to the inescapable problems of group factions in a free republic was to establish a system of representative government to damp down their worst excesses, and to enlarge the potential for the mutual control of the groups by each other. By enlarging the republic, Madison believed that it would make American freedom more secure because it would reduce the likelihood of a majority faction ever taking form.

> Extend the sphere and you take in a greater variety of parties and interests; you make it less probable that a majority of the whole will have a common motive to invade the rights of other citizens; or if such a common motive exists, it will be more difficult for all who feel it to discover their own strength and to act in unison with each other ... it may be remarked that, where there is a consciousness of unjust or dishonourable purposes, communication is always checked by distrust in proportion to the number whose concurrence is necessary.[17]

The implication of this point is that Madison was prepared to forego the prospect of majority government in preference to a system which would openly rely instead upon minority politics, in a system formally designed to produce a form of reciprocal restraint between active groups. In this respect, the chief architect of the United States Constitution would appear to be giving his imprimatur to pluralism and to be establishing the foundation upon which twentieth-century pluralist politics would emerge in its finished form. 'The pluralist characterisation ... thus has a long and respectable intellectual history.' Beginning with the Founding Fathers and 'carried into effect by the provision of the document they produced, it is little wonder that this image should have such ideological power by now, or that it should be effective in shaping the American political style'.[18]

Critics of pluralism complain that Madison's statements have been misunderstood. His remarks are said to amount only to a set of partial recommendations, prescriptions and even hopes. They were not part of some comprehensive theory of political activity or the description of an iron law of political experience. Accordingly, it is quite misleading to try to substantiate modern conclusions with false notions of the Founders' original intentions.[19]

Other critics believe that the pluralists' view undermines the 'classical conception of democracy'. There has been a good deal of confusion over what this term means and whether it has any validity in modern political theory. Nevertheless, the term is used to condemn pluralism's brand of bloodless and impersonal democracy in favour of a democracy with a greater ethical and moral content. 'Classical democracy' is portrayed as a model democracy in which individuals are obliged to assume the responsibility of active citizens fully engaged in widespread political participation. The sort of civic involvement propounded by political thinkers like Jean-Jacques Rousseau, John Stuart Mill and A. D. Lindsay would amount to a constant educative process for the citizenry and one in which virtue and moral development would thrive. Pluralist democracy, by contrast, stresses the functional value of positive allegiance and the unnecessary nature of mass participation. In doing so, it is said to undermine and devalue the idea of democracy as an objective in citizenship and human fulfilment, and to replace it with a largely value-free conception of democracy[20] – i.e. one in which it becomes merely a governmental process for arriving at decisions with a minimum of popular participation.[21]

By way of reply, pluralists argue that their form of democracy is the only feasible expression of democratic rule which is available in a large and advanced society. It is said that pluralism simply extends liberal democracy from the scale of the individual to that of the group and that it optimises America's democratic norms in an age of large organisations and bureaucratic centralism.[22] Competition among social groups for advantages in the fragmented system of government helps to maintain the dispersal of power in the government and, thereby, perpetuates the competitiveness for positions and benefits. A government of multiple and interacting minorities is seen by pluralists as providing not only an enhanced form of representation, but an assured means of preserving the democratic character of the regime.

The second group of objections come from those who believe that the pluralist vision of American politics is quite simply false. Although pluralists take pride in believing their conception of public life to be based firmly upon empirical investigation, it is precisely according to this criterion that they are criticised most by those who claim that the pluralists have misunderstood the evidence. The alternative view centres upon a belief in a much more monolithic view of society. According to this perspective, society is basically divided, firstly into elites who possess power, wealth and privilege, and secondly into an undifferentiated mass which is increasingly susceptible to the manipulation and control of ever-more centralised and insulated organisations.

Elitists do not see society as a set of atomised groups. They see society as dominated by centripetal forces, large organisations and integrated networks of direction. The true basis of society is claimed to be a solid bedrock of concentrated wealth, corporate power and monopoly capitalism. The pluralists, therefore, are accused not only of being taken in by the appearances of diversity and competition, but of ignoring the modern tide of centralised power and of helping to perpetuate the myth of a multiplicity of ruling groups.

The most celebrated and scathing assault upon the pluralist position comes in *The Power Elite* by C. Wright Mills.[23] Mills asserts the existence of a power elite in the United States based upon modern institutional dynamics. As national power has become increasingly centralised, it has become increasingly institutionalised, with the result that power has become monopolised by the leaders of the three fundamental institutions of American society – namely the economic sector, the political sector and the military sector. The occupants of these three hierarchies occupy the 'pivotal positions' of American society and 'have most of what there is to have'.[24] Due to the similarity of their status and the close affinity they have with one another by way of background, education, marriage and family connections, the leaders of these three separate institutions collectively constitute an interlocking power elite. While Mills does not claim that the elite decides upon everything, he does assert that the course of important national and international affairs usually rests upon the decisions of these identifiable cliques. He describes them as 'those who decide whatever is decided of major consequence'.[25]

Mills agrees with the pluralists that small groups are important components of a democratic society. The problem from Mills' point of view is that they no longer exist or, at least, not in sufficient numbers to make pluralism a viable theory of modern American society. Pluralism and its dynamics is only relevant to the middle levels of society.[26] This level of small property owners, consumers, wage-earners and white-collar workers – a level traditionally epitomised by the professional party politician – is the only sector in which the old theory of social equilibrium still operates. What Mills calls 'romantic pluralism', by which groups interact with one another through the checks and balances of the legislative process, occurs only at this middle level.[27]

The dynamics of the middle level do not influence the power elite. The trend is all the time away from such traditional devices of reciprocal control. The rise of the bureaucratic state and the corresponding decline of legislative politics and the party politician bears witness to the withering away of pluralism at the top, where it matters most. To Mills, any attempt to apply pluralistic theories to the economic, political and military command posts of society serves only to obscure the real power structure in a masquerade of fiction. C. W. Mills' book spawned a whole genre of critical studies of American society. Many were far less inhibited in their open dependence upon the established sociology of elites (cf. Gaetano Mosca, Vilfredo Pareto, Robert Michels, Joseph Schumpeter) and in the rise of explicitly Marxist categories, in the effort to identify and to measure the effects of what was taken to be America's governing elite or ruling class.[28] The ensuing debate between pluralists and elitists has been one of the most intense controversies in American political science over the last thirty years. It has aroused fierce disputes over the comparative methodologies, over the relative merits of criteria of empirical validity, and over the ideological basis of operational assumptions and definitions.

While pluralists, for example, have laid great emphasis on studying how decisions are actually made, elitists complain that this is too one-dimensional an approach. It is said to ignore the role of dominant ideologies, corporate realities, structural constraints, objective interests and social consciousness in conditioning the nature of the issues requiring decisions.[29] Robert Dahl's view, for example, is that differences in the objective interests of separate parties to an issue can only be demonstrated by actual disagreement. Elitist critics object that this view obscures the fact that popular consent can be managed through an opinion structure geared only to provide acquiescence. The mainstream ideology that rationalises private property, capitalism, individualism and material acquisition is seen not so much as a declaration of widespread values, but as an instrument to preserve the status quo and the position of the classes occupying the commanding heights of American society.

Although the central pluralist position is to deny the existence – or at least proof of the existence – of an integrated elite, pluralists have, nevertheless, adapted their perspective to incorporate the evident disparities of power and influence between those at the senior levels of organisations and the masses which are purportedly served by them. Pluralists concede that there are elites: not one or a few elites, but many of them. They head responsive and open-ended organisations in which personnel can rise and fall, ideas can circulate, and opinions can be brought to bear at the top. Each elite, therefore, is a democratic expression of the people and interests within its organisation. Instead of taking elites as proof of a horizontal integration of hierarchies, the 'democratic-elitist', or 'polyarchical' position is to see elites in their vertical context of separate and competitive democratic organisations.[30] It is these multiple elites which are said to secure the liberal nature of the regime and to make the potentially dangerous disruption from illiberal mass participation less of a threat to the political equilibrium.[31]

Pluralism's detractors remain unimpressed and claim that 'polyarchy' amounts to an inversion of classical democratic theory because the 'masses not elites, become the potential threat to the system and elites, not masses, become its defender'.[32] The conjunction of democracy with elitism strips away any remaining pretence that pluralists may have had towards democracy.

> The political passivity of the great majority of the people is not regarded as an element of democratic malfunctioning, but, on the contrary, as a necessary condition for allowing the creative functioning of the elite ... While embracing liberation it rejects, in effect, the major tenet of classical democratic theory – belief and confidence in the people.[33]

Criticism of even the revised forms of pluralism continues unabated, fired, as it is, by the belief that pluralism is so closely analogous to the traditionally liberal objectives of the contemporary equilibrium, that it cannot assimilate the unpredictable and assertive character of the public will.

This debate between pluralists and elitists is significant in several respects, but one of the most outstanding features of it is the intensity with which it is conducted. This is largely because in American culture such central ideals as liberty and democracy are presupposed to exist as achieved objectives by virtue of the generative properties of American conditions. This means that empirical theory has tended to have a higher priority than normative political theory. The questions which are raised come to revolve around issues like the ways in which, and the extent to which, democracy, for example, can be said to exist in the United States. The objective is to elucidate what is already there against a background of popular expectation that social reality should – and will – correspond to the democratic ideal in one form or another.

Given America's asserted affinity with liberty and democracy, the controversy over pluralism and elitism has an added significance. The debates are conducted with a sensitivity, and even gravity, appropriate to a greatly extended realm of meaning. This is due to the belief that the empirical and behavioural assessment of America's liberal and democratic credentials may well determine the very feasibility of such ideals elsewhere. If the existence of democracy, for example, can be disproved in the United States, especially in conditions thought uniquely to favour its presence – then the sombre conclusion must be that it is a doubtful objective in any conditions and perhaps even something of a lost cause. Moreover, it is precisely because the physical reality of democracy is regarded as so important in the United States that the potential for damaging criticism is so great. In a country which tends to believe that its social features and political arrangements represent a material bequest from a past designed to ensure the country's modern democratic credentials, any attempt to tamper with the meaning of the present jeopardises the democratic integrity of the past – and in so doing, further undermines the democratic properties of the present.

Whether by conscious design or not, the pluralist vision succeeded in protecting the authority of both the past and the present by portraying American politics in terms of a continuous and autonomous equilibrium, geared to public order, limited government and political stability. The pluralists were also able to rationalise the regime without the appearance of resorting to ideology. This made its appeal all the more potent in a society with an avowedly non-ideological outlook and with a deep attachment to the idea of spontaneous historical and social forces.

It was the elitists, in particular, who sought to show that the pluralists' empiricism dovetailed into normative prescription. Their position was said to be ideological in content and motive. The elitists tried to demonstrate that there are no value-free definitions of democracy and that there are no non-ideological theories of history and society. Even the pluralists' attempts to be purely empirical were considered to be fundamentally suspicious, not only because it could be construed as an attempt to disguise a dominant ideology in the sheep's clothing of mere social dynamics, but because, as empiricists, pluralists would inevitably come to approve of what they took to be a working physical truth. This satisfaction would make them even less likely to cast doubts over their own objectivity in arriving at such an explanatory framework in the first place.

It can be said that the elitists have won a number of the intellectual arguments in the debate – certainly enough for a leading figure like Robert Dahl to shift his position and become considerably less assured of America's democratic properties than he was in his early writings.[34] But while it is true that pluralism has been subjected to intense analytical criticism,[35] this does not mean it has lost its broad appeal. 'Relatively few political and social theorists would accept it in unmodified form today, though many politicians, journalists and others in the mass media still appear to do so.'[36] This is the crux of the matter, for while pluralism may well have been seriously compromised in respect of its own analytical categories, it has retained that rapport with America's prevailing political culture which gave it its early and immediate appeal.

Despite the intellectual challenges, pluralism has remained the predominant conception of American politics. It is far from being the only conception, but it does portray American political activity in a way that is not only amenable to American principles, but readily familiar with the common-sense experience of the outward forms of American political life. In some respects, it can be said that pluralism is now a more convincing characterisation of American politics than it was in the 1950s when many of the pluralist accounts were first written. Blacks, women, environmentalists and consumers, for example, were not conspicuous participants in the pressure-group politics of the time. Today, they are prominent in the political disputes of the nation. They are part of a new pattern of group politics which, with the decline in the organisational cohesion of American parties, have led to the rise of highly organised 'single-issue groups'. These bodies move group conflict directly back to the public through their strategy of creating pressure by mobilising large numbers of people to vote in elections on the basis of a high-profile issue like school prayer or abortion.[37]

New and powerfully-organised groups have also arisen to contest the power of business interests. These 'public interest' groups, like the Ralph Nader organisation, claim that their objective is to make the political system more genuinely pluralist in character. They seek to achieve this by encouraging greater citizen-participation in industrial policy, by establishing greater public accountability in the corporate sector, and by ensuring a countervailing force to the power of business. These groups became so successful in the 1970s that industrial interests were forced to organise counter-measures against the wave of increased governmental regulation.[38]

In the final analysis, the status of pluralism as a quintessentially American view of politics rests not just upon its intellectual accessibility or its factual persuasiveness, but upon those characteristics which make Americans exceptionally susceptible to its appeal. These would include its ambivalence over the state, the priority given to social and economic forces over political institutions and the faith in a self-regulatory form of political stability and social justice provided by the interplay of group interests. It is often said that political thinking in the United States tends to be drawn directly from its economic thinking . Pluralism appears to bear out this old maxim to the fullest extent. Pluralism's assumptions of an 'invisible hand' guiding group conflict towards the unintended social benefits of market dynamics has the closest of connotations with the principles of capitalism. In a society lacking any strongly-supported alternative conceptions of social justice – especially those requiring concerted state action or strongly redistributive policies – the pluralist vision, even if only by default, has always been tailor-made to American dispositions.

> The pluralist solution is ... a descriptive term for the way in which American government is structured to cope with ... problems (e.g. majority rule versus minority rights, the problem of concentration of power and the problem of faction) and is, further, a set of value statements expressing the preferred American approach to such issues.[39]

What this preferred approach amounts to and what pluralism justifies is essentially a way of dealing with problems by ignoring them – i.e. by assigning them to the spontaneous benevolence of freely interacting interests. The subsequent licence afforded to group aggression regularly produces a prodigious amount of politics and a strong belief in the efficacy of politics. What it does not provide for in any great measure is the means of conscious change and adaptation. It is this inclination to define political problems in terms of group solutions – together with the tendency to derogate the role of any external and active agency in the process of political accommodation and to diminish the legitimacy of such guiding principles as the public interest and the general welfare – which subjects those advocating serious reform to the severest of problems.

6

Liberalism

AND THE APPEAL
FOR REASONABLE REFORM

It is entirely appropriate that American liberals should suffer from a lack of identity in a country whose prevailing ideology is that of liberalism. Liberalism in this latter context is a generic term used to denote America's historical and cultural attachment to such principles as liberty, democracy, the rule of law, individualism, progress, political equality and limited government. These principles have traditionally been seen as both a source of historical inspiration and an affirmation of social fact. Liberal optimism in reason and in the emancipation of a natural and self-sustaining order of freely-moving interests have legitimised the principles of both a free-market economy of private property and a pluralist system of political competition. So entrenched are these principles and values in American society that they risk becoming conventional to the point of being axiomatic formalities, immune to changing circumstances and conditions and, ultimately, jeopardising the very existence of a liberal society.

Those who are termed liberals and that which is known as liberalism in this contemporary context refer to those individuals and to that spirit which regards the old liberalism of self-regulating equilibrium as complacent, myopic and conservative in effect. Modern American liberals believe that traditional American values and procedures are sound; nevertheless, these values and procedures have become so overgrown with the effects of vested interests and philosophical atrophy that they are in danger not only of generating a damaging state of public disillusionment, but also of validating, in the image of freedom, social conditions which embody objectives quite contrary to those of the original founders of American liberty. Modern liberals are reformers who believe that conventional American thought on capitalism and pluralism serves to deny the critical and emancipatory roots of old liberalism and to prevent the adaptation of liberal principles to the changed conditions of modern society.

Liberal reform comes from the impulse to dissent from the inequities of the political and social order, from the aggregations of privilege, power and wealth, from the limits placed upon individual opportunities and from the racial, ethnic, regional and economic divisions that afflict society. Liberal reformers seek not the repudiation of American values, so much as their full realisation. Contemporary capitalist–pluralist society is seen as failing to live up to its avowed values of freedom, opportunity, democracy, progress and equality. It is even seen as directly militating against such objectives and as imposing a closed order of vested interests and explanations, in the name of openness, upon a rapidly receding open society. Furthermore, this traditional liberal society cannot transcend its own limitations without the external stimulus, or conscious agency, of governmental direction. The autonomous processes of capitalism and pluralism cannot generate of their own accord the necessarily strategic perspective by which purposeful change can be planned and achieved. This is not least because the very autonomy of the established economic and political processes is widely regarded to be one of the chief virtues of those self-same processes.

Reform liberals believe that the American political system is designed to leave problems in an unresolved state. The pluralist outlook is one which regards democracy as simply a process of conflict management by which the competing demands of group interests produce amoral accommodations. These partial solutions amongst private interests are, to reformers, merely superficial measures which reflect the imbalance of power in American society and perpetuate the spiral of conditions that is responsible for the permanency and depth of America's social problems.

It is the very proficiency of the liberals' critical faculties and diagnostic skills which throws into relief their plight of being reformers in a society that tends to see itself as already libertarian in character. As reformers rather than radicals, and as realists intent upon avoiding the fate of American socialists, liberals do not step outside the political and economic system, so much as step back from it. They remain in the liberal mainstream through their attachment to civil liberties, reason, individual opportunities, private property and even pluralist democracy. Their drive to open up the processes of government, to increase participation, to restore the balance in a capitalist economy, and to remove injustices in favour of a more substantial equality within society is tempered by the need to work within and through the prevailing system, and by the need to contend with the profound equivocation that has traditionally surrounded American dissent and reform.

In studying the ideas that move Americans, it is clear that America possesses a tradition of political criticism and reform. But it is equally clear that this reform tradition reveals an extraordinary diversity in the usage of ideas both in the mobilisation of dissent and in the acquisition of solutions. Nothing better demonstrates the ambivalence that lies behind the motivations, intentions and ideas of the reformers than the nature of America's major reform movements – namely the Populist Party, the Progressive Movement and Franklin Roosevelt's New Deal.

The Populists rose to prominence in the 1890s, by which time the United States had been conclusively transformed from a rurally-based agrarian order to that of an intensively industrialised society. In a very short period of time the United States had undergone a series of convulsive changes in its social nature. The aftermath of the Civil War coincided with an industrial revolution that accelerated America's continental expansion and settlement, drew millions of immigrants to its shores, generated the growth of cities in places where before there had only been villages, and stimulated the rise of gargantuan corporations and trusts displacing individual entrepreneurs and competition with monopoly powers spanning a continent. The cultural changes wrought by such a revolution were correspondingly severe. Populism was the 'first political movement of practical importance in the United States ... to attack seriously the problems created by industrialism'. It was also the first movement 'to insist that the federal government has some responsibility for the common weal'.[1]

There had been other reformist impulses in American history. The Jeffersonians had railed against the mercantile and industrial pretensions of the Hamiltonians and had sought to pit the principles of majoritarian democracy and states' rights against the vested privileges of banks, tariffs and bounties. The Jacksonians also fought against monopoly privileges and used the national bank of the United States as the *bête noire* to be humbled by western insurgency. And in a different vein, the abolitionists before the Civil War engaged in a moral, economic and political campaign against slavery which had the most far-reaching consequences. Nevertheless, it was the Populists who embodied a concentrated response to a process of saturated industrialisation which had reached a point where its revolutionary social implications could no longer be accommodated by bland incantations of liberal capitalism and economic freedom.

Populism marked a new era in which the consequences of an irretrievably industrialised and urbanised society were causing sufficient strain to produce political dissent and protest. It was also generating an intense debate into the meaning, value and challenges of modernity in the new world. In this context, it was entirely appropriate that the Populists should represent that section of America which had experienced the most severe disruption to its identity and status – i.e. those whose livelihoods and living patterns were dependent upon the farms and agricultural communities of the South and the West.

The farmers in these areas were being progressively squeezed into a condition of permanent indebtedness and chronic insecurity. Between 1870 and 1900 the amount of farm land in the United States doubled. Land was a capital asset that appreciated in value and permitted farmers to use it as security for loans to buy the sort of machinery that would make marginal land profitable. Farmers, especially in the South and on the plains, needed the high return from cash crops for interest repayment and for future expansion. They were repeatedly confronted, however, by a set of conditions that continually threatened their position.

Apart from the natural and climatic challenges (droughts, sandstorms, insect plagues), the farmers in these regions were hostage to the profiteering activities of the railroad, banking and merchant interests. Whether it was the high rates of interest, mortgage foreclosures and land seizures of the banks, or the suspiciously varied rates charged by railroad carriers, or the corrupt practices of the middle men, the farmers felt increasingly victimised by large-scale impersonal forces. Their position was further exacerbated by the steady decline in the prices of farm produce during the 1870s and 1880s, and by the seasonal fluctuations in the value of the dollar which was low at selling time and high when goods, services and loans needed to be paid for. By the late 1880s, even the land boom had slumped. This left farmers in the position of having to work harder and to risk greater amounts of capital merely in order to stay solvent and to remain on farms whose land values were falling, whose produce was undervalued and whose profit margins were continually being cut by non-farmers.[2]

The smouldering discontent that had produced the Farmers' Alliance and a variety of co-operative purchasing and marketing schemes eventually produced a conflagration of dramatic protest that culminated in the formation of the Populist Party in 1892. The new party's progress was sweeping in its condemnation of those contemporary conditions which permitted 'the fruits of the toil of millions' to be 'stolen to build up colossal fortunes for a few ... [who] in turn despise the republic and endanger liberty'.[3] The programme was equally radical in its proposals. It included plans for a graduated income tax, the nationalisation of the railroad, telegraph and telephone systems, a reduction in working hours, the unlimited coinage of silver, and a scheme in which all land held by corporations 'in excess of their actual needs' should be reclaimed by the government and 'held for actual settlers only'.[4] Among the political proposals were a system of secret ballots, the direct popular election of senators and the limitation of Presidential incumbencies to one term only.

The Populist party attracted over a million votes in the Presidential election of 1892. This was enough to disturb the two main parties. The Populist campaign progressed under the influence of masterly agitators and propagandists like 'Pitchfork' Ben Tillman, Tom Watson and 'Sockless' Jerry Simpson. By 1896 it was the Democrats who had co-opted enough of the Populist cause to kill off the new party. The Democrats not only endorsed the principle of free silver which had become a near-obsessional issue to the debt-ridden

Populists, but also nominated William Jennings Bryan whose rural background, agrarian rhetoric and western prejudices were guaranteed to appeal to Populist voters. The Populists endorsed the Democratic platform and promptly disappeared as a political organisation. The Democrats succeeded in drawing off the Populist sting but, in doing so, alienated much of its working-class urban constituency. This in turn led to a sectional division of the national party system and to a prolonged period of Republican hegemony.[5]

The Populist movement illustrates a number of the problems which have afflicted the tradition of liberal reform in the United States. Firstly, because the Populists were primarily a provincial movement of rural indignation, they encountered great difficulties in enlarging their constituency of oppression and deprivation.[6] In their original declaration of 1892, the Populists sought to cultivate a joint rural and urban constituency based upon a conception of labour common to agricultural and industrial workers. This reciprocity, however, was always very difficult to develop without endangering the Populists' natural supporters in the western and southern farmlands. The scale of popular agitation in these areas was in itself attributable to a deep and habitual suspicion of the city. To an indebted farmer, it was the city that symbolised the impersonal forces of corporate capitalism and the depraved character of much of contemporary American society.

The radicalism of the Populist farmers was firmly rooted in a conspiratorial view of society. City interests were thought to impoverish rural clients by deliberately engineering booms and slumps and by maintaining the high price of money through the gold standard. In the end, the mutual interests of the agrarian Populists and the urban proletariat could not overcome the geographical, cultural and sectional barriers to their political integration. Apart from 'free silver' not being particularly beneficial to eastern city workers, the Populists could not overcome their suspicion of an urban workforce, which in so many respects represented another facet of precisely that trend towards urban organisation, combination and centralisation which the Populists resented so much.

The second problem posed by the Populists was the fact that their radicalism was mobilised around a desire to return to a golden age

– or at least the vision of such an age – when American yeomanry, honest toil, family farms and agrarian riches were the life-blood of the republic. This was the appeal of an era when the farmers were not only acknowledged to be Jefferson's 'chosen people of God,' but were celebrated as the source of natural and righteous wealth, and the basis of Protestant virtue and American individualism. Despite the apparently progressive content of their programme, therefore, the Populists' reforms were largely driven by a wish to retreat from modernity. It was this Populist nostalgia for a superior age and a superior society which served to further the distance between the country and the city. It also gave considerable licence to the Populists' mixture of liberal reform and illiberal nativist prejudice against the recent surges of urban immigrants from Catholic countries in eastern and southern Europe.[7] This intolerance was given clear expression in the Populists' 1892 programme which condemned the way that America had been opened to 'the pauper and criminal classes of the world'. Accordingly it demanded 'the further restriction of undesirable emigration'.[8]

The last noteworthy facet of the Populists' relationship to liberal reform was their sudden decline in the face of a rapid upturn in the farming economy from 1898 through to the First World War. As farmers experienced an unprecedented period of prosperity, their radicalism turned to an endorsement of group politics. The farmers' lobby ultimately became one of the privileged established 'interests' in American society and government which the Populists used to condemn. To a critic of liberalism like Christopher Lasch, the Populists were 'incurable individualists who did not see the need for counter-organisation against the power of organised wealth'.[9] They lacked a sense of ideology by which they could comprehend their position and their wider social role. Because of this deficiency, the Populists believed that their 'dissidence' could be accommodated and absorbed by the corporate system, while leaving the system essentially intact. As a result, they were 'easy prey to disillusionment when hopes of speedy change turned to dust'.[10] But to Richard Hofstadter, the foremost historian of American liberal reform, the Populists' limitation of social conflict to the sphere of interests rather than that of culture or class was a reflection of their own inner conformity to the tradition of American capitalism. 'It was an effort on the part of a few important segments of a highly heterogeneous capitalist agriculture to restore profits in the face of much exploitation.'[11] In contrast to historians like Frederick Jackson Turner and John Hick who regarded Populism as another expression of frontier idiosyncracy and pioneering primitivism,[12] Hofstadter placed Populism in the more universal American mould of entrepreneurial capitalism. This view tended to be borne out in subsequent developments when twentieth-century affluence, business techniques of organisation and marketing, and a permanent relationship with government resolved the farmers' identity fully in favour of commercialised agriculture and capitalist values.

The Progressive era refers to the first two decades of the twentieth century when America was in a ferment of social criticism and political agitation. It is difficult to detect any single strands of Progressive thought and action because the Progressives were normally entangled in a profusion of objectives, motives and priorities. Because of this very diversity, it is doubtful whether the Progressives even constituted anything so coherent as a political movement. Nevertheless, the Progressives did possess a number of distinguishing characteristics. They were predominantly drawn from the middle classes of small businessmen and independent merchants. They were orientated to city life and, as such, they were particularly sensitive to those urban ills which were threatening to subvert both the fabric of the new cities and the ideals of the American republic. Progressives were dismayed at the social and cultural disruption produced by the millions of new immigrants who flooded into the cities in record numbers between 1905 and 1914. Progressives were concerned over the 'merger boom' when individual corporations began to dwarf not merely their competitors but also the financial structure and political authenticity of state governments. Progressives were further alarmed by the raw power and corrupt practices of the city-wide political machines. These were highly proficient at consolidating the new sources of political power in the vote-ridden slums and at exploiting their relationships with business interests to produce unprecedented levels of corruptly procured political funds.[13]

These concerns and anxieties bred a belief amongst the

Progressives that the capitalist order was a highly productive machine, but one that was in a dangerous condition. Progressives were affronted just as much by the squalor, vice, disease and crime of the slums as by the bloated wealth of the industrial barons and speculators. But because the middle-class Progressives felt morally obliged and materially able to do something to correct the degeneration, they were prompted to engage in political campaigns that would redirect and even redeem an affluent yet ailing society.

The Progressives were noted in particular for their passionate interest in exposure and revelation. This was not confined to the famous 'muckraking' articles of Lincoln Steffens and Ray Stannard Barker. It was extended to a general fascination for the realism that lay behind the formalities of social principles and practices. While the edifice of American history was being stripped away by Charles Beard's revelations of the conflict of economic interests and by Vernon Parrington's exposure of a continuous ideological conflict between the forces of enlightened progress and the forces of blind reaction,[14] American law and even the Constitution were being similarly reduced to the new realism of economic drives and vested interests. The assault upon formalism was such that politics was no longer seen as the medium of individual rights and popular self-government. It was increasingly perceived to be a system in which underlying group interests generated the material substance of political activity and the mutual adjustment of such interests embodied the reality behind the institutional processes of the political system.[15]

Alongside the revelation and condemnations were sets of prescriptive and normative schemes by which the American world would be righted. Publicists like Frederic C. Howe and William Allen White produced popular works advocating reform. Analysts and theorists like Louis Brandeis, Walter Weyl, Herbert Croly and Walter Lippmann attempted to combine contemporary material conditions with current intellectual perspectives to produce accounts of social explanation and guidance for reform in an age increasingly collectivist in character and, therefore, requiring conscious and purposeful action.[16]

The intellectual arguments were conducted against a background of concrete reform. The era was characterised by an army of reform practitioners ranging from social welfare workers and city missionaries devoted to the social gospel, to public administrators and activists intent upon revising the structure of city, state and national governments. Whether the motives of all these Progressive elements were drawn primarily from a human concern for the poor, or from a moral outrage at city life, or from a desire for a more efficient use of resources, the end result was a reform-conscious era. It produced a stream of legislation in such areas as working conditions, maximum hours, minimum wages, child labour practices, unemployment, social insurance, the municipal ownership of utilities and direct taxation. These social and economic reforms by which government sought to provide a more equitable distribution of wealth were accompanied by several changes to the political structure (e.g. secret ballot, primary elections, women's suffrage, the initiative recall and referendum) in an effort not only to secure reforms but to prevent government itself from coagulating into blocks of aggregate interests.[17]

Like the Populists, the Progressives were beset by varied cross-pressures which have served to complicate the nature of liberal reform. For example, the Progressives have been described both as fervent democrats seeking to widen political participation and enhance the value of citizenship, and as elitists intent upon deploying techniques of public administration and the force of executive government to provide technocratic means of advancing the public interest. Progressives have also been described as reformers and as conservatives, for while advocating social change in the name of progress, Progressivism 'was also an effort to realize familiar and traditional ideals under novel circumstances'.[18] It was always difficult to ascertain whether the Progressives viewed the past as an open objective to be retrieved, or simply as a disguise under which a new age would be levered into place. As a result, there are always problems in determining whether old or new means were being used in an old or new spirit to further old or new principles.

Nowhere was this confusion more acute than in the central problem of what was to be done with those industrial, commercial and financial conglomerates known at the time as 'the trusts'. On the one side were those who believed that the trusts were the inevitable consequence of technological progress and capitalist development. Because they provided the base of American prosperity and social advance, they should be recognised as legitimate and, thereupon, regulated by government in a co-operative partnership.

> Competition and group struggle for power produced not efficiency but waste, waste of natural resources, of human lives, of human energy used for selfish ends rather than for the public interest. The social problem could be solved not by quarrelling over pieces of the pie but by 'baking a bigger pie'.[19]

Theodore Roosevelt supported this corporatist outlook. His programme in 1912 was duly entitled the New Nationalism.

Roosevelt had been particularly influenced by Herbert Croly's *The Promise of American Life*.[20] Croly typified that facet of the Progressive movement which drew its inspiration from Hegelian historicism and idealism. Croly believed that America was declining into disorder and that it was essential to regenerate America's social unity out of the corrosive forces of alienation, fragmentation and inequality. Croly sought to combine America's traditional attachment to democracy with the conscious development of a popular sovereign will embodying the ideal purpose of an underlying absolute and all-inclusive American community. A co-operative commonwealth would be created through the absorption of the individual within the natural and moral fact of the nation's higher reality, and through the central planning and direction of individuals by a government representing their collective purpose and their totality as a national entity. Croly implied that the old libertarian aims of Thomas Jefferson were now to be achieved through the centralist means of Alexander Hamilton's statism.[21] Theodore Roosevelt regarded this strategy as the only way forward and, as a result, sought to align Progressivism with vigorous federal government, with enhanced nationalist fervour and with enriched executive leadership.[22]

The other view was shared by Woodrow Wilson. Wilson was Roosevelt's rival for the loyalties of the Progressive reformers. He believed that for government to attempt to regulate the trusts was sheer folly. It would condone and ratify the trusts' position which had been built up unfairly and inefficiently through every possible technique for evading fair and free competition. Moreover, it would require a mammoth state apparatus to regulate the expanding monopolies. This would not only further endanger American liberty through a concentration of governmental power, but would make it likely that the trusts would acquire even greater power – enough to ensure that the corporate poachers would always be able to maintain control of the government gamekeepers.[23]

Wilson believed that Jeffersonian liberty could only be revived by *reversing* the process of combination and by seeking to return to a fairer and more competitive age of smaller units. 'When I am fighting monopolistic control, therefore, I am fighting for the liberty of every man in America.'[24] Wilson won the 1912 Presidential election with his New Freedom programme. Although he had beaten Theodore Roosevelt, it is instructive to note that during his administration, Wilson departed from his *laissez-faire* principles and came to adopt the New Nationalism of his rival. By the end of his administration, Wilson had built up an extensive regulatory structure at the federal level. He had had to come to terms with the necessity of 'big government'. Even though he claimed that it was merely the best route back to individualism, competition and opportunity, he could not deny that government was being made compatible with, and even integral to, the cause of personal liberty.[25] Wilson would not be the last reforming President to become more radical with the experience of government.

In the end, the Progressives succeeded in passing much of the Populists' agenda into legislation. The Progressives never approved of the sectional motivations or the divisive and acrimonious style of the Populists. Their battle with 'the interests' looked to the Progressives too much like a battle between class units. As long as the Populist programme seemed fired with prairie vitriol, then the Progressives were not inclined to support it. But once the content of that programme was cast in the light of the Progressives' own rational analysis and moral judgement, then the proposals looked to be necessary and sensible. It was this dispassionate rationality and the concern for a nebulous 'public interest', however, that became the chief criticism of the Progressives. The middle-class nature of the Progressive movement failed to root its reforms deep into popular consciousness and public sympathy. The Progressive middle-class wish was to suspend the conflict between corporate capitalism and working class radicalism by reference to a 'neutral state' and to the existence of an overriding common interest, which would be represented quite naturally by the moderate middle classes. The Progressives' emphasis was on preventative measures and deferring difficult choices, rather than on any systematic and positive adjustment to a new industrial age. Progressivism, therefore, remained a series of separate responses to an industrial order whose problems were offensive but which, in such affluent times, hardly seemed potentially chronic.

The momentum for social reform was abruptly ended by the revival in dogma during the 1920s. After World War I, the reaction against the centralised direction of the war effort was extended to embrace many of the measures passed by the Progressives before the war. The sweeping renunciations of governmental disciplines, together with the onset of the prosperity of the 1920s led to a reaffirmation of individualised liberty expressed in terms of freedom of contract and minimal government. This dramatic reinstatement of immutable natural balances within society and the economy proved to be only an Indian summer for economic libertarianism, and not the triumphant victory of emancipation over aberrant governmental intervention which it had seemed during the boom times of the 1920s.

The Wall Street Crash of 1929 followed by the Great Depression was nothing short of an economic and social catastrophe. The absolute confidence in the capacity of the capitalist system to generate full employment, with ever-increasing economic growth and social progress, was suddenly shattered by the sort of unequivocal disaster that not only devastates an economy, but fundamentally alters social convictions and principles. By the time Franklin Roosevelt entered the White House in 1933, unemployment had risen from 3 million to 13 million (i.e. 25 per cent of the workforce), five thousand banks had failed, the Gross National Product had slumped by a half, investment had all but ceased, and wages and salaries were being cut everywhere to save costs. Farmers could not afford to ship their produce to the cities while urban workers could not afford to buy what the farmers had grown or raised. The ensuing poverty and destitution was further exacerbated by the primitive forms of relief and social welfare provisions available in the states. In many areas, the social dislocation was chronic with shanty towns, bankrupt governments, starvation and malnutrition, the internal migration of unemployed indigents, and the threat of violent mass action – even the possibility of political revolution. Never before had American society been in such acute need of reformist innovation.[26]

In a storm of frenetic experimentation and improvisation, Franklin D. Roosevelt's New Deal reform programme changed the landscape of American twentieth century history. The New Deal's relentless application of reasoned ingenuity and governmental intervention produced a volume of national regulatory power unequalled since World War I. The market in stocks and securities came under government supervision through the Securities and Exchange Commission. Bank deposits were insured by the Federal Deposit Insurance Corporation. The National Industry Recovery Act sought to restore industrial production by government-sponsored codes of competition that allowed whole industries to fix prices and wages. The Agricultural Adjustment Act aimed to stimulate America's rural economy by paying farmers to limit their production, and thereby to break the cycle of over-production and under-consumption.

The New Deal also engaged in enormous public works schemes to stimulate industrial production (e.g. the Civil Works Administration) and to provide jobs for the unemployed (e.g. the Civilian Conservation Corporation). Relief for the destitute was provided by expanded public assistance and, ultimately, by the landmark Social Security Act which established the provision of both a contributory social insurance scheme and a non-contributory set of welfare arrangements for the needy, the aged, the blind, and for families with dependent children. The New Deal also led to the full recognition of workers to organise into unions and to bargain collectively for improved pay and conditions.[27]

In essence, the New Deal conclusively altered the government's position in American society. It marks the time when the federal government came to assume a basic responsibility for the state of the American economy and for the welfare of the citizenry. The vast expansion of federal power was widely interpreted as a redistribution of political power in favour of a national democracy capable of liberating government from the concentration of corporate wealth, reducing the property rights of vested interests and responding to the needs of the underprivileged.

> The New Deal made liberalism a positive force for the betterment of the human condition; it saw freedom as more than the absence of restraint. Freedom was characterized by a better life, better homes, better education. Government was to be more than the protector and the regulator, it was to be a partner, a constructive force, in improving the nation and helping the individual.[28]

The legitimacy of the positive state was strengthened still further by the centralising and organisational imperatives of both the Second World War and the cold war. As a result, the New Deal's legacy was never seriously challenged. As deficit spending, government regulation and social welfare became facts of American life, the New Deal became widely acclaimed as a cultural watershed marking the irreversible liberalisation of American society.

It is precisely because the New Deal is seen as a pivotal period of American history that it arouses such fierce debate amongst different advocates each desiring to claim the programme, and to establish its legitimacy, for their own political purposes. The problem of the New Deal is heightened by its very association with American liberal reform. Just as the New Deal is regarded as the watchword of American liberalism, so the nature of that liberalism is closely bound up with the character of the New Deal and of the society it brought into being. This dual identity, however, serves to clarify neither party. Put bluntly, there remains so much controversy over the origins and purposes of the New Deal because there is so much argument over the meanings and aims of contemporary liberalism. Likewise, the debate over the latter is fuelled by the ambiguities of the New Deal programme which supposedly represents the fullest expression of liberal reform.[29]

Many questions are raised by the New Deal. For example, whether there was one continuous New Deal or two quite separate New Deal programmes – the first based upon economic recovery and institutional stability (e.g. the National Industrial Recovery Act), and the second geared towards social radicalism in the form of expanded social provision (e.g. the Social Security Act) and increased industrial restrictions. Another question hinges upon whether the New

Deal ever contemplated economic planning, or whether the emphasis always lay inevitably upon emergency and experimental measures. Another debate centres upon the New Dealers' attitudes to corporate capitalism. The New Deal seemed to swing between the faction (Rexford Tugwell and Adolph Berle) representing the New Nationalism approach which accepted economic concentration but called for its supervision in the public interest, and the faction (Thomas Corcoran and Felix Frankfurter) adhering to the New Freedom approach of reversing trends in an effort to restore competitive markets.[30] As a consequence, Roosevelt's legacy in this area has remained a mixed one. Lastly, there is an intense dispute over the extent to which the New Deal represents the culmination of a continuous reform tradition encompassing both the Populist and Progressive movements, or a decisive break from that tradition into an altogether more modern and more social-democratic dimension.[31]

All these questions remain unanswered. Within the New Deal there were visionary planners as well as exponents of 'meat and potatoes' liberalism. There were also pragmatists and technocrats and moralists. Franklin D. Roosevelt's own ideological ambiguity further served to complicate the nature of the New Deal. Some measures were evocative of the class-based radicalism of the Populists (e.g. the rights of labour, progressive taxation), while others seemed more like derivatives of the Progressive concern over business concentration and the prevention and punishment of its abuse (e.g. the dissolution of the holding companies in public utilities). On the other hand, the New Deal's emphasis on realism, organisation, technology, efficiency and practical results gave it a distinctive character all of its own. The programme had a free-wheeling quality of breaking down barriers in the cause of material improvements, rather than being overtly concerned with the righteousness of techniques or with the aesthetic defects and moral costs of large economic or political organisations.

The end result was a massive government structure of regulations, controls and provision which, for all its positive achievements and popularity, had never been fully thought through or rationalised in terms of a conscious or coherent revision of public philosophy. Liberalism's golden hour had not produced the golden egg of a complete metamorphosis in the popular conception of the state's role in modern society. Instead, it bequeathed a proliferation of assorted programmes and agencies whose only *raison d'être* was the usefulness of their functions, the public acceptability of their objectives and, subsequently, the physical fact of their established presence. By the end of World War II, the infrastructure of the New Deal was simply accepted as a towering necessity devoid of solid reflection or a reasoned foundation. Its apparent success and indispensability was its own justification.

The continuing relationship between the historical meaning of the New Deal and the social nature of American liberalism creates profound problems for the latter. In some respects, the New Deal can be seen as revolutionary in that it ushered in a Keynesian structure of economic management, a welfare state, a modern system of social and economic regulation and a centralisation of power within the American federation. But because such a transition was made under the anaesthetic of emergency measures, unpremeditated proposals and temporary solutions, the revolution – if such it was – came more by sleight of hand than by any conscious assimilation of collective action and social purpose.[32]

In another respect, the New Deal was a straightforward conservative response to the greatest crisis in American capitalism. The character of the New Deal and of its modern bequest was dominated by a desire to work with business to save capitalism from itself and to preserve the prevailing structure of private property, free enterprise and the profit system. Roosevelt himself was always quite adamant that this was to be the overriding objective. Quite naturally, this outlook has made the New Deal very susceptible to radical criticism. According to Barton Bernstein, for example, the New Deal's 'experimentalism was most frequently limited to means, seldom did it extend to ends'. Its orientation towards corporate capitalism precluded any interest in structural critiques or structural solutions. As a result,

> The New Deal failed to solve the problem of depression, it failed to raise the impoverished, it failed to redistribute income, it failed to extend equality and generally countenanced racial discrimination and segregation. It failed generally to make business more responsible to the social welfare or to threaten business's pre-eminent political power.[33]

Ira Katznelson and Mark Kesselman conclude that the 'ultimate significance of the New Deal era was to strengthen corporate capitalism and postpone a thorough confrontation of its inequities'.[34]

This inner conformity at the hour of crisis highlights the equivocation that characterises much of the American reform tradition. In their desire for change, reformers are prompted into action by reasoned diagnosis of society. But in coming to know the scale, depth, and systematic nature of the problems, the reformers' solutions do not appear to match the severity of the disorder. Liberals are often accused of stepping back from society in order to see its defects, but of being unable to step away from those cultural loyalties that would enable them to provide far-reaching proposals to remedy the defects. More harshly, the complaint is that liberal reformers know enough about society to be fully aware that their partial and compromised solutions will only succeed at nibbling at the totality of a dominant system of economic and social organisation. Furthermore, because their marginal reforms succeed in defusing the strength of more radical political forces, liberal reforms simply make serious reconstructions more remote than ever.[35]

Liberals defend themselves as having to engage in negotiation and bargaining within a political system that features a profusion of checks and balances and, thereby, requires extensive coalition-building to secure any changes in public policy. Liberals claim that they are effective in affording the citizen a vast amount of protection, assistance, support and opportunity with the objective of ensuring that everyone has the basic rights and opportunities to secure his/ her own potential. Liberals claim that all this state provision has been possible *within* a capitalist order. Their position is that, given the ideological ambivalence and structural mutability of American capitalism, it is possible to achieve substantial change while still conforming to the general ethos of capitalism. Liberals have shown that capitalist values (e.g. individual liberty, freedom of opportunity and human progress) can be deployed against ostensibly capitalist interests for the purposes of collective action and social reform.

Even if the American welfare state is known as 'welfare capitalism', it has not prevented a massive rise in the scale of government provision over the past forty years. In 1950, for example, the number of federal social security recipients amounted to 3 million. By the middle of the 1980s , this number had grown to 66 million. Nearly 30 per cent of the entire American population was receiving benefits from one or more social security programmes. When the scale of these entitlements is added to the numbers of those on means-tested public assistance like food stamps (20 million) and medicaid (23 million), the overall effect has been for social welfare, in its broadest sense, to account annually for over 18 per cent of the United States Gross National Product. In spite of these achievements, liberal reform still suffers from a basic lack of an alternative ideological conception of society. The post-war strength of liberalism came primarily from the concrete inheritance of the New Deal, which had become so integral to American society by the 1950s that the new Republican administration of President Eisenhower ratified it instead of reversing it. The New Deal had set the agenda and provided the apparatus. All that was required of President Truman's Fair Deal, President Kennedy's New Frontier and President Johnson's Great Society to satisfy the criterion of reform was the successive progression of public policy in the direction established during the New Deal.[36] Liberalism had become conventional by default. The 1950s was a period which, to many, marked the end of ideology and with it the objections to liberalism's inheritance and guiding standards. By the 1960s, liberalism had 'become so pervasive since the New Deal ... that it represented mainstream American political thought'.[37] Nevertheless, the problem of liberalism's philosophical anchorage remained. Liberalism in these years depended – and depended most successfully – firstly upon the forces of specific democratic pressures and secondly upon a broad public consensus. But this dependence contained within it the seeds of an acute vulnerability, by which the conditions and prospects of liberal reform in America became hostages to the changing fortunes of political interests and to fluctuations in the public's mood.

Firstly, liberal administrations became penetrated by so many interested parties that, far from representing the public interest, they appeared to embody a composite of special interests. This had been a problem even in the New Deal. In order to maximise his political base, Roosevelt would refer to the New Deal as a 'concert of interests'. Accordingly, 'the word that appears most frequently in the writings of New Deal theorists is "balance".[38] The New Deal's success in acting as a broker state, mediating between powerful organised interests, meant that it drew these interests into the orbit of government. However, it also meant that the government – a government purportedly dedicated to autonomous rationality and social direction – could become exclusively dependent upon its supportive interests. The New Deal has often been criticised on precisely these grounds. It has been accused of not only ignoring the plight of the unorganised (e.g. sharecroppers, migratory workers, tenant farmers, unskilled workers, slum dwellers, farm labourers, unemployed blacks and the destitute), but of being so accommodating to the highly organised vested interests in society that it effectively undermined its own independence and freedom of action. The New Deal may have 'marked an important advance from the "single interest" administrations of the 1920s' but 'Roosevelt's predilection for balanced government often meant that the privileges granted by the New Deal were in precise proportion to the strength of the pressure groups which demanded them'.[39] Lyndon Johnson's Great Society programme was similarly criticised for imprisoning itself with its own support. Johnson's budget may have contained liberal measures but, in attempting also to service major interests at the same time, those interests very often counteracted the reformist intentions of the liberal proposals. Even at the height of the Great Society in 1965-66, Johnson's budget was described by Samuel Lubell as extraordinary because 'no previous budget had ever been so contrived to "do something" for every major economic interest in the nation'.[40]

The writer who has done most to draw attention to the atrophying authority of liberal governments is Theodore Lowi. In his book, *The End of Liberalism*, Lowi describes how reformers in government do not so much exercise power as parcel it out to special interests.[41] This buys support and co-operation, but it leads ultimately to a vacuity of public policy and to a culture of dependence within government upon congeries of large institutionalised and unassailable interests. According to Lowi, the liberal attachment to pluralist theory leads to a complacency that relies upon spontaneous, natural balances to secure the common interest. The consequence is a disillusioning, and even corrupt, disarray within government which results in administrations of declining competence and diminishing public trustworthiness.

The second pillar of liberal support – namely, the broad public consensus on established liberal goals – has also undergone a severe challenge since the 1960s . The era which witnessed the greatest expansion of liberal programmes since the New Deal also experienced the progressive dislocation of American society. The convulsive effects of the Vietnam War together with inflation, drug abuse, crime, pornography, race riots, urban decay, campus dissidence, and political radicalism espousing direct and often violent action produced a backlash against liberalism.[42] Social evils were widely perceived to be attributable to liberal experimentation in social reform.[43] 'In the broad American public, there was a widespread sense of breakdown in authority and discipline that fed as readily on militant political dissent as on race riots and more conventional crime.'[44] Although many of the critiques of American society were directed towards liberal values and programmes, the mere existence of such ferocious criticism tended to shift middle-class opinion away from a defence of the liberal establishment and towards a loss of confidence in its authority for having generated such denunciation of American culture. It appeared that as Lyndon Johnson's reformist consensus was splitting apart, the New Deal coalition itself was breaking up. It seemed as if the American consensus was crumbling away under the corrosive forces of political disruption and social polarisation. The noble causes and inflated promises of liberalism had apparently sunk into a morass of body counts in Saigon, ostentatious sex, psychedelic escapism and an 'imperial Presidency'.[45]

It is fashionable to regard 1968 as marking the end of American liberalism. In that year Robert Kennedy was shot and Richard Nixon's law-and-order disciplines were enough to secure the White House for the Republican party. Liberalism had reputedly been tried, and the United States was so afflicted with the costs of its apparent failures that a succession of conservative administrations was the conclusive result. Even during the periods of recession and stagflation in the 1970s, there was little sign of a liberal renaissance. If anything, liberal disenchantment with government experience was prompting the formation of a jaundiced and 'neo-conservative' outlook upon the New Deal legacy.[46] The collective memory of the

1960s together with the spectre of spiralling government costs, exponential rises in entitlements, and prodigious evidence of maladministration and incompetence by government were sufficient to deter the rise of a viable liberal candidacy.

The liberals themselves were in disarray with Senator Paul Tsongas leading the movement for a revision of liberal attachments away from the New Deal legacy and towards more innovative means of acquiring liberty, justice and rights. Modern liberals in the mould of Paul Tsongas and Gary Hart placed emphasis upon the need to give priority to the problem of America's economic health in a world of finite resources, de-industrialisation and budgetary constraints.[47] These sorts of liberals not only distanced themselves from established New Deal politicians like Walter Mondale, but aligned themselves to new issues (e.g. bureaucracy, environmental protection, industrial planning, consumer choice, deregulation, drug abuse, technology and nuclear power) that cut across the old dualities of the New Deal.[48]

In 1981, the liberal requiem seemed complete when Ronald Reagan's rhetoric against 'big government' (i.e. liberal government) won him the Presidency and allowed him to launch a full-scale assault on the New Deal configuration of American government. In the 1980s, the term 'liberal' had such a stigma attached to it that it was used as a deprecating smear amongst politicians. In the Presidential election of 1988, the Democratic candidate – namely the heir to the New Deal/Great Society legacy – refused either to defend liberalism, or to be asociated in any way with what had become known as the 'L-word'. After repeatedly denying that he was a liberal, Governor Dukakis dropped his non-ideological guard at the very end of his campaign. For purely electoral reasons, he suddenly saw fit to declare that he was, after all, a liberal. Although he had finally connected himself to the 'L-word', Dukakis had displayed a 'disastrous inability to express any definition of "liberal values" likely to allure voters or even persuade them that here was a man of principle'.[49] The terms of Dukakis's endorsement of liberalism seemed like the final affirmation of a post-liberal age.

And yet, while it is common to hear of the demise of liberal reform, it is just as fashionable to point out that liberalism is not nearly so vulnerable as it is often portrayed. It can be claimed that liberalism is entrenched in the vast social security entitlement programmes that dominate the budgetary priorities of America's non-defence spending. These programmes support such powerful constituencies that their budgets have become politically and legally unassailable. This established New Deal/Great Society sector grows in response to its ageing clintele and provides a constant inducement to widen the net of government provision. This has been an inducement which the permanent Democratic majority in the House of Representatives has been constantly unable to resist. Even in 1988, when the Democratic leader was trying to live down the liberal reputation of his party, the Democratic Congress impressed itself upon the policy agenda with a far-reaching programme of reform (e.g. aid for the homeless, the provision of health care for catastrophic illness, a civil rights measure and a $20 billion clean water programme). President Reagan's inability to draw resources away from these citadels of government spending effectively stymied his budgetary revolution. The towering deficits of the Reagan era were the ultimate testament to the impregnability of established liberal programmes. Reagan preferred to go into mountainous debt rather than to take on Roosevelt's structural legacy.[50]

All this is fair comment but it still does not really refute the proposition that the liberal state in America is highly vulnerable to an attack on its legitimacy. It is true that large social insurance programmes – which benefit mostly middle-class Americans, which are funded by regressive taxes and which give its recipients the appearance of rightfully drawing upon their own invested capital – are associated with the sort of political influence that can exploit the inflexibility and inertia of the American system to the full. Nevertheless, it is just as true that those individuals in the most precarious social position are precisely those who are most at risk from changes in the public's mood. Reagan's fulminations about wasteful public expenditure and indulgent social programmes may not have touched Medicare or pensions, but it did hit the disadvantaged and those on welfare. Programmes involving child nutrition, food stamps and student loans, for example, were prime targets for government savings. Over the 1980s, the poorest tenth of the country became poorer still by 10 per cent. In 1988, for example, 37 million Americans had no health insurance – a figure which translates into one in five children having no assured means of health care. The liberal state could not protect its poorest sector from the fluctuations in public attitudes or from the rhetoric of politicians drawing upon the frustrations of low economic growth.

It is common in such arguments over liberalism to point out that polls regularly show that while Americans are always predominantly against the abstract vision of an affirmative state intervening to secure a positive conception of individual liberty, they nevertheless approve of the concrete services provided by 'big government'.[51] This duality of attitudes can sustain a Republican Presidency and a Democratic Congress at one and the same time.[52] It can also be seen as proof of a basic empathy with practical liberal assistance.

In the final analysis, however, it has to be conceded that liberal reformers – traditionally the most intellectually disposed of America's mainstream political participants – have tended to lose the intellectual arguments in favour of the American state. Liberals have depended on, or have had to depend upon, the interest-group politics of bargains, pay-offs and group benefits wrapped in consensus and preserved in bureaucracy. As a result, they have not succeeded in conclusively transforming public attitudes enough for the welfare state to be a fully accepted and assimilated component of American life.

While the idea of a neutral state can be exploited to accommodate social benefits and provisions, it can also cut the other way and provide very little defence against a backlash intent upon cutting such government expenditures. As a result, the welfare system has only a tenuous and provisional status in America. It can even be claimed that there is 'a fundamental hostility in Congress and public opinion to the idea of an American welfare state, especially one that gives money to poor people'.[53]

Liberals in America are continually accused of being insufficiently radical to secure their own objectives. Liberal programmes are commonly described as containing 'no hint of radicalism, no disposition to revive the old crusade against concentrated economic power, no desire to stir up class passions, redistribute wealth or restructure existing institutions'.[54] If this is true, it is also true that liberal reformers have to work within a culture that is not readily amenable to large-scale and premeditated social reform, or to the deep and concerted criticism of society with which such reform is necessarily associated. While liberals have always been noted for their use of ideas, they have had continually to be careful not to over-rely upon sweeping evaluations and principled prescriptions. This is not because the style of American politics is especially non-ideological in character. Some of it undoubtedly is, but less than is often claimed to be the case. It is much more because there is a rich store of alternative ideas – or rather of alternative constructions, meanings and usages of ideas – in American politics. In a country where there is still so much heated debate over the existence and legitimacy of the state, liberal reformers and their facility with ideas can by no means be assured of prevailing over, or even of seizing the initiative from, their opponents.

Conservatism

AND THE PRIZE
OF AMERICAN EXPERIENCE

In 1964, the United States was presented with an unequivocally conservative candidate for the Presidency. In that year, Senator Barry Goldwater led a crusade against what his followers regarded as the effete and elitist establishment of the Republican party. In their view it had for a generation wilfully compromised the principles of the party by endorsing the innovative structures of the New Deal and by maintaining a subversive complicity with the Democratic party's progressive centralisation of governmental power. To all those who felt that the basic issue of the New Deal had been resolved and that its inheritance of a mixed economy, social security and humanitarian assistance had become incorporated into the American way of life, the right-wing purists pledged themselves to refute such an apparent consensus and to reveal a deeper set of conservative attachments and convictions.

The crusade culminated in their take-over of the Republican party and in their nomination of a man who had never come to terms with the governing principles of the New Deal. Goldwater had denounced farm subsidies, criticised welfare programmes, suggested selling off the Tennessee Valley Authority, called for the closure of the National Labor Relations Board, ruminated on whether the social security system should be reorganised on a voluntary basis, and in foreign policy renounced the limited war strategy of communist curtailment in favour of total victory against the forces of world revolution. Goldwater's message was one of fierce determination to change the agenda and to reverse the direction of American politics away from what he took to be a progressive slide towards federal paternalism and social decadence.

Goldwater believed in the mobilising power of pure principles, righteously asserted and adhered to without exception.[1] In the acrimonious and fratricidal atmosphere of the Republican party convention held at Cow Palace, Los Angeles, the right's frustration with thirty years of 'appeasement' boiled over into a seething hatred of the party's eastern establishment and into a headlong rush to engage in an extraordinary display of ideological politics. In his desire of offer the people 'a choice and not an echo', Goldwater dispensed with compromise and consensus. His guiding theme was that of giving the people back their freedom. 'Freedom, under a government limited by the laws of nature and of nature's God. Freedom, balanced so that order, lacking liberty, will not become the slavery of the prison cell; balanced so that liberty, lacking order, will not become the licence of the mob.'[2] Goldwater proclaimed that it was the cause of Republicanism to 'insure that power remained in the hands of the people'.[3] He concluded his address with the stark declaration that 'extremism in the defence of liberty was no vice'.[4]

In the election, Goldwater came to be identified with such precipitous policies as a winding down of the social security system and a winding up for a full-scale nuclear war. Goldwater may well have provided a choice, but it was one which was not merely rejected, but was emphatically repudiated by the electorate. The Republican party was humiliated in the ensuing Johnson landslide. Goldwater's adventure into explicitly ideological politics hung like a pall around the Republican party. Books and articles were written speculating upon whether the party was finished as an electoral organisation, or even as a viable source of alternative perspectives. The Goldwater débâcle was seen as a bitter lesson on the need to keep to the middle ground and never again to stray into the extremities of conservative zeal.

For many years after Goldwater's empty triumph at Cow Palace, it became conventional to discuss American conservatism as electorally redundant and philosophically bankrupt. It was characterised as only a restraint upon the progressive increase in governmental services, budgets and power. Conservatives were seen as offering merely less than liberals rather than anything qualitatively different from them. And yet in 1980 Goldwater's protégé, namely Ronald Reagan, not only took over the Republican party, but won the Presidency with a radically conservative programme comparable in nature and scope to Goldwater's own programme in 1964.

Reagan's brand of nostalgic optimism and idealism, combined with sunbelt economic panaceas and aggressive patriotic expectations, fired an enthusiasm for social self-assertion – for making not merely the world, but also the federal government, come to terms with the American people. As Reagan explained in his 1981 inaugural address, 'government is not the solution to our problem. Government is the problem.'[5] Like Goldwater, Reagan was committed to liberating the people from their own government and to sustaining that liberty against outside threats through a large and equally threatening military establishment. Accordingly, Reagan advocated an extensive build-up of America's military forces, while insisting at the same time that government spending should be cut back by an assault upon the welfare state and by cutting the supply of money at source with large tax cuts. Through the sheer exertion of will, Reagan believed that the inertia of federal programmes could be stopped, that the priorities of the New Deal and Great Society could finally be changed, that the cycle of stagflation could be broken and that the cold war could be won.

It can be argued that Reagan's triumph was not exclusively attributable to his conservatism. Voters referred to many reasons for supporting him. His conservatism was not noticeably more salient than any other factor.[6] This in itself does not prove very much one way or the other as it is quite possible – even probable – for a conservative reaction to be expressed through issues rather than through abstract statements of a candidate's ideological position. What is significant is that Reagan's undoubted conservatism did not deter voters from electing him. Being a conservative did not disqualify him from office in the same way as it had done with Barry Goldwater in 1964.

Many developments and changes in conditions had occurred in the intervening sixteen years but not the least of them was the general shift in public attitudes towards more conservative ideas and sentiments. This had been accompanied by the emergence of several conservative movements (e.g. the National Conservative Political

Action Committee, the Conservative Caucus, the Moral Majority Christian Voice) engaged in developing the arguments in favour of conservative ideas and in raising the public's consciousness over conservative alternatives.[7] Whether or not Reagan himself contributed to, or simply rode on the back of the public's increasing receptivity to conservatism, the fact remains that Reagan's victory was regarded by conservatives as their triumph – the culmination of a long process of rehabilitation.

And yet Reagan's electoral success gave only the impression of a unified conservative force supporting his candidacy. In reality, the Reagan campaign and his subsequent administration exemplified the various and often conflicting strands of American conservatism. Reagan drew upon all the available sources of conservative support but, in doing so, he betrayed the existence of a remarkably unstable mix of conservative sentiments and allegiances in the United States. While Goldwater's defeat merely revealed the existence of conservative forces, Reagan's victory exposed American conservatism's full dependence upon widely different traditions of thought and practice.

One strand of American conservatism is that characterised by the term *organic* or *traditionalist conservatism*. This term describes those conservatives whose basic conception of society is that of an integrated whole. While the separate parts and categories of society can be discerned and even analysed, a society's basic nature can only ever be comprehended as an organic unity from which each part derives its function and purpose. In this way, the components of a society are likewise only to be understood in terms of their relation to the whole. The basic consequences of this conception is that society is regarded as a corporate entity, not only historically prior to the individuals within it, but ethically superior to them as well. Societies, like organisms, are products of history or experience. Their very existence is proof of their evolutionary success and of their moral virtue in a world of constant turbulence and danger. The traditional structure and behavioural conventions of such societies, therefore, are to be valued in their own right as embodiments of survival. Guiding principles are derived from history, religion, natural law and tradition. They are sustained through instinct, sentiment and practice.

This type of conservative thought has always been strongly associated with European politics. Drawn from the social forms and certainties of various *ancien régimes* European conservatism has had a strong tradition of accepting the historical bequest of classes, ranks and hierarchy within society. Such stratification is believed to be essential to the very continuation of society. This does not mean that traditionalist conservatives believe in the perfection of their hierarchical societies or even in their eventual perfectability. On the contrary, their belief in man's inner drives towards greed, violence and destruction and in the limitation and fallibility of human reason leads them to the conclusion that the human condition is inherently imperfect. On this basis, traditionally-minded conservatives adhere to the security of order, obligations and custom. They refute the claims of reason, progress, rights, democracy and equality as delusions serving only to threaten the delicate bonds of civilisation and to risk a subsequent descent into the barbarism of anarchy or tyranny.

The values and principles defended in this sort of conservatism have generally been thought by Europeans to be common to western civilisation as a whole. However, in the United States it appeared that this assumption could not be easily substantiated. American experience and conditions appeared to fly directly in the face not just of this conservative tradition, but of any conservative tradition. America's political independence and cultural autonomy, together with its avowed principles of liberty, progress, democracy and reason, and its celebration of natural rights, contractual government and the self-made man in a self-made society, seemed to be wholly incompatible with the spirit of conservative sentiment.

In *The Liberal Tradition in America*, Louis Hartz pounced on the apparent deficiency, and even the illogicality, of a European-style conservative tradition, to assert the existence of a single philosophical consensus, centred upon Lockian liberalism. Hartz claimed that American conditions had effectively merged conservatism into liberalism, so that a secular unity had been produced in which American conservatives were condemned to conserving liberal traditions. 'By being "born equal", by establishing liberalism without destroying feudalism, it had transformed the rationalist doctrine of

Locke into the traditionalist reality of Burke, so that anyone who dared to use conservatism in order to refute liberalism would discover instead that he had merely refuted himself.'[8] Because America lacked a feudal conception of class relations, it was devoid of an anti-industrial right wing and of a class-conscious peasantry or proletariat. Whatever existed in America, therefore, was predetermined to be liberal, for conservatives could do nothing other than conserve the liberal past, while liberals would have no reason to challenge that which was preserved.[9]

Hartz's treatment of American conservatism may be effective in characterising American history and society in terms of an impregnable consensus. But it cannot refute the existence and international currency of conservative instincts and traditions. Neither can it discount evidence that such instincts and traditions have been present in the United States to the extent of providing a distinctive and articulate commentary on the need for Americans to conform to certain fixed principles of conservatism.

The most conspicuous attempt to infuse American life with traditional European conservatism was that made by Russell Kirk. Kirk prescribed the full gamut of organic conservatism, mystique and prejudices to cure America's ills. He favoured a virtuous and ennobling aristocracy over the self-obsessed individualism of changeable business elites. And his concern for the stability of social orders led him to make remarks on the need for rank and hierarchy, which sound quite extraordinary in an American context.

> Genuinely ordered freedom is the only sort of liberty worth having: freedom made possible by order within the soul and order within the state. Anarchic freedom, liberty defiant of authority and prescription, is merely the subhuman state of the wolf and the shark, or the punishment of Cain, with his hand against every man's.[10]

> A political democracy may attain a tolerable balance between the rights of the talented natures and the claims of the average natures. But it also is possible for a monarchy to achieve that balance, or an aristocracy, or some other frame of government. Respect for natural and prescriptive rights is peculiar to no single set of political institutions.[11]

> Poverty, even absolute poverty, is not an evil; it is not evil to be a beggar; it is not evil to be ignorant; it is not evil to be stupid. All these things are either indifferent, or else are occasions for positive virtue, if accepted with

a contrite heart. What really matters is that we should accept the station to which 'a divine tactic' has appointed us with humility and a sense of consecration.[12]

Fellow-conservatives felt that Kirk's 'conservative manifesto' belonged to a different time (i.e. the eighteenth century) and to a different place (i.e. Europe). According to Clinton Rossiter, for example, Kirk was a man who had 'lost all patience with the course of American development in almost every field'.[13] In the attempt to provide a comprehensive statement on the way tradition can and should act as the guiding principle of social conduct, Kirk had shown just how problematic such a proposition could be in the American context. Kirk's vigorously organic form of conservatism led paradoxically to a dissociation with the American experience and to an 'unhistorical appeal to history' and to a 'traditionless worship of tradition'.[14]

It was Clinton Rossiter who devoted special attention to the problems of conservatism in such an ostensibly liberal culture. In his desire to bed American conservatism directly into the traditions of the American experience, Rossiter investigated the possibility of extricating a separate and truly conservative traditon from Hartz's ubiquitous liberal consensus. The results were mixed. Rossiter had to acknowledge that the American political tradition was a basically liberal tradition giving emphasis to such ideas as progress, liberty, equality, democracy and individualism. Nevertheless, Rossiter asserted that if the faith were truly liberal, 'then somewhere in it lies a deep strain of philosophical conservatism'.[15] This strain was embodied in the American adherence to such conservative principles as tradition, loyalty, unity, patriotism, morality, constitutionalism, religion, higher law, property and community.

Without this conservative element in American history, the attachment to liberal principles would not have been tempered into the stability and order for which America has been renowned. America's conservative instincts formed a 'stubborn dike'[16] that kept liberalism 'from spilling over into..full blown radicalism'.[17] Rossiter was not prepared to go any further than this. His analysis of American conservative thought found little consistency or logic to its development. It had been forced to adjust too much and too often to the flood of democracy and industrialisation. American conservatives found it culturally impossible to reconcile themselves to such traditional conservative principles as the uncertainty of progress, the fallibility and limited reach of human reason, the inherent tragedy of history and the idea of the primacy of the community. Rossiter could neither make the American consensus conservative in nature, nor satisfactorily disestablish American conservatism from the liberal mainstream enough to give the American conservative tradition an autonomy and an identity completely its own.

It was Peter Viereck who probably provided the most satisfactory response to the desire by American conservatives for their political temperament to be given direction and legitimacy. Instead of being concerned with trying to tie American conservatism into an overall western conservative dimension complete with fixed moral and social absolutes; and instead of being excessively concerned with basing American conservatism upon an indigenous historical continuity which the nature of American history would not support, Viereck gave emphasis to the habits of mind that were drawn simply to what were taken to be traditions in a contemporary context. What was important to Viereck was not what traditions *were* in some objective sense, but what they had *become*. In the context of organic conservatism, Viereck pointed out the importance of the adaptation of tradition, in order for tradition to be preserved in a changing world and especially in America, whose world was always changing faster than anyone else's.

As a consequence of this adaptive and assimilative outlook, Viereck was prepared to approve of what had become an 'increasingly conservatised New Deal liberalism'.[18] In his view, the true conservative ought to cherish the New Deal reforms because they had become an integral part of American society. Time had lent legitimacy so that a 'now middle-aged New Deal' had 'become conservative and rooted'[19] and, therefore, worthy of preservation as a development of integral value.

Viereck's conservatism epitomised the post-war conservative endorsement of the New Deal and of the political agenda it bequeathed to the nation. Viereck himself felt that the New Deal had become altogether less radical with the passage of time and that it was quite consistent with America's traditions, which were admittedly liberal in principle, but only minimally so, and had in practical effect been as much conservative as liberal in nature. Viereck's self-consciously organic approach to conservatism was designed to appeal to those who believed that the conservative ethos was rooted in the realism of accumulated experience. It was also designed to confront another and very different strand of American conservatism which to Viereck, and to those who thought like him, was rootless, radical and reactionary.

This second strand of American conservatism is known as individualist conservatism because its supporters believe in the primacy not of the community and its traditions but of the individual and the rights of personal liberty. Individualist conservatives look back to a particular period of American history (1875-1910) when the United States seemed, in retrospect, to be more than fulfilling both its economic potential and its capacity for political freedom. This was the era of *laissez-faire* when the overriding principle of government was to intervene in the economy as little as possible. Minimal government would not only reduce the chances of political authority being abused but would allow the natural dynamics, productive forces and social benefits of the market to be maximised to their fullest possible extent. The degree of economic liberty was regarded as the litmus test for all other liberties to the extent that political liberty was assumed to be dependent upon the amount of economic freedom, as embodied in a freely competitive market and in the absolute freedom of contract between any two parties.

Modern individualist conservatives take this era as their point of reference because to them it provides absolute standards of social and political prescription. According to this type of conservatism, these criteria of economic organisation and social conduct are universal and timeless in their validity. The United States' deviation from them over generations of improvised and disjointed liberalisation, therefore, does not mean that the principles of early capitalism have become redundant. On the contrary, their appeal has been enhanced by the increasing evidence that the positive state has not only failed to provide solutions to America's social economic problems, but has in fact served to exacerbate them.

The 'true faith' of *laissez-faire* capitalism was kept alive during the post-World War II period by such disciples as F. A. Hayek, Milton Friedman and Barry Goldwater. It was their work which was to provide the inspiration to the renaissance in market economics and political individualism during the 1970s and 1980s. F. A. Hayek, for example, rigorously reasserted the existence of natural forces that could create and sustain order, growth and justice in society by spontaneous means. In particular, Hayek pointed to the role of the market as a self-regulating mechanism that would ensure the most efficient use of the factors of production. The market remained the only means by which the sheer volume of information or changing individual demands could be systematically processed in an immediate and responsive way. Furthermore, the market represented the most viable form of economic organisation and also the most attractive means of avoiding what Hayek took to be its oppressive alternative – namely, a planned economy which would inevitably involve coercion and, ultimately, totalitarianism.

The market, to Hayek, was more than a receding ideal of economic exchange. It was a beacon of light in a darkening world of pernicious central planning and political direction. It was Hayek's fear of the ferocity of European governments following their abstract, and necessarily subjective, formulas of social justice that led him to eulogise the free market and to adopt as his conception of freedom the highly negative outlook of an absence of coercion. In Hayek's eyes, coercion was divesting an individual of his mental and evaluative faculties for choice. It amounted to the

> control of the environment or circumstances of a person by another that, in order to avoid greater evil, he is forced to act not according to a coherent plan of his own but to serve the ends of another. Except in the sense of choosing the lesser evil in a situation forced on him by another, he is unable either to use his own intelligence and knowledge or to follow his own aims and beliefs.'[20]

This is a very narrow conception of freedom in that it is concerned wholly with the absence of restraint and not with the provision either of choices, or with the means to make them. Hayek's liberty has no connotations of power. As such it avoids any implication with schemes for the redistribution of wealth by governments.

Hayek's stark categories of liberty and the threatening state, set in a context of universal and timeless conceptions of man and

society, were given a distinctly American orientation by Milton
Friedman. According to Friedman, a free market and a free political
order were interdependent entities. The former relied upon the latter
for its functional effectiveness. Friedman referred to Adam Smith's
description of the markets as an 'obvious and simple system of
natural liberty' in which,

> the sovereign is completely discharged from a duty, in the attempting to
> perform which he must always be exposed to innumerable delusions,
> and for the proper performance of which no human wisdom or
> knowledge could ever be sufficient; the duty of superintending the
> industry of private peoples and of directing it towards the employment,
> most suitable to the interest of society.[21]

As part of a wider social freedom, economic liberty should be valued
in its own right and as an end in itself. On the other hand, political
liberty was also dependent upon economic liberty.

A free economy served both to diffuse economic power, and to
separate it from political power, thereby helping to ensure a similar
diffusion of power at the political level. In Friedman's view, political
power has a natural tendency towards centralisation. Because it
seemed to Friedman that there was only ever a fixed amount of
political power, once that power had become concentrated then no
new sources of political power would be available to relieve the
concentration, let alone to reverse it. Economic power, by contrast,
could grow and be widely dispersed. Its very capacity for diffusion
helped to keep it separate from political power and to increase the
chances that the latter would not succumb to the condition of
centralisation.[22]

Although Friedman states that the economic and political sphere
are dependent upon one another, it is quite clear that the major
dependency relationship is the reliance of political freedom upon
economic freedom. Political liberty to Friedman, as it is to Hayek, is
freedom from coercion. Individuals are assumed already to have
liberty, and therefore the main social objective is to leave people free
to make their own decisions on how they should use it. *Laissez-faire*
capitalism is both a direct expression of such liberty, and also the
chief means of its preservation. The checks and balances of capitalist
competition, together with the separation of economic and political
powers, would ensure that American individuals would flourish in

natural harmony with one another's interests and that the American state would maintain freedom through its own physical limitations.

The individual who probably did most to channel these sorts of ideas and sentiments directly into the political arena and thereby into public debate was Barry Goldwater. From his position on the right wing of the Republican party, Goldwater was able to sustain an interest in individualist *laissez-faire* conservatism even when it was chronically unfashionable during the Great Society era. In the early and mid 1960s, Goldwater appeared to be a prophet crying in the wilderness. His book, *The Conscience of a Conservative*, was an unrepentant assault upon post-war liberalism and an uncompromising defence of the conservative principles of laissez-faire capitalism.

According to Goldwater, the conservative looks upon politics as the 'art of achieving the maximum amount of freedom for individuals that is consistent with the maintenance of social order'.[23] Conservatism recognises the essential differences between men and acknowledges that their potentialities are diverse and can only be fulfilled in a variety of different ways. Central government in Washington not only wastes public money in unnecessary administrative layering, but decreases liberty by redistributing wealth and by issuing standardised social directives to the nation. Apart from failing to recognise that material welfare is only a part of each person's individual needs, such practices override local traditions and preferences, undermine a proper sense of individual responsibility and militate against the development of a genuinely democratic community. In return for the benefits of the welfare state, the citizen 'concedes to the government the ultimate in political power – the power to grant or withold from him the necessities of life as the government sees fit'.[24] In Goldwater's view, when the state relieves the individual of the responsibility for his own welfare together with that of his family and locality, it 'takes from him the will and opportunity to be free'.[25]

By the 1970s, Goldwater's description of government as 'a leviathan, a vast national authority out of touch with the people and out of their control'[26] no longer seemed so fanciful. Because of its association with the economic stagnation and social malaise of the period, the record of liberal 'big government' was now far more

vulnerable to attack. The apparent intractability of society's problems, together with the growth in federal expenditures and bureaucracy, enabled a figure like Goldwater to come in from the cold
as the United States indulged in a ferment of conservative discussion
and debate. Goldwater now claimed that his brand of conservatism
had become the 'conscience of the majority' and it revealed itself in
the call for individual liberty.

> In all of this liberal organizational activity aimed at any and all social
> and domestic problems, the individual is most often ignored. He is there
> just to be manipulated. He is there to be submerged, to be swamped, to
> be treated as something you can mold into a social pattern.'[27]

Goldwater and the increasing number of other conservative publicists reflected a growing groundswell of opinion that favoured a
review of even the New Deal in the search for new policy approaches
and new reasons to engage in radical U-turns away from established
patterns of government provision.

It is a measure of the general interest shown in this form of
conservative thought at the time that a work of political philosophy
by Robert Nozick should have acquired such widespread prominence. His *Anarchy, State and Utopia*[28] was essentially a systematic
re-enactment of Locke's theory of individual rights, private property
and the state. Nozick's premise – that everything begins with, and is
consequently rooted in, individuals and their rights – led him to
sanction the inequalities that inevitably attend the exercise of
personal liberty. Nozick gives primacy to the individual over the
community. So long as individual property is fairly acquired and/or
fairly transferred, then any ensuing inequalities should stand.

The alternative of government intervention to redistribute property-holdings in pursuit of a desirable 'end-state' is illegitimate. This
is because the state's only moral basis is that of protecting individuals from those who would wish to infringe their rights. To
sustain its legitimacy, the state has to maintain the least capacity for
force consistent with the maintenance of rights. If a state were to
intervene to reduce inequalities, therefore, it would have nullified its
raison d'être. It would have destroyed liberty by unjustly infringing
upon property rights in order to bring about a state of affairs different
from that produced by the free trade of property holdings.

Although Nozick left a number of important questions unanswered (e.g. the extent to which it is true that the size of the modern state is entirely due to its efforts at redistributing wealth; the degree to which any society is viable that elevates individual rights and property-holdings to such absolute heights), his philosophical scheme for society was significant in the extent to which it was taken seriously and discussed at length. One reviewer believed the book gave 'intellectual respectability to the reactionary backlash' within the United States. Nozick's conclusions articulated

> the prejudices of the average owner of a filling station in a small town in the Midwest who enjoys grousing about paying taxes and having to contribute to 'welfare scroungers' and who regards as wicked any attempts to interfere with contracts, in the interests, for example, of equal opportunity or anti-discrimination.[29]

Anarchy, State and Utopia is in many respects an unconservative tract of political thought. It is highly libertarian in content and rationalist in its manner of construction. It eschews any ideas of justice based upon religion or natural law and it dispenses with any concern for the social bonds of mutual and collective obligation. Nevertheless, the book was seen and used as a fully-developed expression of individualist conservatism in a period when such conservatism no longer seemed reactionary or shameless, but appeared to present logical alternatives and even the prospect of solutions.

This individualist conservatism, together with the organic form of conservatism referred to earlier, are the two predominant sources and expressions of conservatism in the United States. Their prevalence, however, is qualified by their obvious differences in approach and content. American conservatism has been characterised by a more or less continual tension between the traditionalist wing emphasising community, order, authority and obligation, and the libertarian wing laying stress upon personal rights, private property and minimal government. Traditionalists like Peter Viereck see the Goldwater–Reagan brand of conservatism as a form of rootless materialism and anarchic libertarianism dedicated merely to strengthening the established patterns of wealth and of widening those social and economic differences that threaten the social fabric of America.[30] Richard Hofstadter has labelled them 'pseudo-conservatives' because of their rejection of accumulated experience and their desire to overturn tradition in favour of a return to an idealised past.[31] Likewise the individualist conservatives have tended to regard the traditionalists as liberal fellow-travellers, who are blind to their own elitist prejudices and who are too timid to engage in the counter-revolution against government. Various attempts have been made to achieve a genuine and sustainable synthesis between these two sets of conservative ideas and attachments.[32] What have made these efforts so much more difficult is the intrusion of a third, highly disruptive element in the nature of so many of America's conservative movements.

The element in question is populism. The term has many meanings and it can be used to define a variety of political phenomena. As such, it is not exclusive to conservatism – still less to conservative thought. Populism is more a form of behaviour than a scheme of ideas. Nevertheless, American conservative movements have often been characterised as being populist in nature because of the way that their support is mobilised and because the arousal of mass feelings is often seen not only as the conservatives' central objective, but also their final solution to complex problems.

In general terms, populism refers to the origins, behaviour and politics of mass movements. A populist movement is usually an impulsive uprising, generated by an unequivocal belief in the righteousness of the cause, the solidarity of support behind it, and the virtue of any proposed solutions. Populist movements are driven by temperament rather than ideas. The motive force is usually provided by those sectors of society who feel a strong identity with the nation's history and ideals, but who believe that their society, and their place in it, is being subverted and corrupted from within. When the level of frustration and alienation and powerlessness experienced by these forgotten people reaches an intolerable level, they become susceptible to calls for an emphatic reinstatement of their interests and principles by direct means.[33]

The populist impulse, therefore, is an expression of the social frustration and resentment within a society which, while dedicated formally to the principles of popular sovereignty and democracy, appears to many of its citizens to be controlled by manipulative groups working against the public interest. The democratic structure of elections and consent, therefore, is seen as part of the affliction in that it provides a covering of democratic legitimacy to the continuation of the economic, social and cultural impoverishment of the populace. As a result, populist insurgency often represents an idealised appeal to popular government, at the same time that it expresses a denial of the customary institutions of democratic government. Fired by the legitimacy and moral superiority of the people's will and by the need for it to be directly and forcibly expressed – rather than transposed into distant consent – populists tend to threaten the social order and political liberties of democracy, in the name of a righteously authoritarian expression of popular sovereignty.

This populist underside to American democracy has been exposed on many occasions throughout the nation's history. There have been populist movements associated with left-wing causes and objectives but, in the American context, it is true to say that populism is associated far more with right-wing impulses and prejudices. The right has provided some of the most notorious examples of how populism can degenerate into nothing more than organised expressions of nativist intolerance, racial discrimination, religious bigotry and chronic xenophobia.[34]

One such movement was the Ku Klux Klan which had its origins in the racial divisions of southern society after the Civil War, but which grew into an altogether broader movement of resentment in response to the disruptive changes to rural and small-town life in America after World War I. The Klan was more or less an open secret society, which attracted those who felt that they, and their conception of America, were being displaced by alien elements. In the cause of a higher moralism and patriotism, the Klan became a vehicle of White Anglo Saxon Protestant fundamentalism. Its animus was widened from simple racial prejudice into a self-styled redemptive force against Jews, Catholics, liberals, socialists, communists, homosexuals and hyphenated Americans (i.e. recent immigrants). The Klan was the political embodiment of the social strains exerted upon traditional Protestant communities by rapid urban and industrial growth and by the influx of millions of European Catholic and Jewish immigrants.[35] The Klan's violent excesses were always justified by the scale and malevolence of the subversion believed to be directed to the true American conditions. Although the Klan has now declined in importance since the 1950s, it retains a presence in areas of high tension and its rituals of intimidation continue to be employed as a warning to what it regards as social deviants.

Another populist phenomenon was McCarthyism. This refers to the period in the early 1950s when the United States was overrun by a public paranoia that fixed itself upon the belief that American institutions and government were infested by communist agents. Senator Joseph McCarthy was the most notorious publicist of this belief and he used it to generate a heightened state of anxiety which allowed him to engage in an indiscriminate witch hunt. Unsubstantiated accusations, smears and innuendos led to blacklists, deportations and loyalty oaths. Despite the fact that there was no evidence of an invisible communist government or even of any widespread communist espionage and infiltration, the McCarthyite hysteria prevailed over mere fact. McCarthy was left free to browbeat and humiliate not only left-wing organisations and labour unions, but also such previously sacrosanct elements of Washington's liberal establishment as the civil service, the State Department, the Army and the Presidential record of Franklin D. Roosevelt.[36]

Although McCarthy's personal bubble burst in 1954, its spirit has lived on in the form of the John Birch Society. The Society is organised around the premise that a subterranean conspiracy exists in the United States. Blacks, Jews and communists are undermining the nation's freedoms and security. Because of the severity of the threat, John Birchers believe that the usually complex procedures of political reconciliation have to be circumvented. The higher truth of the presence of a communist conspiracy makes the compromises and negotiations of normal democratic politics quite inappropriate to dealing with such a menace. Robert Welch, the creator of the John Birch Society, made it quite clear that his brand of populism, was consistent with authoritarianism.

> I am thoroughly convinced ... that we cannot count on politicians, political leadership or even political action ... Actually we are going to cut through the red tape and parliamentary briar patches and road blocks of confused purpose with direct authority at every turn ... What is not only needed, but is absolutely imperative, is for some hard-boiled,

dictatorial, and dynamic boss to come along and deliver himself as follows: '... You fellows, over there, all of you, get the heaviest clubs you can find, spread yourself out no more thinly than you have to along the whole length of this wall, and don't hesitate to break the heads of any saboteurs you find monkeying with it. Don't even hestitate to break the heads of those you find creeping towards the wall, if you are sure of their evil intention, just as a warning to the rest of the dirty gang.[37]

The most recent example of a mass-based right-wing populist movement was George Wallace's American Independent Party. Wallace appealed to the 'little people' whose 'hard won gains ... seemed threatened on the one side by Negroes and on the other by the federal government'.[38] Wallace's explicit racism appealed to Ku Klux Klan members, while his sweeping denunciation of the liberal establishment along with the federal government and its taxes drew support from the John Birch Society. In some respects, Wallace was a Burkean conservative seeking to defend the interests of his low-income supporters by endorsing the federal government's social benefits and entitlements. But in many other respects Wallace was a spokesman of the radical right. He appealed to those who had been most affected by change – i.e. those who 'were upset ... by pressures toward integration, who were concerned about law and order, who reacted strongly to the changes in moral values as reflected in sexual behavior, use of drugs, the liberalization of the churches, and the like.'[39] As a result, Wallace's party was in essence a populist backlash directed against those forces in society that had made his supporters feel dispossessed, displaced and disaffected.[40]

Populist movements like these invite all manner of speculation on the origins of, and motivating forces behind, the phenomenon of populism. For example, it is possible to speculate on the extent to which there is a natural empathy between conservative attitudes and populist impulses. It may well be that the conservative disposition towards instinctive tradition, national pride and nostalgia for an idealised yet declining social order can lend itself to the nativist passion of what Seymour Martin Lipset and Earl Raub call the 'politics of unreason'.[41] Whether or not populism can be seen as a visceral extension of the conservative temperament, and whether or not conservative issues and techniques of persuasion are peculiarly susceptible to populist excitement, the fact remains that right wing populist movements have had close associations with the right-wing of the Republican party. Populist groups have been, directly and indirectly, openly or covertly, bound up with the radical anti-establishment, and libertarian themes of the Taft–Goldwater–Reagan style of individualist conservatism.[42] This has made any lasting reconciliation between this form of conservatism and the organic form of conservatism very difficult to achieve. Their similarities in historical roots and doctrine are constantly pulled apart by differences in values, outlooks, issues, strategies and objectives – even by differences in the personal backgrounds and characteristics of their respective supporters. These differences are accentuated by the often raw populism that inhabits one side of the American conservative equation, and which allows critics to claim that 'America lacks an intellectually respectable conservative tradition'.[43]

Conservative movements in the United States reflect the strains and tensions within American conservative thought and action. The Religious Right or the New Christian Right movement, for example, represents an uneasy alliance of all three types of conservatism mentioned above. Firstly, it is dedicated to the idea of a fixed moral order to which society should conform both in deference to God, and in order to save itself from its own internal disintegration. According to this view, American society is faced with the corrosive forces of secular humanism that have promoted abortion, women's rights, gay liberation, racial quota systems, busing, pornography and even the abandonment of prayers in schools. The New Christian Right is committed to turning the tide back to what it sees as the traditional Christian principles of America.[44] While it is questionable whether the millennial and apocalyptic visions of what is primarily a Protestant fundamentalist movement fits into or breaches the organic conservative tradition, the Religious Right does lay particular emphasis upon the virtues of an older America and one more settled in a definable public philosophy.

In the economic and military sphere, the Religious Right – to the extent it is concerned with such areas – is supportive of the Goldwater–Reagan attachment to the minimal state, the character-building disciplines of the market and to the grandeur of America's armed might to project the righteous truth of American Protestant values on to the world. Lastly, the Religious Right has clear populist overtones of elite conspiracies, moral subversion and the personalisation of interests, issues and politics. The movement offers attractive and, above all, simple solutions to the complex problems of American decline, technological failure and economic limitation. It encourages a vengeful attitude towards those sectors of American society (e.g. homosexuals, Jews, liberals, blacks, pacifists and feminists) which are identified as being responsible for the economic and social discomfort of the forgotten millions of lower-middle-class Americans and for the subsequent dislocation of American society.[45]

One of the most vociferous groups in the movement is suggestively entitled the Moral Majority.[46] It mixes traditional evangelism with the most modern techniques of mass mobilisation (e.g. satellite broadcasting, sophisticated market targeting, cable television, computerised mass mailing) to generate a message that the will of the people is being unfairly frustrated by godless elements in the higher echelons of American society. It is claimed by critics of the New Christian Right that the movement uses religion as a vehicle of popular frustrations and resentments, and that it exploits the absolutist character of religious truth to justify social and cultural intolerance. The New Christian Right, therefore, embraces all three elements of American conservatism but, in doing so, it suffers from immense internal strains between tradition and renovation, libertarianism and authoritarianism, individualism and collective purpose and between conservatism and radicalism.

The tensions within one conservative movement are increasingly magnified when an attempt is made to combine conservative movements together into a national administration. This is precisely what Ronald Reagan attempted in 1980. Although he won the Presidency, the Reagan administration became an object lesson in the difficulties of keeping the diversity of America's conservative impulses together for any extended period of government. The Reagan coalition was constantly jeopardised by the friction (i) between the religious fundamentalists and the conservative traditionalists; (ii) between the east coast patricians and the Californian *nouveaux riches*; (iii) between Wall Street's Keynesian conservatives who were generally moderate, interventionist and even progressive, and Main Street's traditionalist dogmas against cities, bureaucracies and size in general; (iv) between the internationalism of big military budgets and the projection of American forces overseas, and the isolationism of American self-interest through strategic independence and national freedom of action; (v) between the intellectual critiques and measured prescriptions of ex-liberals disillusioned with past government practice (i.e. 'neo-conservatives') and the populist backlash against the welfare state; (vi) between free-traders and nationalistic protectionists; (vii) between the economic 'supply-siders' seeking to stimulate both the economy and government revenues, and the free-market libertarians who wanted the economy to be stimulated in order to reduce government spending; (viii) between the free-marketeers, and those businessmen who did not want their enterprises to be liberated by 'deregulation'; (ix) between the conservative working class 'Reagan Democrats' who were critical of the abuses of the welfare state, and the individualist *laissez faire* ultras who wished to turn a campaign against abuse into a holy war against the positive state which provided much of the working class with its long-term financial security.

Ronald Reagan's difficulties were symptomatic of a President who wished to base his administration firmly upon conservative principles. He found not only that such principles were many and varied, but that in order to transform even a fraction of them into law he necessarily had to be selective over which conservative principles he would adopt and which ones he would reject. He also had to confront the paradox of having to centralise power, in order to implement a radical programme of concerted decentralisation.

Coupled with these problems was the difficulty of simply being a conservative within the formal liberal culture of American history and politics. In such a context, it is politically difficult to propose the reduction of government services and entitlements when such action can be interpreted as a withdrawal of recognised rights and a contraction of personal liberty. Reagan sought to resolve this problem by constant references to his support for Franklin Roosevelt in the 1930s and to his belief that he was continuing the liberating spirit of the New Deal. This was by no means convincing, but it did allow Reagan the appearance of squaring the circle – of attempting to dismantle the liberal past by claiming to conserve it. In the end, the real conservative achievement was more attributable to the structural conservatism of America's complex political and constitutional system of separated powers, checks and balances and pluralist coalition-building.

The much-heralded Reagan revolution never occurred. Apart from attacking the soft targets of generally unpopular programmes serving the marginal sectors of the 'undeserving poor' (e.g. food stamps), the Reagan years left the basic configuration of government expenditure untouched. The forces of continuity were too strong for Reagan's radical right crusade. The only way of overcoming such forces would have been to take on the entire framework of the political system. While some of the religious populists would have relished such a confrontation, Reagan was always enough of a politician to know that such a crusade would have been self-defeating, as it would have represented the ultimate denial of American conservatism.

Equality
AS AMERICA'S GUARDED IDEAL

Within the revolutionary rhetoric of the Declaration of Independence lies the inspirational assertion that, as far as America was concerned, it was a self-evident truth that 'all men are created equal'. The denial by British imperial authority that American colonists had rights comparable with, and even equal to, other Englishmen generated a revolutionary fervour in the 1760s and 1770s. That fervour expressed itself in an intense and broad-ranging evaluation of the origins and nature of political authority. When the technical and jurisdictional arguments against British authority had been exhausted by the ultimate constitutional sanction of parliamentary sovereignty, the Americans resorted to the sweeping categories of natural law.

Building upon a principle that had become quite conventional in the eighteenth century – namely a basic equality before the law by which justice was thought to require equal procedures for all men – Americans ventured to claim that each individual had equal rights. In the words of Bernard Bailyn,

'Rights' obviously lay at the heart of the Anglo-American controversy: the rights of Englishmen, the rights of mankind, chartered rights. But 'rights', wrote Richard Bland – that least egalitarian of Revolutionary leaders – 'imply *equality* in the instances to which they belong and must be treated without respect to the dignity of the persons concerned in them' ... This emphasis on social equivalence was significant, and though in its immediate context the remark was directed to the invidious distinctions believed to have been drawn between Englishmen and Americans its broader applicability was apparent. Others seized upon it, and developed it, especially in the fluid years of transition when new forms of government were being sought to replace those believed to have proved fatal to liberty.[1]

It was because equal rights presupposed a basic social equality that the political implications were so profound.

The American assertion that their rights were equal to those of the English led to the revolutionary conclusion that they possessed the same authority as Englishmen in resisting what they regarded as the subversion of the British constitution by George III. The rallying justification of the Declaration of Independence expressed both the meaning of America's revolution and the sources of its national autonomy and identity in terms of an international equality of rights. Such a declaration, however, proved to be double-edged.

The formal dedication to equality in the very act of American independence bequeathed a potent vein of egalitarian intent to the stated principles and purposes of American society itself. The notion of equal rights was by 'its very nature corrosive to the traditional authority of magistrates and of established institutions'.[2] The clarion call in 1776 that all men were created equal and that government was derived from their consent confirmed such iconoclasm. The Declaration at the outset established an attachment to egalitarianism which was to influence political ideas and to motivate political movements throughout American history. In the view of Straughton Lyrd, for example,

> the Declaration of Independence is the single most concentrated expression of the revolutionary intellectual tradition. Without significant exception, subsequent variants of American radicalism have taken the Declaration of Independence as their point of departure and claimed to be the true heirs of the spirit of '76.[3]

But its significance has by no means been confined to radical movements. The Declaration allowed equality to occupy a central position in the nation's established system of values.

The profusion of egalitarian impulses that have sought legitimacy in the language of 1776 have given American politics a special quality. Some commentators would go further and say that the moral fervour and emotional intensity generated by the equality issue is a distinguishing characteristic of American politics. According to J. R. Pole, who has written the definitive history of American egalitarianism, the idea of equality has a 'tenacity' and a 'vitality' which owed much to 'the fact that equality had entered into the language of justice in a more explicit and more public manner than in most contemporaneous political systems'.[4] 'As a social ideal, then as a constitutional principle, the idea of equality' in Pole's view 'has a primacy in America that it generally lacks in other Western democracies'.[5] Ronald Dworkin agrees and points out that American 'politicians have never ceased to invoke equality in the aid of their policies'. According to Dworkin, the force of the Declaration of Independence and later the Fourteenth Amendment – which made 'a requirement of equality part of the fundamental law' – was not an answer to the question of what equality meant, so much as an insistence that the 'question never be set aside, so that politicians and courts had to defend, not only particular policies, but some theory of equality as well.'[6]

The centrality of the egalitarian principle in American society is unquestioned. What does remain open to question is how that centrality is both conceived and expressed. If the United States has had wide experience of egalitarian ideas in its political culture, then it is just as true that America has had every opportunity to come to know the prodigious complexities of equality as both a concept and as an ideal. Equality is one of the most elusive of political terms. It can assume different meanings to different people at different times. There can be different dimensions of equality applied to different categories of society. Principles like equality before the law, political equality, equality of opportunity, religious equality, sexual equality, racial equality and economic equality all have separate implications which can lead to conflicts between different forms of equality.

For example, an equality of opportunity may allow for a rudimentary equality at the starting gate of life, but in doing so it can be used to justify the greatest of inequalities that ensue in the subsequent race for possessions and status. Alternatively, the effort to achieve even a modicum of equal opportunity will require forms of political intervention that will almost inevitably restrict the liberty of some individuals and lead to charges that they are being subjected to unequal treatment by the state. The relationships between varying dimensions of equality, therefore, can be highly problematical in terms of logical analysis, practical arrangement and social attachments. Given that the United States has traditionally given equality a position of high natural prominence, then it is true to say that America has had more experience than most with the many ramifications of egalitarianism.

American attitudes towards equality and towards the problems raised by it have been many and varied, but they can be reduced – without undue oversimplification – to three basic positions.

First, equality is simply incorporated into the litany of other American values. Any inconsistencies or contradictions are nullified by the belief that such traditionally American principles as liberty, individualism and democracy are not only compatible with equality, but generically related to it. The result is that equality is often simply regarded as part of a set of values that are interdependent upon one another to the extent of forming an integral whole of American principles. They are seen as fitting together with one another by virtue of the American experience. America's social consensus, in other words, translates into a consensus of values. The values may not be fully in accord with one another on an abstract level, but they are rendered compatible in American life by their assimilation in a unified American culture.

It is common, therefore, to find potentially conflicting values spontaneously and unselfconsciously woven together in an American context. For example, according to Henry Steele Commager, 'The New World possessed not only the most favored of natural environments; it had constituted for itself the most favored of social environments – one of freedom, toleration and equality.'[7] Daniel Bell is similarly reassuring: 'In the United States, the tension between liberty and equality, which framed the great philosophical debates in Europe, was dissolved by an individualism which encompassed both. Equality meant a personal identity, free of arbitrary class distinctions.'[8] Alexis de Tocqueville used democracy and equality in America as interchangeable categories. The equality of American conditions was to him the embodiment of democratic development.[9] But perhaps the most celebrated example of America's fusion of equality with other political principles came in Abraham Lincoln's Gettysburg Address (1863), which joined together liberty, equality and democracy into a composite American ideal. In the space of a few lines, Lincoln first gave full recognition that the nation had been 'conceived in liberty, and dedicated to the proposition that all men are created equal'. He then went to link this hybrid to a democratic conception of government which was 'of the people, by the people, for the people'.[10]

This type of accomplished conjunction of equality with other American values is not without some foundation. From a logical point of view, it is possible to argue that liberal individualism presupposes a devolution of responsibility and power outward to all persons on the basis of their equal status as citizens. Liberties in this sense follow on as a corollary of equal rights. Democracy similarly can be seen as an extension of the equality of individual rights and as the necessary expression of the belief that all individuals possess an intrinsic worth and a right to share in their own government. Equality, to W. H. Riker, is 'simply an insistence that liberty be democratic, not the privilege of a class'.[11] According to these terms of reference, egalitarianism has been an American ideal, and like other American ideals, it has been achieved as part of a collective package of principles without the evident need for choices or priorities to be made between the respective components.

The *second* view of equality which is common in the United States is to see it not as an achieved ideal but as a condition yet to be acquired. The egalitarian terms of the Declaration of Independence are seen as a substantive promise of equality in American life. The assertion evoked at the birth of the nation that 'all men are created equal' has acted as a continuing standard of social evaluation, as a crusading manifesto of protest and reform and as an agenda for American progress. This view of American equality does not regard egalitarianism as a descriptive generalisation of American society, so much as a requirement to rekindle the radical spirit of 1776 in the context of current conditions.

Egalitarianism, according to this perspective is a living ethical idea with profound political implications. As a value requiring sustained and intensive social activity to ensure its translation into reality, the proponents of substantive egalitarianism realise that such an ideal demands the recognition that other American political principles may not always be consistent with the drive towards equality. To press for equality in America, therefore, can be controversial for it can risk the appearance of damaging rifts amongst American ideals, and generate a need for choices to be made between them.

Historical experience, for example, has shown that democracy can be used not merely to reflect the equality of individual rights, but to restrict such rights in the cause of a social equality that limits and even denies personal liberty. In the same vein, the pursuit of equality can fly directly in the face of a democracy content with an established structure of inequality in society. The same de Tocqueville who regarded American equality as being synonymous with American democracy was under no illusion that either of them could always be consistent with political liberty. 'The taste which men have for liberty, and that which they feel for equality, are, in fact, two different things; and I am not afraid to add that, among democratic nations they are two unequal things.'[12] De Tocqueville believed that the equality-cum-democracy of American conditions posed a direct threat to liberty. To de Tocqueville, the 'almost irresistible' force of American democracy raised 'very formidable barriers to the liberty of opinion',[13] to say nothing of the restrictions upon the liberty of action.

If egalitarianism can be dangerous to America's liberal democratic consensus, it can also be attractive as an instrument of political complaint – especially when it can be claimed to be an active derivative of the American revolution. Egalitarian principles have been frequently invoked by American dissidents for this very reason. Egalitarian rhetoric has successfully animated such political movements as the Jacksonian Democrats, the slavery abolitionists, and the Populists. The desired states of equality (i.e. equality of opportunity, legal equality, economic equality) and the manner of their acquisition may well have varied greatly, but this does not detract from the fact that egalitarian principles can and have been effectively used to mobilise American protest and to define reform objectives.

After the promise of equality comes its denial. This represents the *third* common conception of egalitarianism in the United States. The allusions to the prospect of, and the aspiration to, a condition of equality are normally mixed with a recognition that there exists in

America a glaring discrepancy between the ideal and the fact of equality. The abstract attachment to egalitarianism does not translate easily into concrete measures of equality in a society which, in every other respect, is renowned for its emphasis upon individual incentives, private aspirations and personal liberties. This does not necessarily mean that the American commitment to equality is fraudulent. It means that it is conditioned and qualified at any time by expressions of equality – each one of which is susceptible to a variety of meanings sufficient to accommodate the social existence of diversity, hierarchy and even inequality within a construction of general equality.

The American ambivalence towards its own ideal of equality was even evident during the revolutionary period when Americans appeared to be most dedicated to the precepts of egalitarianism. At the very time when the American revolutionaries were dedicating themselves to the principle of republican equality, it was clear that the equality they had in mind was a general equality of moral esteem. The revolutionary leaders had no intention of denying what they regarded as the inevitability of natural inequalities and the consequent formation of a natural hierarchy of talents, skills and virtues. 'By republicanism the Americans meant only to change the origin of social and political pre-eminence, not to do away with such pre-eminence'.[14] Even the Founding Fathers, who have often been accused of serving their own propertied interests by devising a central and protective government, were so concerned that a strong government could be corrupted into creating unnatural, unwarranted and undesirable inequalities that they saw it was as much in their interests to have a government of limited powers, as it was to have one of extensive powers. Equality in this sort of context referred to the equal accessibility of rights that would allow individuals to rise and fall in station in such a way as to reflect their true merit and natural capacity. 'The peculiarities of social development in the new world had created an extraordinary society, remarkably equal yet simultaneously unequal, a society so contradictory in nature that it left contemporaries puzzled and later historians divided.'[15]

The puzzlement and divisions have remained. In some respects, late eighteenth century America can appear to be thoroughly egalitarian in spirit. The era witnessed the destruction of the

American Tories, the prevention of an established church, the formal abandonment of separate social orders, the prohibition of any titles of nobility or other forms of hereditary privilege, and the provision of guaranteed equal liberties against government in the various charters of rights included in the constitutions of the new states. In other respects, the period can be said to be far removed from being egalitarian. Voting was limited to white males with a variety of age, property and residence qualifications. Women were excluded from all political activity. Slavery was condoned by the Constitution. The indigenous Indian population was regarded as being outside the law. And indentured servants might have to survive as semi-slaves for many years in order to fulfil their contractual obligaticns. This cultural duality over equality was epitomised in the American attitudes to rank and hierarchy. Americans found the pretensions of social distinction quite detestable, yet at the same time it was undeniable that they coveted the symbols of social status and prestige.[16]

It could be said that 'the American revolution introduced an egalitartian rhetoric into an unequal society',[17] where it has stayed ever since. While this rhetoric has not been without long-term significance, its immediate effect was to emphasise equality for the purpose of a libertarian rush for the new sources of individual inequalities in the social and economic spheres of a rapidly developing country. To a historian like Martin Diamond, it is important that we should not be misled by the language of the Declaration of Independence into believing it ever had anything at all to do with a call for equality. To Diamond, it was always first and foremost a charter of political liberty: 'The Declaration does not mean by 'equal' anything at all like the general human equality which so many now make their political standard ... The equality of the Declaration ... consists entirely in the equal entitlement of all to the rights which comprise political liberty, and nothing more.'[18] Notwithstanding the debates over the meanings and motivations behind the Declaration, the history of much of the nineteenth century leaves little doubt as to how the 'equality' of the Declaration was interpreted and used at the time.

In the early nineteenth century, 'equality of opportunity' rose in prominence to become an accepted orthodoxy. In a period of industrial and commercial development, such equality acquired a validity which was drawn directly from the social mobility and economic expansion of Jacksonian America. By the late nineteenth century the die of corporate capitalism had been cast. Free enterprise and competition had been extended – or been corrupted – to produce vast economic empires and natural monopolies, along with well-established business and financial elites and a burgeoning industrial working class. Notional equality had surrendered to huge inequalities in wealth, status and prospects. The original egalitarian impulse of liberal capitalism had been turned in on itself and America's greatest achievement of economic growth had come to coincide with the country's most vivid contradiction of equality.

The American ambivalence over equality is illustrated by these three outlooks upon the subject. No single view of equality exists in the United States. This is partly because of the elusive nature of what equality means in any unified abstract sense. As noted above, equality can alter in relation to any category of society (e.g. economics, religion, race, gender, etc.). 'Equalities' can clash with other 'equalities'. The mercurial nature of American equality, however, is also due to the fact that the United States' experience of equality as an ideal and as an issue has varied so much over its history. In contrast to some of the other central values in American politics (e.g. liberty, individualism, democracy), the status of equality has fluctuated quite markedly during America's development.

To J. R. Pole, equality in the first half of the nineteenth century was reduced to an equality of opportunity – 'an imperfectly digested notion which actually conflicted with other egalitarian precepts'.[19] After the Civil War, the idea of equality 'advanced far beyond the heroic rhetoric of revolutionary times'[20] only to fall away as 'egalitarians lost their grip on American developments more completely than ever before'.[21] After World War II, equality was 'out of its box again'[22] and given close attention as 'a central and definitive object – a social aim to be achieved'.[23]

Equality as a driving political force appears, therefore, to wax and to wane in American society. This further compounds the complexity attached to the idea of equality, as its meanings become heavily dependent upon its changing salience as a political issue. At different times, it is more likely than not that equality will be construed as (i) simply an integral feature of the American consensus, or as (ii) a promise of substantive change, or alternatively as (iii) a promise more honoured in the breach than in the observance. In this respect, it is just as plausible for the same group, and even for the same person, to concur with each of the three views of American equality at different times, as it is for any group or individual to hold consistently to one or other of these three perspectives.

Nothing exemplifies better the complexity surrounding the meanings of, and attachments to, American equality than what has been not only the most fundamental dispute in American history and society, but the most grievous challenge to America's egalitarian credentials. The dispute in question is known as America's 'racial problem'.

The problem has remained rooted in the fact that America's black population is derived from its original condition of enforced enslavement. As the only sector of American society which had patently never opted voluntarily to emigrate to America and which had arrived in the new world as officially designated forms of property, the historical position of black Americans has been uncertain, provisional and, at times, precarious.

One of the great ironies of the Declaration of Independence was that it included a charter of universal rights propounded by the great libertarian, Thomas Jefferson, who himself kept slaves. Jefferson opposed slavery in theory but believed that the security of the whites and the preservation of republican government required the continuation of the South's 'peculiar institution'. Jefferson thought emancipation would come, but that the two races would never form a single society. 'Nothing is more certainly written in the book of fate than these people are to be free. Nor is it less certain that the two races equally free, cannot live in the same government. Nature, habit, opinion has drawn indelible lines of distinction between them.'[24] The emancipation eventually came in the middle of a Civil War which was a conflict between the social and economic interests of American sections, occasioned by, and symbolised by, the issue of slavery. The Emancipation Proclamation was declared by Abraham Lincoln in 1863, but it contained none of the egalitarian tones of the Declaration. Despite his reputation for having freed the slaves,

Lincoln never expressed any support for the principle of a social or political equality between the races. The terms of the Emancipation Proclamation made it quite clear that the motive had been one of military and diplomatic necessity.

The Civil War bequeathed a notional equality and freedom upon a race which had been remorselessly conditioned to systematic subordination. Thereupon began a process by which Americans sought to reconcile old habits with new expectations. In the end, the transformation was stillborn. The new consciousness of equal rights and liberties, which the Civil War had done so much to promote, declined into a steady acceptance of a social structure characterised by impregnable privileges, inviolable property rights and entrenched inequalities.

At first, the prognosis looked very promising. The radical forces in Congress succeeded in the most thorough revision of the American Constitution since its inception. The Thirteenth, Fourteenth and Fifteenth Amendments were intended finally and conclusively to raise the ex-slaves to a position of equal citizenship with guaranteed rights and, in particular, the right to vote, by which other rights might best be maintained. To drive the point home the Fourteenth Amendment contained an unprecedented directive to the states not to 'make or enforce any law which shall abridge the privileges or immunites of citizens of the United States'; nor to 'deprive any person of life, liberty, or property without due process of law'; nor to 'deny any person within its jurisdiction the equal protection of the laws'. These amendments were designed to prevent the South from slipping back into its old prejudices. The 'Black codes', pursued by the old confederate states immediately after the Civil War, had already limited the property rights of blacks and prevented any ex-slaves from holding public office, from voting in elections and from serving on juries. The Civil War amendments and the federal army of occupation in the South helped to provide an environment in which America's new black citizens might exercise the rights of citizenry. It was in the late 1860s and early 1870s that the course of black advance flourished in the South. The states of the old confederacy even sent thirteen blacks to the House of Representatives and two to the United States Senate – an achievement that has never since been repeated.[25]

Within ten years, however, the South was permitted to lapse back into racism. The North had passed its constitutional and legal measures and, as time went on, had lost interest in the immensity of the South's problems. Once federal troops were withdrawn in 1877, the South was allowed to act out what the North took to be its regional nature – namely, a backward, impoverished, ingrown and thoroughly regressive backwater of an otherwise industrial and progressive America which was passing it by.

By the end of the century, the South was awash with 'Jim Crow' laws through which blacks were effectively disenfranchised and reduced to segregated second class citizenship. The Supreme Court had effectively gutted the Fourteenth Amendment of its meaning and force.[26] Most significantly in the *Plessy* v. *Ferguson* (1896)[27] decision, the Court condoned segregation by stating that the races could be constitutionally separated as long as the facilities provided were equal. As the Court showed very little interest in determining *how* equal they needed to be, the South was able to provide separate facilities that were equal instead to the level of esteem that blacks were held in by the mass of southern whites.

In the early twentieth century, the South had become the dark continent of the American mind.[28] Behind the official edifice of legal segregation lay a vast hinterland of unofficial restrictive practices, social discrimination, administrative trickery, selective treatment and outright intimidation. The brutality of white supremacy was most chillingly symbolised by the local practice of summary lynch law for 'troublesome niggers'. It is estimated that between 1880 and 1917 over 2,000 blacks were put to death in ritualised violence – very often orchestrated by the Ku Klux Klan. 'Some of the black victims were children and pregnant women; many were burned alive at the stake; others were castrated with axes or knives, blinded with hot pokers, or decapitated ... Throughout the carnage, the Federal government remained blind and mute.'[29] There could be no clearer manifestation of the extent to which blacks had been subjugated by a white community totally secure in its assumption of superiority, and in its local power to convert that assumption into violent activity.

Although the South's pattern of social discrimination and economic exploitation continued largely undisturbed into the 1940s

and 1950s, there was, especially in the North, a greater consciousness of, and even concern for, the deprivations of southern
blacks. American consciences began to be disturbed by what Gunnar
Myrdal termed the 'American Dilemma'[30] – the dilemma of the
coexistent commitment to equality and to white superiority. The
inconsistencies, contradictions and even hypocrisy of such a dichotomy began to become uncomfortably evident as knowledge of
southern practices became more widespread and, thereby, more
open to outside condemnation. Where there was interest, so also
was there opportunity.

The person who did most to exploit that opportunity and who
came to embody the strategy most widely employed by black
reformers was Martin Luther King. Dr King supported the legal
assault upon segregation conducted by organisations like the
National Association for the Advancement of Colored People. They
had been successful in undermining the structure of 'separate but
equal' facilities for different races by proving that the facilities offered
were usually far from equal and were occasionally non-existent. In
the celebrated *Brown* v. *Board of Education of Topeka* (1954)[31]
decision, the Supreme Court had even overturned the *Plessy* v.
Ferguson formula in public education by declaring that separate
educational facilities were 'inherently unequal' and, therefore, were
a denial of 'the equal protection of the law guaranteed by the
Fourteenth Amendment'.[32] Despite these victories, Dr King felt that
the protracted process of legal reform was a necessary but not a
sufficient means to achieve change. He believed that the examination of legal meaning was no substitute for a political challenge to
segregation.

Dr King's Southern Christian Leadership Conference in conjunction with organisations like the Student Nonviolent Coordi-
nating Committee and the Congress of Racial Equality believed in
direct collective action against segregation in an attempt to mobilise
public opinion, to change attitudes and to undermine the political
foundations underpinning segregation. As an avowed pacifist and as
a realist who knew the limits of black power in the South, King's
main tactic was that of passive resistance. His boycotts, 'sit-ins' and
'sit-downs' were very effective in placing the onus of response on the
authorities. If nothing was done the protesters would achieve a

moral victory over local segregation ordinances; alternatively, by enforcing the law, the authorities exposed the normally concealed violence of racism in beatings and arrests. King became a master of publicity, juxtaposing non-violent piety on the part of the defenceless and dispossessed with the traditional southern discipline of police dogs, whips and water cannon. The results of these televised set-piece confrontations outraged white middle-class opinion in the North and prepared the ground for action by the federal government.[33]

Martin Luther King succeeded in projecting the civil rights issue, with its egalitarian overtones, into a position of national prominence in the late 1950s and early 1960s. The issue succeeded in claiming mass attention and King determined that the mobilisation of political interest and sympathy should be turned into concrete legislative achievement at the highest level. He knew that the power of the white majority in the South could only be limited, to the advantage of the black minority, by a prevailing national majority in the federal government. King succeeded in appealing to this wider audience by couching his radicalism in conservative terms. He had an astute sense of how American history and American values could be made to serve the cause of civil rights. He regularly wrong-footed the opposition by seeking to 'out-Americanise' them with reference to the Declaration of Independence, to the role of universal rights in the American Revolution, and to the Bill of Rights.

In his celebrated 'I have a dream' address to the great civil rights rally in 1963, King assured his listeners that his dream was 'deeply rooted in the American dream':

> This sweltering summer of the Negro's legitimate discontent will not pass until there is an invigorating autumn of freedom and equality ... I have a dream that one day this nation will rise up and live out the true meaning of its creed: 'We hold these truths to be self-evident; that all men are created equal.' ... I have a dream that one day every valley shall be exalted, every hill and mountain shall be made low, the rough places will be made plains, and the crooked places will be made straight.[34]

King's renewed revelation of the radical implications of America's traditional principles prompted a previously reluctant President Kennedy to work for the most ambitious civil rights bill in a hundred years. In addressing the problem of civil rights, Kennedy himself found that it was difficult to avoid the egalitarian ramifications of the issue.

> This nation was founded by men of many nations and backgrounds. It was founded on the principle that all men are created equal, and that the rights of every man are diminished when the rights of one man are threatened. We are confronted primarily with a moral issue. It is as old as the Scriptures and is as clear as the American Constitution. The heart of the question is whether all Americans are to be afforded equal rights and equal opportunities; whether we are going to treat our fellow Americans as we want to be treated ... Now the time has come for this nation to fulfill its promise. The events in Birmingham and elsewhere have so increased the cries for equality that no city or state or legislative body can prudently choose to ignore them.[35]

It was said that 'no other chief executive had ever talked that way about human rights in America'; and that 'no President had ever before so forcefully recognized the moral injustice of all racial discrimination'.[36] Dr King and his followers, therefore, had succeeded not only in establishing civil rights on America's political agenda, they had set the terms and vocabulary of the ensuing political debate.[36]

Martin Luther King's objective was that of integration. He regarded the United States race issue to be not merely a social problem for America's black community but a moral problem for American society as a whole and, in particular, for the integrity of its avowed political principles. American freedom and equality – not just black freedom and equality – would be secured by the full admission of blacks to the mainstream of American society. In criticising white behaviour, therefore, King was not condemning the principles of American democracy but offering the opportunity of their total vindication by allowing blacks their rights to full and equal participation in a basically sound and – in every respect other than race relations – even an admirable society.

King's plea for special treatment for a sector of the population that had suffered generations of special discrimination – and which as a result had produced a frightened, passive and apathetic people quite ill-suited to the aggressive self-assertiveness of pluralist politics – was a request which raised a host of difficult problems over the meaning and place of equality in the United States. His opponents felt that the civil rights campaign was divisive both just because it drew attention to the inequalities in American life, and because it attributed such inequalities to a structural and deliberate practice that conferred continuous advantages on some to the direct detriment of others. This was offensive to many white Americans. It amounted to a flat denial of the basic egalitarian assumptions of American life. More significantly, it sought to discredit the diversities in wealth and social position that were seen as endemic in a free society and the natural result of an interplay of different skills and talents. They pointed out that *inequalities* were a condition and consequence of freedom and that to try to convert them into a singular state of *inequality* was an attempt by black people to evade personal responsibility for their own position.

Dr King, for his part, always insisted that he wanted blacks to be assimilated into America's liberal democratic culture as individuals. Even up to the point of his assassination in 1968, Dr King maintained that the ultimate demand of the blacks was their acceptance by whites into American society.

> The American racial revolution has been a revolution to 'get in' rather than to overthrow. We want a share in the American economy, the housing market, the educational system and social opportunities ... What is needed is a strategy for change ... That will bring the Negro into the mainstream of American life as quickly as possible.[37]

But, in order to acquire the entry qualification of equality of opportunity, it was necessary for blacks to be helped collectively by government intervention. King always sought to escape from the paradox of seeking unequal treatment in the pursuit of an equality (i.e. equality of opportunity) that would justify sustaining a system of inequalities. Although he attempted to tie his appeals for equality to demands for liberty, it was always a difficult hybrid to keep alive. If he gave emphasis to equality, he threatened the liberty of those who would be required to accommodate such equality. If he stressed liberty, then the equality argument always risked being turned on its head and for equality to be seen as nothing more than the equal availability of a right to be unequal.

It has to be pointed out that the measured arguments and assured optimism of the integrationists were not shared by all sectors of the black community. Those who experienced the *de facto* segregation and discrimination in the racial ghettoes of America's northern cities were impressed neither by Dr King's appeals to Christian love and to the better nature of whites, nor by the assault upon the *de jure* segregation provided by the Civil Rights Acts of 1964, 1965 and 1968.[38] On the contrary, they believed that white racism was a deeper and far more endemic cultural condition than any civil rights legislation could ever relieve. To these embittered victims of hard-core urban racism, the problem of race was not a product of the failure to translate American values into actuality. It was, instead, the natural extrapolation of such values. At a time (i.e. the mid 1960s) when white sympathy for black progress was already waning in the light of urban violence and race riots, many blacks felt that racial equality was a chimera and that as soon as blacks showed signs of improving their position, white tolerance of equality subsided into a backlash.

This fertile ground of disaffection produced the 'black power' movement which had many variations but which was united in a condemnation of white American society. It drew its inspiration from Marcus Garvey's Universal Negro Improvement Association which had attracted widespread black support in the 1920s for its dedication to black pride, black consciousness and the need for blacks to disavow America and return to Africa. The followers of black power in the 1960s identified with contemporary revolutionaries in Africa and Latin America, who were engaged in what were described as racial wars against imperial power. The black power movement projected the same struggle on to America, and regarded the black community as a colony needing to wrest its independence from the white imperialism of the United States. Instead of integration with what was seen as a degenerate and even fascist white culture,[39] the black power ethos was centred upon a rejection of American values and the need for a physical separation of the black race into self-governing communities, where the superiority of its culture and virtue would be secure from the contamination of white greed and cruelty.

The black power movement enjoyed the licence of a sweeping and comprehensive indictment of American society. Its articulate leaders (e.g. Malcolm X, Huey Newton, Eldridge Cleaver)[40] could engage in Pan-African romanticism and in calls for armed insurrection without the need to balance interests or to accommodate other principles.

Their avowal, and threatened use, of violence ultimately served to fulfil their own prophecies of a white backlash. The hope of transforming a caste consciousness into revolutionary effect proved to be ill-founded. Diminishing white interest in the collective aspirations of blacks – combined with the onset of new issues and conditions, the growth of a black middle class, and the rise of the black vote – all led to a decline in radical black politics.

Although the various and often exotic visions of the black nationalists never materialised, it is said that they were successful in showing that the drive for racial equality could assume forms different to that provided by the prevailing conception of integration. To an extent this is true. Nevertheless it is also true to say that the black power movement raised just as many questions over equality as the integrationist position. It is arguable, for example, that the black nationalists revealed an ambivalence, and even a discomfort, over egalitarianism that ultimately propelled them into a flat rejection of equality on the grounds of the racial superiority of blacks and the need for the races to be kept apart from one another.

The issue of black rights shows that the cause of equality in America is a continuing process and not a fixed condition. The process has often been long and protracted. By the end of the 1980s, the growth of black voting power had enabled over 6,000 city- and county-level posts to be won by black politicians. In relation to the position in the 1950s, this is a considerable achievement, but in relation to the total number of such elective posts (i.e. 490,000), then the pursuit of equality appears to have only just begun. The same is true for wealth. Blacks have become more affluent and yet the median income of white families is still nearly twice that for black families. Accordingly, 28 per cent of black families (compared to 9 per cent of white families) remain below the federal government's designated poverty line. As a consequence, 43 per cent of black children (compared to 15 per cent of white children) live below the poverty line. Many do not live at all, as the rate of black infant mortality remains double that for white infant mortality.[41]

The process of black equality can not only be slow, it can also be intermittent and even reversible. In the 1960s, the Supreme Court under Chief Justice Earl Warren repeatedly endorsed the principle that the federal government should not simply be confined to eliminating the negative features of inequality and discrimination, but should be acting as the chief instrument through which a positive condition of equality might be secured.

> Its concern was to serve the value of equality and to incorporate that value more deeply in the Constitution. While the structure was never completed, the blueprint was clear. The Court was moving toward the creation of constitutional guarantees of national basic minimums in education, housing, subsistence, legal services, political influence, birth control services, and other facets of the modern welfare state for all persons regardless of race.[42]

Furthermore, the Court gave constitutional sanction to 'affirmative action' programmes like the busing of school children to achieve racially integrated schools. It also gave encouragement to a variety of equal-opportunity schemes in the fields of government employment and government contracting. 'This drive toward equality'[43] on the part of the Warren Court slowed in pace under the succeeding Burger Court (1969-86). Although the main principles established under Warren remained largely intact, the reduced pressure for equality allowed litigants a greater opportunity to challenge the ways in which equality was being pursued by the courts.

The most notable case in this respect came in 1978 when Allan Bakke challenged the University of California's rules on the admission of students from minority groups. The University's Davis Medical School had set aside sixteen out of every 100 places for disadvantaged minority students, whose grades could be considerably lower than the rest of the candidates. The scheme was an attempt to compensate for past discrimination by affording unequal advantages to minority groups with the intention of widening the equality of opportunity available to such groups. As a white candidate who had failed to acquire a place in medical school on two occasions – despite having better grades than many of the disadvantaged students – Mr Bakke claimed that the affirmative action programme amounted to reverse discrimination, and therefore was a denial of 'the equal protection of the law'. Conservative commentators and politicians agreed. George Will, for example, believed that such schemes were a denial of America's social order.

> The premise behind reverse discrimination is this: an unfair start can be inferred from an unequal outcome. The traditional American premise is

this: the equal status of citizenship is the basis on which a structure of inequality *should* be built by a population in which talents are neither equally distributed nor equally rewarded. Reverse discrimination is a betrayal, not a fulfillment of American values.[44]

The irony of a white using a Civil War amendment to claim he was being discriminated against by a measure designed to alleviate the inequality of a minority was not lost on the public. The case aroused fierce controversy over the meaning of equality, and what was fair and equitable in seeking to alleviate inequality in the United States. In the end, the Supreme Court found that it had to equivocate.[45] It secured Bakke a place at medical school on the grounds that the university's quota system was too rigid. On the other hand, the Court did approve of the principle of race being taken into consideration in the admissions process. The Court may have endorsed the *principle* of 'affirmative action', but it also served notice that its *practice* would always be liable to challenge, should it ever be successful enough for aggrieved students to claim that some races were being afforded a higher degree of protection against unequal treatment than others.

Controversies like these serve to confirm that the passage of equality is at best intermittent. Some would claim that it is reversible. But what may have been lost in terms of pace over the last twenty-five years has more than been made up for in terms of proliferation. The ideas and arguments of equality that were originally formulated and popularised in the civil rights campaigns of the 1950s and '60s have been used to great effect by other minorities in search of group rights. Once the idea of equality had been re-established in the public domain, 'it multiplied and divided like the sorcerer's apprentice's broom'.[46] The pursuit of equality has ramified out to Hispanics, Asian Americans, American Indians and, not least, to women.

The current feminist movement, for example, originated in the 1960s when the civil rights campaign led to a heightened awareness of discrimination in other areas. Women's groups press not merely for equal pay for equal work, but for a re-evaluation of the comparable worth to society of different jobs, and particularly of those occupations traditionally dominated by women (e.g. teaching, nursing, office work). The cause of equality in hiring and promotions within the work-place has already progressed with the Supreme Court's willingness to accept sex discrimination cases under the rules of the 1964 Civil Rights Act. The Court has approved of Congressional measures viewing women as a 'protected class' requiring affirmative assistance. The chief objective of the women's lobby over recent years has been the Equal Rights Amendment which is intended to change the Constitution so as to assure that equality of rights is not derived or abridged by any form of sexual discrimination. Although it is unlikely that this charter of equality will be passed in the near future, it is almost certain that sex-based specifications in employment will continue to be eroded away by the courts.

These diversified appeals for equality may be couched in similar terms but their practical effects may not be consistent with one another. Each category of proposed equality inevitably gives rise to its own peculiar problems of interpretation and application. The roads of equality may have increased in number, but there is no way of ensuring that they are all directed to the same point, or that they do not intersect one another's purposes and objectives.

The most obvious example of just such an intersection in the American context is the clash between equality of opportunity and economic equality. It is arguable that all forms of inequality are in one way or another derived from the conditions and influences of economic inequality. Be that as it may, it is the disjunction between equal opportunity (with its individualistic assumptions of ambition, competition and achievement by merit and application) and the dedication to equality (which in an economically self-conscious society has a strong inference of the need for some measure of equal shares) which represents one of the most vivid anomalies in America's experience of equality.

Every study of American equality begins by acknowledging the exceptional degree to which Americans endorse the principle that all people are inherently equal. Opinion polls show that Americans are not easily diverted from sweeping endorsements of human equality. A study by Sidney Verba and Gary Orren demonstrates that there is a stronger commitment to political equality than in any other developed nation.[47] And yet Verba and Orren go on to disclose that American principles and policies produce one of the highest levels of

economic inequality in the world. This commonly observed phenomenon is largely attributable to the capacity that the equal opportunity principle has for accommodating values like personal freedom,
individual development and rewarded effort, which are hostile to
most notions of economic equality, or equality of result.

The extent to which equality of opportunity embodies a Trojan
horse inside the American citadel of egalitarianism can be gauged by
Verba and Orren's figures on the American attitudes to the distribution of wealth in society.[48]

Commitment to income equality by liberal groups in the United States

| | Those who call themselves 'far left' or 'very liberal' among | | | |
Commitment	Democrats	Union	Blacks	Feminists
Favor equality of results(%)	20	14	9	10
Favor equal pay (%)	26	23	23	25
Favor top limit on income(%)	45	32	22	37
Fair income ratio of executive/ elevator operator[a]	12·0	9·8	12·2	8·2
Proportion of group far left and liberal (%)	23	22	32	46

[a] The leaders were asked what would be a fair income for people in
different occupations. The above ratio is based on what they thought the
president of one of the top hundred corporations should earn compared
to what they thought an elevator operator ought to earn.

These findings reveal that amongst even the most liberal and
potentially radical sector of America's leadership, there is considerable tolerance of wide differences in income and conspicuously little
support for such differentials to be reduced. The satisfaction with the
present distribution of wealth is underlined still further when
American attitudes are compared to those in a country like Sweden.

While 68 per cent of union leaders in Sweden favoured equal pay
and 51 per cent approved of a top limit on incomes, only 11 per cent
of American union leaders favoured equal pay and only 13 per cent
agreed with a top income limit. Furthermore, Social Democrat
leaders in Sweden believed that a fair ratio between the income of an
executive and the income from a menial job should be in the region
of 2·5. On the other hand, Democratic party leaders in the United

States believed that such a ratio should be in the region of 15•0. The American allegiance to equality, therefore, cannot easily withstand the cultural attachments to market principles which, despite being portrayed as a projection of equal opportunity, work to ensure that the United States is 'a far remove from the level of equality that has been achieved in many other industrialised democracie'.[49]

The same pattern of egalitarian principles and inequalities in practice is evident in the operation of America's welfare state. Opinion polls record very high levels of support for the general principles of social provision for the needy.[50] But when attention is directed to specific programmes, support tends to vary depending upon whether such programmes have benefits based upon social insurance contributions, and whether programmes of entitlement appear to be abused by the recipients into providing a means to avoid work and to evade social responsibilities. In short, there is strong support for the social security programmes (e.g. pensions, disability and unemployment benefits) that can be justified as insurance schemes, which assist those who have applied themselves in the past through individual effort and self-reliance. Americans reveal far less tolerance, however, for those programmes like Aid to Families with Dependent Children (AFDC), Medicaid and food stamps which give money and benefits to the poor on a non-contributory and means-tested basis. While Americans always respond generously to the abstract principle of 'welfare', they nevertheless remain highly suspicious of the ways in which welfare programmes are adminis-tered, and of the extent to which public funds are directed to those individuals who deserve to be supported, as against those who are not deemed to be deserving of such assistance.

This duality of response has been particularly prominent through-out the 1980s when the welfare system came under greater attack than ever before. According to popular analysis, the expansion of welfare programmes in the 1960s had led not to the reduction of poverty, but to an increasing population on the welfare rolls and even to an alleged 'underclass' depending permanently on welfare benefits.[51] To the 'new right', this culture of welfare dependency was being passed on from generation to generation. It was actively encouraging such social problems as crime, drug abuse, illegitimate births, juvenile delinquency, slums and family breakdown into female-headed households. It was in effect a threat to civil society. Against this background, the Reagan administration successfully moved to change the welfare system in a way that made welfare payments conditional upon the recipient agreeing to undertake work or training. This 'workfare' provision in the Family Support Act (1988) was based on the assumption that citizenship should be seen not simply as a matter of civil rights, but as a matter of reciprocal, and even contractual, obligations. By affording welfare recipients the educative and social value of work experience, it was believed that it would allow them to improve their self-esteem, to identify themselves with their community and to be treated 'like other citizens in the ways essential to equality'.[52]

But perhaps it is the race question in the end that best illustrates the depth of complexity which surrounds the conjunction of an equality of rights with a corresponding liberty to be unequal. Once again, opinion polls uncover an impressively high rate of support for the proposition that all people are equally worthy and deserving of equal treatment. This egalitarian outlook is translated into substantial agreement that the plight of many blacks is due to poor education and lack of training, and that the best way to improve their position is to ensure that they have better educational and employment opportunities.[53] It is precisely at the point when the practical implications and consequences of such principled diagnoses become evident that the support for egalitarian positions falls away under the pressure of concern for individual ability, effort and merit.

In one poll, 77 per cent of respondents favoured 'government job training programmes for negroes,' while 82 per cent opposed 'giving negroes a chance ahead of whites in promotions where they have equal ability'.[54] In another poll, 76 per cent thought that 'laws requiring employers to give special preference to minorities when filling jobs were unfair to qualified people who were not members of a minority'.

On the issue raised in the Bakke case, only 5 per cent of respondents believed that eligibility standards should be lowered to allow more minority students to be admitted to college.[55] In their study of American attitudes, Herbert McClosky and John Zaller conclude that while 'Americans favour equality of opportunity, including government programmes to promote it, they do not favour equality at the expense of discouraging individual achievement, or penalizing non-minorities'.[56]

This disinction between abstract equality and material inequality is, in the view of Seymour Martin Lipset and William Schneider, symptomatic of the 'contradiction between two core values in the American creed – individualism and equality'.[57] To Lipset and Schneider, race has reflected this contradiction 'more dramatically than any other issue'.[58] The inspirational egalitarianism of the early civil rights campaign proved to be remarkably effective in mobilising support for the movement. The resulting consensus on civil rights, however, began to break down as the issue started to 'come up against the individualistic, achievement-minded element of the American creed'.[59] The emphasis upon imposed integration, affirmative action and preferential treatment for minorities 'forced the sharpest confrontation between egalitarian and individualistic values'. Lipset and Schneider go on to point out that,

> white Americans have been much slower to accept full racial integration in education, housing and social life. White Americans largely see these matters as an individual choice ... Preferential treatment ... probably sounds to most whites like an effort to force equality of results by predetermining the outcome of the competitive process.[60]

Collective government action to improve the life chances of a designated category of citizens prompted whites into a renewed appreciation of the traditional conception of American society, which had always emphasised the factors of individual worth and personal responsibility, rather than those of structural conditions and general discrimination in the constitution of the social order. This shift led many blacks to the realisation that their claims for equality exceeded – and would probably always exceed – what white Americans were willing to concede.

Just as it is customary to begin discussions on American equality with references to the Declaration of Independence, so it is traditional to end them with allusions to the continuation of barriers to complete social equality. But this is, in many respects, an unfair standard by which to evaluate a society's attachment to egalitarianism. It overlooks the fact that no society has ever reached a condition of perfect equality and it ignores the proposition that such a state of existence is physically impossible. It also fails to recognise that many other political principles and values may be jeopardised in any pursuit of substantive equality. Because Americans choose to value equality in conjunction with other norms like individualism, liberty, democracy and capitalism, this does not mean that America's egalitarian attachments are somehow fraudulent and hypocritical or permanently subsumed under a blanket of propertied freedoms.

For J. R. Pole to claim that Americans in the nineteenth century 'wanted a society run on equal principles without wanting a society of equals',[61] or for Verba and Orren to state that Americans today 'can agree on equality only by disagreeing on what it means'[62] is far from being mere sophistry. It accurately conveys the difficulty both of conceiving a fusion between equality and liberty in the abstract, and of describing a society that attempts to give comparable stature to two values which are notorious not only for being mutually exclusive, but also for being absolutist in nature. Because the United States often appears to give greater weight to liberty and its associated values and because equality requires a great deal of conscious and active effort in its pursuit, then it is easy to derogate the importance of egalitarianism in American history and society. It is true that the effort to match social change to the high rhetoric of American equality has often been absent – leaving a conspicuous discrepancy between ideal and fact as a consequence. It is also true that equality of opportunity has often been used as a pretext for the continuation of gross inequalities. Nevertheless, what should not be overlooked is the remarkable extent to which egalitarianism can stir the American spirit and mobilise political forces in its wake. The nature of American politics provides considerable opportunity for the principle of equality to be introduced into the consideration of political proposals. Once part of the debate and once established in the vocabulary of political discourse, its effects are not easily restricted in scope and can be quite unpredictable. Due to the sheer force of this egalitarian tradition in American politics, the United States has been propelled – often inadvertently and even at times unintentionally – into intensive efforts to construct, extend and refine the most prodigiously comprehensive framework known to the world for securing an equality of rights for its citizens.

9

Nationalism

AND AMERICA'S
WORLDLY THOUGHTS

In the 1988 Presidential election, one of the main issues centred upon the American flag. In an effort to embarrass the Democratic candidate, Vice-President George Bush reminded voters that his opponent had once vetoed a bill requiring teachers to lead their classes in the Pledge of Allegiance. This executive decision was taken as long ago as 1977, when Michael Dukakis was serving his first term as Governor of Massachusetts. The decision was also quite consistent with an earlier Supreme Court judgement on the issue. Nevertheless, George Bush was able to inflict considerable political damage on his opponent by accusing him of placing civil liberties before patriotism. Bush was later able to press home his advantage by making a much-publicised visit to a flag factory in New Jersey, by stressing the word 'America' in his campaign speeches, and by claiming the first thing he did each morning was to pledge allegiance to the flag.[1]

In many countries, such a contrived attempt to make electoral capital out of patriotism would have met with little success. But Bush was able to convert 'Old Glory' (i.e. the flag) into a campaign issue because Americans are one of the most devoutly patriotic countries in the international community. When Americans were asked in a recent poll what made them feel good, 63 per cent mentioned spending money and 85 per cent noted family relations. But what made more Americans feel better than anything else (i.e. 95 per cent) was simply 'being an American'.[2] This sort of finding is symptomatic of a society whose integration and sense of solidarity has been, and continues to be, drawn from an accentuated sense of nationhood.

America's pronounced national consciousness can produce waves of uninhibited patriotic fervour. Whether it is the bicentenary of the Declaration of Independence (1976) or of the Constitution (1987), or the celebrated return of astronauts, or the public anguish over American hostages and American casualties overseas, the mood is one of corporate identity and open emotion expressed through the continued visual presence of the Stars and Stripes on battleships and spacecraft, in classrooms and hospitals, waved in parades and draped over the coffins of dead marines. The 1980s witnessed one of these surges in American national pride. The era was personified by President Reagan who openly sought to enhance the state of American belief in its own exceptionalism, superiority and virtue. The crowning moment of Reagan's 'new patriotism' was the 1984 Olympic Games, when the United States indulged in an orgy of national celebration. In between the explicitly American festivals of the opening and closing ceremonies, American athletes swept up medals in a forest of American flags and to the sound of an almost continuous national anthem.

President Reagan saw the Olympics as part of the revival of American nationalism which he himself had helped to generate. As 1984 was also an election year, Reagan had no inhibitions in seeking to reinforce the identity of his Presidency, his party and his own persona with that of the nation. He used the success of America's Olympians as a metaphor for American strength and promise in other international arenas, and tied it all to his election strategy of nationalistic mobilisation. 'We were never meant to be a second best nation,' the President exhorted in his campaign speeches. 'And so, like our Olympic athletes, we're going for gold.'[3] Reagan's appeal to the national spirit of America was extraordinarily effective. He won an emphatic victory over the Democratic challenger, whose complaints that Reagan had co-opted the American nation for his own electoral purposes fell on deaf ears.

Just as these waves of nationalistic fervour can be expressed in positive and optimistic terms, so they can also lend themselves to forms of social anxiety, resentment and intolerance. This negative and darker side of American nationalism has been revealed in various 'nativist' movements like the anti-Irish 'Know Nothings' and the Ku Klux Klan. These types of movements have had a history of resorting to discrimination and intimidation in various crusades to rescue the 'true America' from those forces purportedly undermining its racial, ethnic, religious or political integrity.

Prejudice in the form of national allegiance has not just been confined to fringe or regional groups. The United States government itself has often moved against elements of American society on grounds of national unity or national security. For example, in 1921 and 1924, the United States government passed new immigration laws that established quotas on the numbers of immigrants that different countries could send to the United States. As the quotas were fixed in relation to the proportion of each country's descendants in the United States population of 1910 – changed to that of 1890 for the 1924 revision – the intention was clearly to preserve the predominance of White Anglo Saxon Protestants (WASPs) in American society. Tens of thousands of Catholic and Jewish applicants from southern and eastern Europe were refused entry at the same time that huge British and German quotas were left unfilled.

Another instance of explicit discrimination in the name of the national interest was provided by the forced evacuation and internment of Japanese-Americans citizens in World War II. In the weeks after Pearl Harbour, Japanese-Americans on the west coast of America were suspected of being spies, saboteurs and fifth columnists. As a result of this hysteria, President Franklin Roosevelt signed an executive order designating the west coast as a military area and, thereby, authorising the summary suspension of constitutional rights to all 112,000 Americans of Japanese ancestry. They were arrested and forcibly sent to 'relocation camps' in the interior of the United States.

In many ways, these conspicuous expressions of American nationalism – whether they assume a positive or a negative form – are an anomaly in the new world. The location and composition of America do not lead readily to notions of nationalism. On the contrary, nationalism is usually associated with a single and long-established people who possess a common culture, history and language set within the context of a fixed geographical area. Although the themes and characteristics of nationalism are notoriously resistant to clear definition, the basic idea of nationalism does centre upon the fusion of a singular people with a single place. It is the cultural and ethnic distinctiveness of a people that is expressed through a sense of place. By the same token, it is the homeland which is taken to be the source of a natural community of common ancestry, traditions, history and customs. The culmination of such a fusion is the development of the nation–state, in which the nation is taken as the proper basis for a viable government and the state is seen as an affirmation of the integrity and autonomy of a genuinely national community.[4]

These defining characteristics of nationalism do not at first seem in any way applicable to the United States. Americans are renowned for being a society of immigrants from all parts of the world. These immigrants had in many respects rejected their own nation–states in the act of journeying to the new world. As a result, America had developed into a society which necessarily rejected the idea that its people were bound together by common descent. Americans did not have the advantage of 'a common past with its roots in antiquity or medieval times [or] a common religion or a unique cultural tradition'.[5] They did not even have a sense of being rooted in 'a historically defined territory'.[6] On the contrary, they were a polyglot collection whose ideals and identity had been formed out of a renunciation of Europe's cradle of nationalities. Far from possessing a common consciousness of territory or ancestry, Americans seemed to be distinguished more by a consciousness of *not* having such attributes and of taking a positive pride in their own rootlessness and mobility.

In retrospect, it is difficult to conceive how America ever developed anything in the way of a national identity. It is true that at the outset the United States had some of the ingredients of national development. It had undergone an extended period of colonial government. It had assimilated British traditions and principles of government. And it possessed enough in the way of common experience and identity to engage in a collective declaration of *American* independence and to form a continental army that would fight the *American* War of Independence. After that climactic struggle, however, Americans dispersed into Virginians, Georgians and New Yorkers. Although the Founding Fathers and their federal constitution managed to reverse the process of disaggregation to the point of providing a framework of national government, the mere fact of a federal system did not resolve the problem of the relationship between the nation and the states. In many ways, the Constitution ratified America as an assemblage of separate sovereign entities. A national government existed, but as yet it was without the zeal and passion of an American nationalism.

During the first half of the nineteenth century, the prospects of an integrated American nation were not altogether promising. America not only attracted ever-greater numbers of immigrants from an ever-greater variety of sources, it was growing ever bigger in scale through westward expansion. By purchase (e.g. Louisiana Territory, 1803), by treaty (e.g. Oregon Territory, 1818), by war (e.g. California and the Utah and New Mexico Territories through the war with Mexico, 1846), by annexation (e.g. Texas, 1845) and by the continual clearance of Indians from their lands, America assumed a land mass of continental dimensions. The protean quality of these virgin lands was almost overwhelming to a young, underpopulated and overstretched republic with a weak centre of government, poor communications and a dependency upon both an experimental federalism and a theoretical pluralism untried on such a scale. The huge interior of the new world both exaggerated the absence of any notion that America possessed a traditional and fixed national heartland, and allowed the nature and content of American nationalism to change in time and space as the new western America progressively departed from the old eastern America.

In spite of all these factors discouraging the development of a collective unity around the theme of nationhood, the United States had by the end of the nineteenth century emerged as a highly self-conscious and self-assertive nation. In the view of Marcus Cunliffe, nationalism was 'a strong cement throughout the nineteenth century world', but 'nowhere was it more fervently and idealistically cherished than in the United States.'[7] The country had come to possess a heightened awareness of its own uniqueness as a culture. It had a developed sense of national history and purpose. It filled the interior, which Jefferson thought would last a thousand years, with so many new settlements that the frontier was officially declared closed in 1890. It was integrated by industrial organisation and national communications into a single economic market and, thereby, into a world industrial power. And it even fell prey to the imperial appeal of the rightful extension of national power into colonial possessions.[8]

By 1916, President Woodrow Wilson was able to take the United States into World War I as a major military and economic power in pursuit of the rights of national self-determination. The sense of American national consciousness was sufficiently well developed for it to override the residual national allegiance to Germany of those millions of German-Americans upon whom the German government was relying to prevent America's entry into the war. Wilson was confident that most Americans of German stock were 'as true and loyal Americans as if they had never known any other fealty or allegiance'.[9] This assumption proved to be correct, as America abandoned its traditional isolation and neutrality to re-enter the old world as a distinctive nation, set upon re-making the international community in its own image of republican principles and open diplomacy.

By the end of World War II, the United States had become established not just as a permanent and integral part of the international order, but as the world's first superpower whose popular culture, political values and military priorities came to dominate the West. The cold war which ensued between the United States and the Soviet Union was a war of words, military threats, political ideologies, destructive technologies and unqualified social imperatives. It was a war designed to produce the type of national anxiety upon which xenophobia and blind national solidarity could thrive. In 1961, President Kennedy could call upon his fellow citizens to 'ask not what your country can do for you – ask what you can do for your country'.[10] Although the disillusionment with the Vietnam War reduced the United States' willingness to 'pay any price, bear any burden [or] meet any hardship ... to assure the survival and success of liberty',[11] America's commitment to its national security and to its national values has remained as militant as ever. It was President Reagan in his inaugural address of 1981 who warned the world that America's 'reluctance for conflict should not be misjudged as a failure of will'.

> When action is required to preserve our national security, we will act. We will maintain sufficient strength to prevail if need be ... Above all we must realize that no arsenal or no weapon in the arsenals of the world

is so formidable as the will and moral courage of free men and women. It is a weapon our adversaries in today's world do not have. It is a weapon that we as Americans do have.[12]

His claims seemed to be based on firm foundations, for in a 1982 poll measuring national pride and patriotism in six countries, Americans were revealed as having far more national pride (80 per cent) and were far more willing to fight for their country (79 per cent) than any of the other five more venerable nationalities listed (i.e. France, Italy, Spain, Great Britain and West Germany).[13]

The origins and sources of such a formidable nationalism remain open to question. It is possible to attribute America's national consciousness to the progressive consolidation of political and economic power. The growth of such material frameworks of centralised resources may have afforded the opportunity for the emergence of a national dimension, but it does not in itself lead to the generation of a collective national sentiment.

Another asserted influence is the role of ideas. In this context, it is not uncommon for such ideological schemes as Social Darwinism and Hegelian idealism to be used to explain the depth of America's national spirit. The aggressive dogmas of national survival within a competitive international environment can be used to account for America's national expansion and imperial adventures. On the other hand, the Hegelian tendencies of a writer like Herbert Croly can also be advanced to explain the enhancement of American nationalism. Because he interpreted the nation–state as the realisation of an ethical idea and as the vehicle of a common and collective spirit, Croly has been seen as being instrumental in revising America's *laissez-faire* liberalism into the communal obligation, social solidarity and national citizenship of the positive state. Croly believed that the promise of American liberty and equality could best be secured by fusing the popular sovereignty of Jefferson and the nationalism of Hamilton into one mutually inclusive entity, so that each would be served by the other and a democracy of freedom would become embodied in a nationalist solidarity serving the general welfare.[14] Despite the salience of such doctrines, it is difficult to ascribe national causality exclusively to them alone. Social Darwinism, for example, was always more of an agent of social division than it was an instrument of an integrated American outlook upon the world. As

for Hegel's philosophical idealism, it was known and understood by
very few Americans and actively adopted as a social philosophy by
even fewer in a culture pervaded by the political themes of private
interests and individual rights.

Another attributed source of American motivation centres upon
historical experience. The most celebrated example of an attempt to
establish America's identity exclusively in conditions and experiences peculiar to the United States was Frederick Jackson Turner's
frontier thesis of American society.[15] Turner's assertion concerning
how a frontier of settlements advancing against a wilderness could
have socially and ideologically generative properties proved to be a
popular analysis of American liberty and democracy. It had widespread appeal to a developing nation eagerly in search of an
understanding of what was distinctively American about America.
Although the thesis was ultimately recognised as being too contrived an attempt to lodge American traditions purely within a
domestic context – in particular a western American context – the
Turner analysis exemplified the American propensity for seeing its
own national character as a derivative of spontaneous social
development set within natural conditions and physical forces.

All these sources of nationalism are only partially true. Unified
structures, nationalistic ideas and American experiences are all
important factors, but none of them individually accounts for the
depth of national sentiment that is synonymous with the United
States. What really galvanises a people with a common stock of
experiences, ideas and features of life into a solidarity of national
spirit are those occasions or periods that force all the available
elements of potential nationalism into a lasting bond of national
identity and purpose.

The American War of Independence was one such catalyst of
national consciousness. An even more significant metamorphosis
occurred in the American Civil War. The federal constitution of
1787 had not so much resolved the issue of the relationship between
national and state authority, as deferred it to a process of negotiation
and adjustment. The nature of the federation was, thereby, subjected
to divergent and controversial interpretations. On the one side was
the Federalist construction that saw the federal compact as having
been made by the collective action of the American people. Since

they had made the Constitution the supreme law of the land, the federal government could be regarded as embodying the people as a national community. This view was used to support the idea of national growth and the central development of a national economy. Its opponents believed that the union had never been anything other than a contract between sovereign states, which retained the right to nullify acts of the federal government if any state believed that the terms of the federal contract had been broken.

These arguments over the sources of political authority, the nature of political obligation and the meaning of federalism rumbled on through the first half of the nineteenth century. The conflicting contentions only became chronic when it was clear that Madison's vision of a multiplicity of continental interests had broken down into a polarised sectionalism of northern and southern blocs. The union had encouraged nationalism, but at the price of the threatened secession of the South into a second American nation. As the two sections hardened in attitudes, so their respective constructions of the federation and of the nature of the union became irreconcilable.

In the ensuing civil war (1861-65) the northern forces ground the southern nation into military defeat. In doing so, it conclusively won the argument over the characteristics of the American union. Through the massive mobilisation of men and materials on both sides, the Civil War succeeded in energising the two sections into a heightened state of consciousness concerning their respective nations. The enormous bloodshed and devastation of the conflict ultimately directed that consciousness into the single dimension of the United States. The Civil War ended the fundamentalist arguments over federal authority and state sovereignty and, as a result, cleared the ground for the development of an uninhibited American nationalism.[16] The union was, thereupon, transformed into an indissoluble and indivisible nation. This provided the scale and solidarity of American integration that was later to enable the United States to engage in global conflict as a major international power.

The other major element in the formative processes of America's national spirit was provided by those conditions which led Americans to believe that its people had a divinely-inspired historical purpose. Originally this ideal took the form of a moral example to the rest of the world. The first Puritan governor, John Winthrop, had declared that America was to be 'a city upon a hill' that would provide an inspirational example to the rest of mankind. This notion of America as the chosen ground of excellence and the universal model for emulation had acquired a secular dimension by the end of the eighteenth century. America was now the consummate example of political liberty. It was not only an asylum, but a laboratory within which the feasibility of the republican ideal would be tested and demonstrated to a hopeful world. In the view of Thomas Jefferson,

> A just and solid republican government maintained here, will be a standing monument and example for the aim and imitation of the people of other countries; and I join ... in the hope and belief that they will see, from our example, that a free government is of all others the most energetic; that the inquiry which has been excited among the mass of mankind by our revolution and its consequences, will ameliorate the condition of man over a great portion of the globe.[17]

According to this perspective, America was a social entity that exemplified the full potential of man to recreate a life in accordance with his true nature. America was not merely *a* model or *a* refuge but the only model and refuge left in the world riven with anachronistic and degenerate social structures.[18]

By the 1840s, America was clearly set upon a course of territorial expansion. With the progressive enlargement of the lands under its authority came a renewed affirmation of American social principles and political ideals. The nature of its dynamic progress and the sheer scale of its economic success seemed like proof of America's inner virtue and providential design. As the United States almost effortlessly took vacant possession of vast tracts of the new world, its own sense of example began to take on a more active role. The American appetite to annex new lands became associated with a conscious sense of national mission to spread republican institutions of liberty to the furthermost reaches of the continent. Expansion became synonymous with the ennobling cause, and the onerous responsibility, of ensuring a natural American freedom within America's own state of nature.[19]

For years the United States was able to act out this sense of moulding a malleable and open-ended new world through the force of its own willpower and its inner light of obligation. During the 1840s, however, the American missionary practice was beginning to encounter a sense of political and geographical limitation. Other powers in the new world like the Spanish in Mexico and the British in Oregon were now offering resistance to American expansion. As the momentum of accommodation faltered, the notion of mission was transformed into one of righteous aggression.[20] The progressive and enlightened nature of America's indigenous democracy was now cast as the overriding justification for the borders of the United States to be extended over and against the claims of either the moribund and corrupt powers of the old world (Spain, Britain), or the regressive and savage nature of inferior peoples like the Mexicans and the Americans Indians.

America became prey to the idea that it possessed a 'manifest destiny'. John L. O'Sullivan, for example, proclaimed that through this 'manifest destiny' it was America's fate 'to overspread and to possess the whole continent which providence has given us for the development of the great experiment of liberty and federated self-government'.[21] As a result, Texas had been assimilated into the union as part of

> the inevitable fulfilment of the general law which is rolling our population westward; the connection of which with that ratio of growth in population which is destined within a hundred years to swell our numbers to the enormous population of two hundred and fifty millions (if not more), is too evident to leave us in doubt of the manifest design of Providence in regard to the occupation of this continent.[22]

A contemporary of O'Sullivan's, William Gilpin, was even more flamboyant in his millennial prophecies of America:

> The *untransacted* destiny of the American people is to subdue the continent – to rush over this vast field to the Pacific Ocean – to animate the many hundred millions of its people, and to cheer them upward ... to agitate these herculean masses – to establish a new order in human affairs ... to regenerate superannuated nations ... to stir up the sleep of a hundred centuries – to teach old nations a new civilization – to confirm the destiny of the human race – to carry the career of mankind to its culminating point – to cause a stagnant people to be reborn – to perfect science – to emblazon history with the conquest of peace – to shed a new and resplendent glory upon mankind – to unite the world in one social family – to dissolve the spell of tyranny and exalt charity – to absolve the

curse that weighs down humanity, and to shed blessings round the world![23]

The imprimatur of manifest destiny lent significant support to America's aggressive foreign policy goals in the 1840s. It justified an internal imperialism in which foreign lands were to be made free either by coercion, or by the displacement of its peoples. The establishment of manifest destiny represented a major turning-point in America's national consciousness. In the words of Arthur Ekirch,

the idea of mission, though expansionist, emphasized on the whole the peaceful export of American ideology and the realization of the natural rights of man through the spread of American institutions. In contrast, the concept of manifest destiny implied expansion in a more belligerent manner. It turned the defensive and idealistic notions of isolationism and mission toward the course of a unilateral, nationalist, political and territorial expansion. And, in so doing it also transposed broader, more universal values of genuine international importance – the natural rights philosophy, for example – into a narrower doctrine of the special rights of Americans over and against other peoples.[24]

The idea of manifest destiny elevated the American impulse to expand to the level of an inexorable and providential process, in which Americans were bequeathed both special rights and obligations to extend their sphere of influence over other peoples for the greater good of all, but more particularly for the narrow benefit of the United States.

Following the interruption of the Civil War, but thereafter with the enhanced nationalist spirit coming from that conflict, the United States resumed the pursuit of its manifest destiny with a greater zeal and aggression than ever before. The old notion of righteous and providential expansion was now infused with America's industrial and financial power, with the Darwinian categories of competitive necessity and with the rise of a new imperialist international order. The United States' sense of its universal beneficence now took it into its own imperialist era. The western impetus was carried beyond the natural boundary of the United States into the Pacific Ocean, thereby abandoning the idea that America could have any natural point of limitation.[25] After the Spanish-American War of 1898, the United States acquired Puerto Rico, Guam and the Philippines.[26] This sudden inheritance was construed as renewed validation of America's mission to propagate the message of natural rights, to regenerate lesser nations, to enlighten inferior mortals and to widen the blessings of democratic civilisation. Even when this imperialist impulse to acquire lands had weakened, the nature of America's messianic obligations was simply transferred to the sphere of foreign markets, dollar diplomacy and an economic, military and ideological pre-eminence in world affairs.

These examples of 'nation-building' experiences are highly significant to the contemporary state of American nationalism. Factors like the Civil War and manifest destiny are more than simply contributory factors to a basic sense of American nationhood. They have been central in demarcating the type of nationhood America has acquired. In other words, the Civil War and manifest destiny have not just provided the occasions when Americans developed an enhanced sense of solidarity as Americans; they have been, and still are, instrumental in defining the content and characteristics of current American nationalism.

A case in point is the continuing tension within the American mind over whether American behaviour as a nation follows its own ideals or its own self-interest.[27] This sort of debate is plagued with all manner of conceptual difficulties and yet it remains a permanent fact of American public life and an integral element in how America views itself as a nation. The fusion of territorial expansion with national integration and American political ideals, first achieved in the era of rising manifest destiny, has remained a controlling assumption of national outlook and foreign policy. The nation, which had apparently spread so naturally, had now inherited the duty to promote the spread of America's nature elsewhere. In the words of President Kennedy,

> Other countries look to their own interests. Only the United States has obligations which stretch ten thousand miles across the Pacific, and three or four thousand miles across the Atlantic and thousands of miles to the south. Only the United States – and we are only 6 per cent of the world's population – bears this kind of burden.[28]

This sense of obligation has been shared by men as varied as Dean Rusk, the Secretary of State in the Kennedy and Johnson administrations ('other nations have interests, the United States has responsibilities'[29]) and Henry Kissinger who was the Secretary of State for Presidents Nixon and Ford. Despite being the acknowledged master of the black arts of international *realpolitik*, even Kissinger believed that the United States had a special historical role as 'the embodiment of mankind's hopes'.[30]

America still defines itself as a nation compelled to action by its own principles. In August 1990, President George Bush despatched naval, air and ground forces to the Gulf of Persia to protect Saudi Arabia from possible Iraqi aggression. In launching the greatest deployment of American military power since the Vietnam War, the President made it clear in a televised address to the nation that 'standing up for our principles is an American tradition'. He concluded with the following reassurance: 'America has never wavered when her purpose is driven by principle, and on this August day, at home and abroad, I know she will do no less.'[31] Americans continue to be convinced that they are different to other nationalities in that their motives and objectives are thought to be necessarily superior in virtue because they emanate from a uniquely located and conditioned society and because they are informed by a different set of ideals. According to James Chace, for example,

> Americans are most comfortable with a foreign policy imbued with moral purpose. Even when the pursuit of justice has led to unintended consequences, even when our ideals have concealed from ourselves as well as from others motivations of a darker and more complex nature, we have preferred a policy that at least rhetorically is based on moral purpose rather than self-interest'.[32]

As such, Americans have a propensity to believe that they are 'different from Europeans in having the best interests of the world at heart'.[33]

What this avowed idealism and selflessness can overlook, however, is the way that an attachment to principle can become synonymous with an attachment to self-interest. Just as economic concerns can be expressed in terms of overseas emancipation and enlightenment, so American ideals of individual rights and liberal stability can service the needs of American capitalism. Because of this interrelationship, the celebration of American ideals and American self-interest can become one and the same thing. The sentiments of Senator Albert J. Beveridge, for example, convey America's potential for this fusion of commercial gain and moral right.

The commercial empire of the Republic! That is the greatest fact of the future ... This Nation is to be the sovereign factor in the peace of the world ... As our commerce spreads, the flag of liberty will circle the globe and the highways ... of all mankind be guarded by the guns of the Republic ... We are enlisted in the cause of American supremacy, which will never end until American commerce has made the conquest of the world; until American citizenship has become the lord of civilization; and the stars and stripes the flag of flags throughout the world.[34]

The extent to which self-interest can appear to dominate national drives is a traditional cause of American concern. It can lead to periodic attempts to revive the idealistic element of America's manifest destiny. By the same token, this impulse towards self-conscious idealism can in its own right generate demands that America be more attentive to its domestic welfare and national interests.

The notion that a country needs to be reminded of its own self-interest and of the need for 'realism' in foreign policy[35] is peculiar to the United States and bears witness to America's belief in its idealistic otherworldliness. To Europeans and more sceptical Americans, on the other hand, America's travails over the extent and expense of its own professed innocence and naivety can be seen to be bogus preoccupations that conceal an arrogant national righteousness. This sense of inner conviction can prompt Americans not only to pursue self-interest under the guise of idealism, but even to pervert its own democratic principles in the name of an overriding notion of idealised obligation. From America's destruction of the Philippine national liberation movement after the islands had been ceded to the United States in 1898, through its numerous interventions in Latin America, and on to its recent characterisation of the Contra guerrillas in Nicaragua as 'freedom fighters', the United States has regularly defied its own professed ideal of national self-determination. On those occasions when the principles threatened to produce types of government which were not in accordance with the form and purposes of American government, the United States would seek to overturn them as contrary to America's national interest and therefore, by American definition, contrary to the interests of the countries in question.[36]

The persistence of tensions between ideals and self-interest, between moralism and realism and between libertarianism and militarism has led to a continued American ambivalence towards the world. It has even led to assertions that the 'American mind ... is incapable of coping with modern history'.[37] For example, the United States is known for its capacity for xenophobic isolation and also for its inflated internationalism. Just as America's confidence in its exceptionalism can lead it into global engagements to redeem the world, so it can also lead it to a retreat from the ethical afflictions and intractable problems of what lies beyond America's shores. 'Its absolute national morality' can, in Louis Hartz's words, inspire it 'either to withdraw from "alien" things or to transform them: it cannot live in comfort constantly by their side.'[38]

America's geographical isolation, its wealth of natural resources and the customary assurance of its national security as the new world's most extensive and well integrated power bloc following the Civil War, has allowed the United States to remain a nation apart from other nations – to be *in* the world but not *of* it. While it is true that the United States has become an integral part of the collective security and international alliance arrangements of the post-World War II environment, America is still regarded as being only a half-formed member of the international community. The United States' own sense of nationalism remains rooted in the idea that it is not as irrevocably and as inextricably enmeshed into the world as other nations. Its entry into the world is still conceived as an autonomous act by a nation moving of its own volition and in pursuit of its own destiny.

Accordingly, its collaborative efforts with other countries have often been strained. The United States has a reputation for only participating in those alliances in which it is assured of being the dominant partner (e.g. the North Atlantic Treaty Organisation); for distancing itself from international organisations which it cannot dominate (e.g. the United Nations); and for retaining a licence to act suddenly and alone in the pursuit of its own interests (e.g. Grenada/Reykjavik).[39] America's lack of reconciliation with being an 'ordinary country'[40] in a progressively interdependent world has been most recently revealed in President Reagan's obsession with a missile defence system for the United States (i.e. the Strategic Defence Initiative or 'Star Wars'). To many Europeans, this was yet another attempt by the United States to possess a reserve capacity to disengage from other nations and to take refuge in itself, by using American wealth and technology to replace the old spatial isolationism of the oceans with a new spatial isolationism based in the skies.

Whatever form American nationalism takes, one thing is quite certain – America's view of the world and the world's view of America has always been, and remains, central to the nation's identity. America's sense of itself is rooted in its conception of the position and role that it possesses in the outside world. It is this point of reference that defines America's distinctive and even exceptional properties. It also provides the object upon which America's own contribution to civilisation can be identified and even celebrated. What America believes it means to the world is important to what America means to itself. The significance attached to the idea of America's world role as the outward signs of an inner national character is reflected time and again in US foreign policy.

During President Carter's administration, for example, a deliberate attempt was made to revive the universal moral value of America by injecting human rights considerations into US foreign policymaking. Carter himself led the crusade by stating that America's 'commitment to human rights must be absolute'.[41] Apart from trying to improve the human rights records of third world dictatorships like Argentina and Brazil, the policy had the added benefit of reminding America of its own virtues and ideals. After the national malaise induced by the Vietnam War and the Watergate scandal, Americans were being asked to recall that the system of human rights was 'America's unique and wondrous contribution to mankind'.[42] Carter's overseas evangelism, therefore, was not confined to the world outside the United States. It was very much an effort to restore confidence in American institutions, traditions and ideals by using the world as a mirror to reflect the properties and pride of American nationalism back upon the homeland.

Carter was not unusual in using the Presidency to invigorate the nation's spirit. In many respects, the modern presidency has become synonymous with the American nation, not just because of the central position in foreign policymaking that it affords to its incumbent, but also because of the way that Presidents can provide enough of a focal point in America's mass politics to become the 'personification of the people'[43] and the 'democratic symbol of national unity'.[44] A President's capacity to embody the nation and to arouse the expression of national allegiance through his own office is revealed most dramatically on those occasions when the United States is involved in an international crisis. Studies show that a President enduring low support for his domestic policies, and suffering from all the restrictions implicit in a pluralist system and in a constitutional framework of checks and balances, can suddenly be given a prodigious freedom of action and a high level of popular support whenever America finds itself implicated in dramatic and sharply-focused international events.[45]

This 'rally round the flag' effect is even evident when the President himself is seen as being responsible for a crisis. Events like military interventions, major diplomatic developments and actions leading to international tension, confront the nation as a whole. As such, they generate an intense national loyalty which devolves emphatically upon the only entity capable of giving concentrated symbolic and material reality to the idea of the nation. Alton Frye concludes that

> The pronounced tendency to rally around the president in a crisis is one indicator of the continuing force of American nationalism. However doubtful or self-critical Americans may be about particular foreign policies, they are in no doubt whatsoever that they share a common fate as a people and that, when tested by dangers in the outer world, they must stand together. No international institution, no global values, no appeals to our common humanity demonstrate such power to mobilize American opinion.[46]

Nationalism has proved to be such a palpable and potent political resource that it has not been uncommon for Presidents to establish – or to try to establish – international affairs as the centre-piece of their administrations. Less evident, but no less real, have been the numerous attempts by Presidents to colour domestic issues in nationalist tones. Presidents try to channel the nationalist potential for political mobilisation into internal affairs to give themselves the same leverage as they have in foreign policy. President Eisenhower, for example, used the launch of the Soviet Union's Sputnik satellite in 1957 to shock his political opponents into supporting the principle of federal aid to education. Under the pretext of the need to improve the standard of scientific and technical training, the President was able to secure a broad-based package of student loans, graduate fellowships and school assistance schemes under the title of the National Defense Education Act. Whether it is President Kennedy using the cold war's ideological competitiveness in the third world to force the pace of civil rights in the South, or President Johnson declaring a 'war on poverty', or President Carter describing the energy crisis as the 'moral equivalent of war', or President Bush launching a 'war on drugs', the strategy of invoking national mobilisation for domestic objectives is the same. The fact that this tactic has so often been successful is a further testament to the power of American nationalism.

But perhaps the most remarkable facet of the American national spirit is the way that it can be differentiated from, and then used to oppose, the state. This is not to say that American nationalism has not been successfully deployed to give legitimacy to American government and its actions. From the examples quoted above, it is clear that the federal government has in many ways successfully claimed the right to embody an integrated form of national citizenship and to act on behalf of the nation to promote the general welfare and the national interest. Nevertheless, the fusion of nation and state remains far from complete.

Within the concept of the American nation lies the ancient libertarian tradition of the new world which can still be successfully activated to oppose not merely government policy, but the authority of the state itself. In spite of its democratic credentials, therefore, America possesses a nationalist spirit that generates a dimension of experiences and allegiances that is separate from government. As a consequence, it is possible to be against the state without being against the nation. On the contrary, just as an attachment to the nation is often regarded as being positively synonymous with anti-statist sentiment, so America's periodic crusades against government are normally fired by an arousal of national ideas, faiths and symbols.[47]

The American nation has remained a separate entity from the state largely because the qualities of American nationalism continue to be so elusive in character. According to Hans Kohn, the American sense of nation is founded not upon any ethnic, religious or cultural ties rooted in some ancestral soil, but upon a common allegiance to a set of traditional ideas and principles. 'It was born in a common effort, in a fight for political rights, for individual liberty and tolerance.'[48] What were originally English rights and traditions were transformed by the American experience into universal rights which had the 'strength to transform men of the most various pasts and descents into new men, building a common future in a new land'.[49] This was tantamount to making a nation through the acquisition of common values.

> The United States indeed, virtually alone among nations, found and to some extent still finds its identity not so much in ethnic community or shared historical experience as in dedication to a value system; and the reiteration of these values, the repeated proclamation of and dedication to the liberal creed, has always been a fundamental element in the cohesion of American society. In this respect the United States has always resembled rather a secular church, or perhaps a gigantic sect, than it has the nation–states of the Old World.[50]

With this background, America has become the archetype of 'open nationalism' – a nation of fellow citizens from different backgrounds but with a shared allegiance to certain general principles of social and governmental organisation.

As has already been acknowledged, this 'openness' has not only been questioned by groups convinced of their own exclusion, but has also been simultaneously attacked and exploited by nativist movements seeking to impose a 'closed nationalism' of ethnic and tribal purity on to the United States. To other observers, America's 'open nationalism' *is* based upon an attachment to a common cause of liberal ideas. Nevertheless, the collective loyalty to these principles can make the United States seem as enclosed a nation as any other.

> For an immigrant, to be American was to believe in Americanism, just as to be a Roman once implied neither race nor descent but conformity to a civic religion. A man can even cease to believe in the Bolshevik ideology and still be a Russian. But if he ceases to believe in the American way he becomes literally expatriate.[51]

As the investigations into Un-American Activities during the 1950s revealed, the rational openness of America's principles implied a corresponding expectation of a closed and emotional conformity to their content. But whether America's nationalism has been more closed than open or more open than closed, what is clear is that America's national experience and identity is characteristically discerned and expressed through the medium of rights, liberties and limited government. And nowhere is this equation of nationhood with governing values more evident than in the national veneration afforded to the American Constitution.

Constitutionalism
AS THE MEDIUM OF
AMERICA'S POLITICAL VALUES

If, as has often been claimed, the United States is a secular religion, then there can be little doubt that the Constitution provides the Holy Writ. The Constitution is often referred to as the Ark of the American covenant because of the emotional attachments it evokes and because of the political symbolism it generates throughout American society.

> Written interpretations of it resemble analyses of the scriptures, it comes to prescribe civic virtue and to legitimize good behavior, and an elaborate code of laws and customs build up around it, presumably shaped by the needs of the day. Often the fact that a constitution was originally a political document is all but forgotten.[1]

This 'cult of constitution worship'[2] can lead to the most extraordinary eulogies of dedication and veneration.

> Our great and sacred Constitution, serene and inviolable, stretches its beneficent powers over our land – over its lakes and rivers and forests, over every mother's son of us, like the outstretched arm of God himself ... O Marvellous Constitution! Magic Parchment! Transforming word! Maker, Monitor, Guardian of Mankind! Thou hast gathered to thy impartial bosom the peoples of the earth, Columbia, and called them equal ... I would fight for every line in the Constitution as I would fight for every star in the flag.[3]

It can also lead to an ornate imagery of almost baroque proportions: 'The Constitution has the aura of the sacred about it. It occupies a shrine up in the higher stretches of American reverence. A citizen imagines sunshot clouds, the founders hovering in the air like saints in religious art.'[4] Clearly the United States Constitution is far from being simply a legal charter. It possesses a centrality in American society and culture which is quite exceptional and which is rooted in something far more substantial than mere sentiment or blind faith.

The outstanding appeal of the Constitution to a society not noted for its respect for political institutions is derived from the document's close connection with the identity and development of the United States as a nation. The Constitution not only marked the creation of the American republic, it has also defined the character of its subsequent history and political ethos. As a result, the American nation is conceived in constitutional terms while American nationalism is seen as the derivative of American constitutionalism. National crises are therefore equated with constitutional crises; and American victories are identified as occasions when the Constitution has prevailed over adversity. In the words of Hans Kohn, 'it represents the life-blood of the American nation, its supreme symbol and manifestation'.[5] To Alexander Bickel, it is 'the symbol of nationhood, of continuity, of unity and common purpose'.[6]

Integral to its identity with the American nation has been the Constitution's capacity to absorb and to symbolise those values and ideals with which the United States has been most closely associated. In this sense, it can be said that the Constitution

> draws its lasting strength not from what it says but from what it is: the embodiment of the idea by which the United States was constituted – a nation without even a name to which emotions could cling, like England, France, Italia or Hellas, and yet from its beginning appealing to the imagination of men as the first nation to identify itself and to have been identified by others with an idea. To become an American has always meant to identify oneself with the idea.[7]

The idea or ideas in question – whether the emphasis is given to liberty, or equality of rights, or to individual freedoms, or to popular sovereignty – serve to render the Constitution as a foundation of social and ideological cohesion for a turbulent and rapidly-developing country, whose potential for disintegration would otherwise have been considerable. As Ralph B. Perry put it, 'history affords few parallel instances of a state thus abruptly created, and consciously dedicated to a body of ideas whose acceptance constitutes its underlying bond of agreement'.[8] That initial agreement has been successively reaffirmed with the result that the Constitution now not only 'provides the most important symbol of national regime identity ... it represents – and to some extent is – the regime'[9] itself. In other words, the Constitution's original 'triumph as a pure reflection of the American ideology – the political idea given governmental form' has now been extended to the point where it is actually the 'embodiment of the country's most fundamental political values'[10] and of that level of social consensus which maintains them. Liberals and conservatives may 'disagree over what certain constitutional provisions require, but together they see being "unconstitutional" as the equivalent of being un-American'.[11]

The extent to which the Constitution can be projected into the realm of primary truths and metaphysical constructs is best represented by the work of Daniel Boorstin. In *The Genius of American Politics*, Boorstin attributes the poverty of political philosophy in the United States to the belief that America was bequeathed at its birth with a comprehensive political theory in the form of the federal constitution. This bequest by the Founding Fathers has been adequate for all subsequent social needs. According to Boorstin, Americans find it 'peculiarly congenial to claim possession of a perfect set of political ideas, especially when they have a magical elusiveness and flexibility'.[12]

> Changes in our policy or institutions are read back into the ideas, and sometimes into the very words, of the Founding Fathers ... What is more significant is the way in which we have justified the adaptation of the document to current needs: by attributing clarity, comprehensiveness, and a kind of mystical foresight to the social theory of the founders.[13]

His elevation of the Constitution to that of a scheme of government acquired through America's historical and geographical providence is used to support the contention that the United States possesses such a level of unanimity in support of these original ideas, that they no longer seem like ideas. They appear instead to be the self-evident expressions of a prolonged experience of social agreement in which any ideas or themes can seem unnecessary and superfluous in the American context.

In Boorstin's view, the Constitution is central to the exceptionalism of American culture. The asserted perfection and instinctive validity of the Constitution's ideas mean that alternative ideas are viewed as suspiciously alien and subversive simply because they are given the stigma of being 'ideas' – and therefore not of the Constitution or of America. In this way, 'constitutional history can, and in many ways, has become a substitute for social and political theory'.[14] Boorstin might just as well have added that it was a substitute for social and political history as well because, to an observer like Boorstin, American history was born with the Constitution and has followed a singular, continuous and unchanging course ever since.

Boorstin's celebration of the Constitution typifies the American attachment to the document. But while the intensity of the dedication is undisputed, the reasons for a society's intimate and even obsessive involvement in its constitution is not so evident. At first sight, it is difficult to see why such a constitution should evoke such extraordinary interest. The document is short, ambiguously worded and devoid of any clear programmatic content in which the objectives and purposes of the American nation are clearly stated. In spite of its reputation as a systematic structure of political authority and organisation, the Constitution was the product of a series of bargains and compromises which led to many problems being either unacknowledged (e.g. slavery) or unresolved (e.g. the nature of the federal union). During the bicentennial of the Constitution in 1987, Justice Thurgood Marshall, the only black man ever to serve on the Supreme Court, had the audacity to remind his countrymen that the Constitution had not been the answer to America's problems when it was formulated in 1787.

> I do not believe that the meaning of the Constitution was forever 'fixed' at the Philadelphia Convention. Nor do I find the wisdom, foresight and sense of justice exhibited by the Framers particularly profound. To the contrary, the government they devised was defective from the start, requiring several amendments, a civil war and momentous social transformation to attain the system of constitutional government, and its respect for individual freedoms and human rights, we hold as fundamental today.[15]

Marshall might well have gone on to affirm the view of other critics who believe that the Constitution has not only failed to settle old problems (e.g. the scope of the executive's prerogative powers in foreign policy; the question of who shall be given 'the equal protection of the laws' and how it should be done; the difficulty of determining whether the prohibition on the establishment of religion means that the state can encourage religious pluralism, or no religious practice whatsoever); it has served to generate fresh problems through its chronic inability to adapt to modern conditions (e.g. the extent to which the constitutional system of checks and balances generates so much friction that it reduces and even eliminates the American system's capacity to make coherent policy in areas of urgent public concern like environmental protection, industrial planning, economic management, urban renewal, equitable taxation, economic security and technological development).[16]

In spite of the severity of such criticisms, the peculiar appeal of the Constitution and the compulsive loyalty to its provisions remain undiminished. Its significance and authority continue to belie its apparent content. The reasons for this almost anomalous state of allegiance are many and varied, but three are of particular importance.

Firstly, is the fact that the Constitution is the oldest working constitution in existence. The Constitution's sheer longevity invests it with a historical authority stretching back to the eighteenth century when the United States was formed. The success of the country has been reflected back upon its Constitution. Furthermore, what crises have arisen 'like the civil war, the Indian campaigns and massacres and foreign wars have all been dealt with within the same constitutional structure'.[17]

The brevity and ambiguity of the Constitution has afforded it a capacious adaptability, while at the same time allowing it to retain the prestige of apparent changelessness. The Constitution has revealed a capacity to absorb substantial changes within its terms of reference. Not the least of these has been the development of democracy to embrace categories of people (e.g. women, blacks, the propertyless) previously excluded from participation, the rise of the positive state, and the emergence of the United States as an international superpower. Despite the scale of such changes, the Constitution has been formally amended on only twenty-six occasions since 1789. In form, at least, the Constitution today remains virtually the same as it was at its inception.

The *second* factor relates to the institutional structure of the Constitution. Power was divided amongst spatial (i.e. federalism) and functional (i.e. separation of powers) units of government, in order to generate a mechanism of competitive interplay between institutions that would ensure a self-perpetuating dispersal of power and the preservation of individual liberties. The Founding Fathers' concern that the general welfare and public interest could be endangered by the mobilised prejudices of the general population and by the agitation of the public into turbulent and impulsive majorities led them to rationalise the variously negotiated components of power as a unified scheme of checks and balances in the cause of limited government. The Constitution's chief architect, James Madison, explained that in the 'compound republic of America' the rights of the people were afforded a 'double security'.[18] Power relinquished by the people was 'first divided between two distinct governments, and then the portion allotted to each subdivided among distinct and separate departments' of government.[19]

As a consequence, the federal division of sovereignty between the national and state governments – which was largely the result of both political bargaining and a realistic appraisal of the strength of state authority – was given the same ulterior motive as the separation of powers scheme amongst the legislative, executive and judicial branches of the national government. As M. J. C. Vile, points out, the connection between the organisation of political authority and the objectives of such an arrangement does not have to be declared in order for it to be effective.

> The great theme of the advocates of constitutionalism ... has been the frank acknowledgement of the role of government in society linked with the determination to bring that government under control and to place limits on the exercise of its power ... [In this respect] there are certain demonstrable relationships between given types of institutional arrangement and the safeguarding of important values.[20]

Even though the underlying objective of the Constitution's pattern of powers and institutional dynamics was not stated, the liberal ethos of limited government was quite clear – liberties *from* government were to be as important as any liberties secured *through* government.

The *third* factor that has contributed to the constitution's authority has been the Bill of Rights. These first ten amendments to the Constitution were proposed by the Founders' opponents who believed that the political rights to be defended by the new structure should be made explicit. The Anti-Federalists were not prepared to rely solely on the provisions of the original Constitution or upon James Madison's self-limiting mechanics. As a result, the First Amendment gave expression to a series of positive liberties (e.g. freedom of speech and of assembly, and freedom of religious worship), while most of the remaining amendments laid down traditional common-law rights against the government (e.g. fair trial procedures, the right to bear arms, rights against unreasonable searches and seizures). These stipulated guarantees became the chief monument of American individualism. If American government was to be limited government, then it was these measures that would define something of the freedom to be secured through such constraint.

The Bill of Rights is just as significant for the way that it exemplifies the degree to which the Constitution draws on, and reveals, the depth of the American tradition of higher law. This refers to the belief that legitimate government is one whose authority is derived from, and whose actions conform to, a set of values which are variously described as natural, or eternal, or universal or divine. The validity of these underlying principles provide an alternative dimension to political legitimacy. They imply 'a justice which human authority expresses, or ought to express – but does not make ... It follows that law – in the sense of the law of the last resort – is somehow above law-making. It follows that law-makers, after all, are somehow under and subject to law.'[21]

In the colonial era, Americans had become particularly susceptible to the theories and practices of higher law. They were as accustomed to the textual interpretation of colonial charters as they were of the Bible. They showed as much interest in the various classical and contemporary philosophies of natural law as they did in the idea of a divine law. And as English colonists, they also had that distinctive outlook on customary liberties that had always been the basis of Anglo-Saxon common law. These separate strands came together in the late eighteenth century and prepared the ground for a thoroughgoing constitutionalism of limited government and of guaranteed rights against government. The attribution of the Constitution as 'the supreme law of the land' was based upon these traditions and allegiances that were themselves infused with the concepts of natural law.

The American tradition of a higher law – of a 'government of laws, not of men' – was sustained throughout the nineteenth century in spite of the rise and development of a mass democracy. Indeed, nineteenth-century Americans affirmed 'as the primary doctrine of their democratic faith, that beneath society, its customs and institutions, a law existed that men did not make. This law outlined the patterns of both individual and social life.'[22] Today this tradition of higher law as a challenge to human authority is still expressed in the belief that the Constitution is ethically superior to government and that in comparison to ordinary laws, therefore, the Constitution is the law of superior obligation. Government is seen as subject to and accountable to the Constitution. In this way, the legitimacy of the government is, ultimately, dependent not on its own political record, but on the extent to which it is adjudged to have conformed to the Constitution. The distinction between the Constitution and the government remains central to American politics. The Constitution maintains its distance through its close association with the virtues of higher law. The 'indebtedness of American constitutional law to natural law [and] natural rights concepts for its content in the field of private rights is vital and well-nigh all-comprehensive'.[23]

The government's constitutionality is only in part determined by the fact that it is composed of those institutions and powers provided in the Constitution and by the fact that it has of necessity to conduct itself through the complex and self-limiting procedures laid down in the document. But the American conception of constitutionality is not confined to structural and procedural propriety. It is the Bill of Rights which provides the substantive embodiment of the Constitution's liberal purposes and which epitomises the way that the Constitution is invested with the moral code of a genuine and determinable higher law.

These three contributory factors in the Constitution's remarkable authority (i.e. its continuity, its structure and its tradition of higher law) have together given rise to a peculiar type of politics in the United States. Because the Constitution is accepted as the supreme law of the land, it means that political debate is dominated by the need to justify political positions and proposals by reference to the Constitution. Policies and measures, therefore, need more than merely political support. They require constitutional validity. They need to be seen as being derived from the Constitution's provisions and to be in accord with the pure essence of the American ethos, which the Constitution is assumed to embody in its provisions. As a consequence, every issue, act, law and practice has to be argued out in constitutional terms, as each party in any dispute pursues the mantle of constitutional probity. As a result, political debate becomes entwined in constitutional constructions, while the forms of legal adjudication become heavily penetrated by the arguments and interests of political forces.

Inherent in this fusion of political and legal activity is the common assumption that the law – in the grandeur of its constitutional sense – pre-exists the transient laws of government. In consequence, constitutional law is thought to be not made, so much as discovered by being elicited from the body of the Constitution itself. Because the Constitution is regarded as a particular type of law and because it is accepted that it requires arbitration from an independent and impartial agency, Americans have generally deferred to the principle that it is judges who ought to provide the final answers as to what the Constitution has within it. This is what de Tocqueville meant when he said that 'scarcely any question arises in the United States which does not become, sooner or later, a subject of judicial debate'.[24] The courts, and especially the Supreme Court, are considered to be the ultimate arbiters of the Constitution, not simply because they are last in a long line of constitutional dispute, but because the asserted truth of the Constitution is more persuasively revealed by judges who appear at least to have less political concern than any other sector of society.

The authority of the Constitution has afforded a social status and political power to American judges that is unsurpassed outside the United States. Bertrand Russell once remarked that in the United

States, 'the reverence which the Greeks gave to oracles and the Middle Ages to the Pope is given to the Supreme Court'.[25] These professional custodians of the Constitution attempt to preserve and to extend the principle that constitutionality is not a matter of construction but of elucidation. In the words of Arthur S. Miller: 'The dominant ideology of the American legal profession is "legalism". Law is separated, in this conception, not only from morals but also from politics. Law is considered to be "there" – separate and apart from the rest of society, a discrete entity amenable to analysis as such.'[26] American judges have encouraged their countrymen not only to view the Constitution as an 'ideal floating above [their] heads',[27] but also to accept that only judges can finally transmute the ideal into the material reality of hard decisions and concrete pronouncements.

In laying claim to be the arbiters of the Constitution, the American judiciary has worked to fuse its own identity and its own protection with the solemn majesty of the Constitution. Thus the Constitution has received a voice and an institutional expression. A judge portrays himself as having to 'interpret and apply the constitutional order by deductive decision-making, applying its generalities to the specific problems of everyday life'.[28] This has the effect of continually enhancing the status of law in American society and, in particular, of securing the position of the Constitution as an evocation of high values and supreme authority. The interdependency of the judiciary and the Constitution has meant that while constitutional law is celebrated as 'evidently and necessarily the rock on which the American nation is built',[29] judges are acknowledged as having a similarly exalted status as agents 'participating directly and explicitly and actively ... in the endless process of making the American nation'.[30] In Ronald Dworkin's words, 'the courts are the capitals of law's empire, and the judges are its princes'.[31]

Because the judges assume the role of 'discovering' the Constitution's meaning and because they have the privileged positions, through the practice of judicial review, to act upon that assumption, there is always immense interest in the United States in who the judges are and what they actually do when they are engaged in constitutional adjudication. Controversy rages amongst scholars, observers, lawyers and even among the judges themselves over the nature of the judicial process and over different claims between what judges are supposed to be doing and what they actually do. For example, some theorists believe that during the recent past the Supreme Court has departed from the Constitution in its judgements. Instead of adhering to the text of the Constitution and to making judgements on the basis of a fair reading of the document's content and of the intentions of the Framers, critics complain that Supreme Court decisions have all too often been based upon what the judges felt were desirable policy outcomes. According to this perspective, these decisions have not been drawn from an impartial consideration of the spirit and letter of the Constitution's content. They have come about from a desire by judges to abuse both their position and the standard of the Supreme Court's jurisprudence, in order to exert their own will on the Constitution's meaning and to arrive at decisions indistinguishable from legislative enactments. Such critics advocate the need for 'neutral' principles of adjudication, for a proper respect for the original intentions behind the Constitution and for the recovery of the literal meaning of the text.[32]

Other theorists oppose these views on both empirical and normative grounds. They argue that Supreme Court judgements have not simply been derived from rootless subjectivity but have been necessary and desirable constructions which have allowed the Constitution to remain a living entity of adaptable meanings and applications. According to this type of perspective, the Constitution has neither fixed principles nor static meanings. Judicial self-restraint, therefore, would not only jeopardise the Constitution's centrality as a scheme of government, but would be tantamount to rejecting the possibility that the Constitution had a genuinely normative content of individual rights and social justice. To these theorists, the courts are right to enforce principles of liberty and justice derived from the Constitution's stock of natural law principles. Legal judgement is, and should be, political in nature in so far as it allows the Constitution to be informed by the prevailing beliefs and practices that together constitute a political community.[33]

This is not the occasion to enter into an evaluative discussion of these claims and counter-claims. It is enough simply to recognise that the debate over what judges do and how they do it is a reflection of the problematic nature of the much larger and more significant

question of what the Constitution itself is in terms of composition
and purpose. At first sight, this might not seem to be much of a
problem. The Constitution appears to be a codified framework of
institutions, procedures and rights which reputedly provides a
comprehensive structure of government embodying a thorough
constitutional settlement of all major issues concerning sovereignty,
authority and liberties. But, as has already been acknowledged
above, the Constitution in reality did not resolve, and has not
resolved, many of the most important issues in American politics and
society. The chief reason for this failure is usually attributed to the
fact that the Constitution itself has failed to resolve the questions of
its own meanings and powers as a charter of government. This is
because the Constitution is as noted for its ambiguities, anomalies
and points of friction, as it is for any of its systematic properties.

Nevertheless, it is precisely this element of indeterminacy and
uncertainty that provides much of the Constitution's enduring
virtue. The Constitution's brevity and ambiguity gives the document
a valuable degree of interpretive slack. This in turn provides it with
a huge capacity to absorb different points of view and different
principles within a single unified dimension of presumptive constitutionality. It is the Constitution's lack of definition, therefore, that
provides it with so many contending definitions. This makes it
possible for widely differing parties to argue out their differences
through the common medium of constitutional argument and
construction.

This does not mean that the different parties will come to agree
with one another, but it does mean that they are likely to agree on
how to differ from each other. The very fact that they are both using
the Constitution as a common frame of reference and as a common
standard of legitimacy – together with the language, words and
criteria of proof associated with constitutional argument – means
that in their differences they are revealing a unified deference to
constitutional arbitration.

The assimilative properties of the Constitution, together with its
status as the core of American political legitimacy, has led to the
Constitution becoming the supreme matrix of American ideas and
traditions. It provides the medium through which values and
principles confront one another and through which practical ac-

commodations are arrived at. As ideological and social conflict is transmuted into constitutional dispute, and as political questions are transformed into legal argument, so it is that constitutional adjudication provides the format for political and ideological settlement. In the words of Morton Keller, the Constitution 'however tangentially and ambiguously' has

> defined the boundaries of debate over persistent, never-resolved issues in American public life. The great ongoing contentions between liberty and equality, between individual freedom and social responsibility, between the nation and the states, and between the State and the citizen, have always been expressed in constitutional terms.[34]

Whether it is the case that the Constitution's wording especially lends itself to being construed in politically substantive and ideological terms, or whether it is more that political and ideological differences are simply projected on to the Constitution's language, the end result is the same – namely that conflicting parties and values are reduced to the same level of constitutional propositions requiring adjudication and the provision of solutions in the form of judicial declarations as to what the Constitution contains or means.

Constitutional disputes, therefore, provide the occasions when different components of the American creed or different constructions of the creed come into direct and explicit conflict. In arbitrating between these conflicting perspectives, the Supreme Court has to use the Constitution to weigh not merely the merits of the constitutional argument, but also the contemporary meaning and importance given to the variety of American values accommodated within the Constitution. In this respect, Supreme Court judgements are often in essence declarations of public philosophy in constitutional dress – declarations in which the inherent strains between American values are not so much resolved as reformulated either to reflect current conceptions of, and allegiances to, different aspects of America's liberal democracy, or else to achieve a different balance between the constituent themes of the regime.

In the previous chapter, we witnessed how the rising sensitivity over the bogus equality of segregated schools led the Supreme Court to declare such facilities to be no longer constitutional. The Court chose to infringe the liberty of whites, in order to secure a greater equality for blacks. On other occasions, the Court has sought to enhance individual liberty at the expense of equality and even to the detriment of democracy.

The most extreme example of this permutation of emphasis was probably provided by the Court's attempt to limit the traditionally uncircumscribed powers of the states to pass whatever laws they wished in order to protect the health, safety and welfare of their citizens. In the *laissez-faire* era of minimal government and Social Darwinism, the potential for state government intervention was seen as a perennial threat to the liberal dogmas of individual autonomy and market dynamics. The Supreme Court sought to prevent any excessive or unnecessary state interference in the conduct of business by using the due process clause of the Fourteenth Amendment to restrict the scope of state government activity.[35]

According to the Amendment's wording, no state should 'deprive any person of life, liberty, or property, without due process of law'. The Court proceeded to pack the due process clause with substantive meaning so that it was transformed from a procedural guarantee into a device for maximising economic freedom. The process alluded to in the 'due process of law' was changed into a consideration of the political and economic implications of any statutory measure and, in particular, the extent to which it amounted to an unjustified infringement of individual contractual liberties. In other words, due process was given a social content and the Supreme Court set itself up as the assessor of whether states had complied with this content. On the pretext of examining *how* states had arrived at their decisions, the Court found a way of appraising *what* the states were intending to do with their powers in the light of a purportedly objective standard of evaluation.

The high-water mark of this judicial presumption, to make state actions conditional upon the Court's appraisal of whether they had complied with a particular conception of liberty, came with *Lochner v. New York* (1905).[36] In this case, the Supreme Court directly and explicitly incorporated the principles of market liberalism into the Constitution: 'The general right to make a contract in relation to his business is part of the liberty of the individual protected by the Fourteenth Amendment.'[37] This infusion of *laissez-faire* liberalism into the Fourteenth Amendment contributed towards the crisis over the Supreme Court in the 1930s when the extraordinary emergency of the Great Depression prompted unprecedented governmental intervention. The Supreme Court's inability or unwillingness to depart from its accumulated precedents led to it striking down a whole range of New Deal reforms in part because they did not conform to the established conception of economic liberty and minimal government. The crisis abated when the Court responded to the changing public philosophy, and in particular to the altered conception of liberty. In 1937, Chief Justice Hughes registered the Court's change of outlook from negative to positive liberty.

> The liberty safeguarded in the Fourteenth Amendment is a liberty in a social organization which requires the protection of law against the evils which menace the health, safety, morals and welfare of the people. Liberty under the Constitution is thus necessarily subject to the restraints of due process, and regulation which ... is adopted in the interests of the community.[38]

Implicit in this conception of liberty in the community's interest was a revision in the relative weighting given to democracy and public will over private interests and property rights. It was the community that could best decide its own economic interest. There was no longer the need or the justification for a separate and independent standard of judicial evaluation. As a result, the Supreme Court dropped substantive due process and largely abandoned the field of economic regulation to the public's elected authorities.

In circumstances less exceptional than the now discredited 'substantive due process' episode, the Court normally tries to adopt a more even-handed approach to the task of adjudicating between political principles equally legitimate in the American tradition. For example, the Court has defended the government's right to preserve public order against the rights of free political expression enshrined in the First Amendment – but only if it can be shown that political dissent actually constitutes a direct threat to political cohesion. In *Schenk* v. *United States* (1919), the Court stated the balance between freedom and order in the following terms:

> The question in every case is whether the words used are used in such circumstances and are of such a nature as to create a clear and present danger that they will bring about the substantive evils that Congress has a right to prevent. It is a question of proximity and degree.[39]

The words employed in inciting political agitation together with the manner and intention of their usage had to be measured against the likely consequences of their deployment in arriving at a conclusion as to whether or not to infringe the freedom of expression.

Another example is provided by the conflict between the First Amendment's guarantee of a free press and the nation–state's interest in keeping sensitive information on national security and foreign policy out of the public domain. The Court has generally been supportive of the executive branch's prerogative powers in international affairs. But in 1971 it refused to uphold the government against the *Washington Post* and the *New York Times* when these papers published the Defense Department's own classified history of the United States' involvement in the Vietnam War.[40] The government had obtained an injunction in a federal district court against the *New York Times* preventing further publication of what were called the 'Pentagon Papers'. When the case reached the Supreme Court, the Court was confronted with a clash between the interest of the state together with the values of nationalism and patriotism, and the First Amendment freedom of the press, together with its implications of individual rights and the 'public's right to know' in a democracy.

The Court found in favour of the latter, in the main because the government failed to show that publication would be prejudicial to the national interest. 'The First Amendment tolerates absolutely no prior judicial restraints of the press predicated upon surmise or conjecture that untoward consequences may result.'[41] And yet in what appeared to be a stinging rebuke to the Nixon administration and a celebrated affirmation of the freedom of the American press, the Court clearly implied that had the nation been in a genuine state of crisis, like a war, and had the published material clearly been detrimental to the national interest, then the Court would probably have authorised the restraint of publication.

Perhaps the Court's most ambitious attempt to reach an accommodation of values and interests in recent years came in *Roe* v. *Wade* (1973)[42]. The Court had to negotiate between the claims of women who asserted a right of personal choice over whether or not to have an abortion and the rights of democratically-elected state legislatures to ban abortion within their own areas of jurisdiction. In this highly charged issue, individual rights were confronted by clear expressions of public will within a context of intransigent moral fundamentalism. Even though the Court acknowledged the 'sensitive and emotional nature' of the abortion issue and the way that it aroused 'vigorous opposing views' and 'seemingly absolute convictions', the Justices believed that their task was to 'resolve the issue by constitutional measurement'.[43]

In effect, the Court attempted a middle course by investing both sides of the issue with constitutional legitimacy at different periods of time during a pregnancy. The Court found that in the first three months of pregnancy a woman's right to choice was protected by the guarantees of individual liberty contained in the Fourteenth Amendment. This right of privacy – implied by the individual rights enumerated in the constitution and now extended to abortion – was not, however, an absolute right. As the foetus developed, so the interest of the state grew in respect both to the mother's health and to the 'potential human life'[44] within the womb. From between three and six months, the state could regulate abortion procedures as long as they related to maternal health. The Court felt that the state's interest became compelling after six months when the potential for life outside the womb had been reached. For the final three months of pregnancy, the state 'in promoting its interest in the potentiality of human life may, if it chooses regulate, and even proscribe abortion except where it is necessary, in appropriate medical judgment, for the preservation of the life or health of the mother'.[45]

This decision has generated an intense legal and political controversy. Far from resolving the issue by 'constitutional measurement', the Court seems in many ways to have aggravated it. The judgement has been criticised by constitutional lawyers for gratuitously striking down a series of anti-abortion state laws on the grounds of a contrived right to privacy which is nowhere mentioned in the Constitution.[46] The decision has also aroused a storm of ferocious, and at times violent, political protest. On some occasions, it seemed that the *Roe* decision not only approached the limits of constitutional arbitration, it actually surpassed them. And yet in spite of the legal condemnations and the mass rallies, the decision has stood. The proposed Acts of Congress and constitutional amendments, designed to constrict the jurisdiction of the Supreme

Court and even to remove it altogether from the issue of abortion, have all failed. At no time has there been any serious prospect of solutions being sought outside the Constitution. Intense though the dissent has been, it has always been directed through the Constitution and expressed in the form of alternative constructions of the Constitution.

In the political culture of the United States, the Constitution is both a form of higher law in which fixed truths are there to be revealed and a document amenable to redefinition in the light of changing public convictions. What permits it to perform both these roles is the neutrality of its language. The Constitution may have bequeathed the United States with one predominant and ubiquitous medium of political vocabulary and debate, but in doing so it has also provided the American system with a device of extraordinary adaptability. It is no exaggeration to say that practically any principle or ideal can be cast in terms that are compatible with the Constitution. Likewise, the Constitution's own codified stipulations and provisions can ramify outwards and embrace the great and enduring questions of human affairs.

On some occasions, the neutrality of the Constitution's language can have an ameliorative effect on conflict. This is especially so when taken in conjunction with the Constitution's function of stipulating the powers of, and defining the boundaries between, units and levels of political authority. A demarcation dispute can act as a cover for a dispute over values. Likewise, a conflict over political philosophy can, in constitutional terms, be transmuted into a debate over the balance of governmental powers. For example, the confrontation over whether or not to desegregate public accommodation was argued out in the form of differing conceptions of the federal government's powers drawn from the commerce clause in the Constitution. The egalitarian drive from the centre was similarly disguised and defused in the extension of civil liberties to uniform standards within the states. What has in effect been a nationalisation of the Bill of Rights was fought for and won as a constitutional adjustment to the meaning and scope of the Fourteenth Amendment.[47]

On other occasions, the neutrality of the Constitution's language accommodates such richly differing viewpoints that the vocabulary and conventions of constitutional discourse cannot always conceal the depth of confrontation between various political beliefs and ethical values. At these times, it becomes more apparent that the Constitution was 'made for people of fundamentally differing views'.[48] In such circumstances, legal judgement cannot always avoid explicit choices. According to A. E. Dick Howard,

> The Supreme Court has in the last thirty years become an arena for resolving fundamental issues in political theory and morality. Where political theorists have long disputed, the justices have waded in, choosing among competing theories ... Where philosophers and theologians have failed to agree, the justices have decided questions of life and death.[49]

But whether conflicting political positions are rendered more or less explicit in constitutional debate, the significant point is that they are all reducible in one way or another to constitutional form. It is this virtuosity in constitutional contention that underlines the extraordinary level of constitutional consciousness in the United States and the extent to which the Constitution is regarded as an icon of the nation's traditions and purposes – prompting opposing parties to contest their differences in terms of diverging legal constructions of the central and ultimately unifying theme of America itself.

Conclusion

The place of political ideas in American society normally evokes one of three responses.

First is the view that dismisses the significance of ideologies both in America's historical development and in its current political practice. This perspective is supported by historians like Daniel Boorstin who insist that America's chief distinguishing feature is the way its political forms and processes have emanated spontaneously and organically from the geography and experience of the new model. Because tradition has conferred an indigenous hierarchy of values upon America, 'no nation has ever been less interested in political philosophy or produced less in the way of theory'.[1] Such a conception of American history lends strong support to the traditional notion that America's social consensus is both a contributory cause and a direct expression of the country's lack of ideological orientation.

These claims concerning the non-ideological outlook of American society are given considerable empirical support by recent social surveys on the systems of mass belief. In his seminal study of the structure of beliefs within mass publics, Phillip Converse asserted that members of the American public were grossly deficient in their ability to understand political issues, and to structure their positions on different issues according to a coherent set of organising principles.[2] In Converse's view, most American citizens do not possess a clearly defined scheme of conceptual reference that would allow diverse issues to be sorted in a consistent and logical alignment of response. On the contrary, most voters neither define nor use ideological terms to evaluate political parties and candidates. Their political preferences not only remain unrelated to one another, revealing a lack of 'constraint'[3] in their political belief systems, they are also highly unstable, which lends weight to the suggestion that voters are largely devoid of any substantive political beliefs at all. Other studies have produced similar findings on the tenuous relationship between the issue positions of the American public and the existence of larger and overarching points of reference that might shape and organise such attitudes. The conclusions are often couched in terms of hard realism. The genre is typified by the authors of *The American Voter* who remark that their 'failure to locate more than a trace of "ideological" thinking in the protocols of our surveys, emphasises the general impoverishment of political thought in a large proportion of the electorate'.[4]

The *second* response to the role of political ideas in the United States is the very reverse of the first response. The emphasis is placed on the centrality of ideas and on the salience of interpretive and evaluative schemes of thought. During the 1960s, in particular, the United States suddenly seemed beset by political polarisation, social disarray and ideological conflict. The turbulence engendered by radical criticism, street violence, political assassination and a brutal war seemed to mark the end of the American consensus and to transform the 1950s notion of an end to ideology into a grotesque delusion. America had experienced the sort of propulsion into ideological awareness that revealed issues to be nothing less than serious social divisions. In this atmosphere, even the Marxism of the Frankfurt school was transformed from a fringe interest into such a fashionable perspective that Herbert Marcuse became a public celebrity.[5]

Although the intensity of ideological experimentation and critical introspection waned in the 1970s, the convulsions of the earlier political debates have reverberated throughout the succeeding period right up to the present day. The ferocity of the 1960s has given way to a more sustained sense of enquiry, scepticism and awareness. The 'end of ideology' is now recognised to be not only a chimera, but an expression in its own right of a dominant ideology. In the prevailing mood of examining society's presuppositions and controlling assumptions, and of revealing the depth and extent of ideological allegiances, it has become commonplace for revisionist historians to interpret the New Deal or the cold war in the light of the imperatives of a capitalist order. It has become uneventful for the conduct of American foreign policy to be perceived in the harsh light of an ideological orientation that could include outright racism and a persistent opposition to social revolution.[6] And it has become thoroughly unremarkable to point out that the McCarthyite episode of American history had very little to do with the threat of international communism and a great deal to do with nativist intolerance towards 'the unassimilated alien, the hyphenated American still carrying the contagion of old world socialism, that creeping gradualist Fabian New Dealism, which posed so insidious a threat to unbridled business, big or small'.[7]

The renewed interest in the ideological drives behind social movements and behind the nature and power of the state has led to an enhanced appreciation of political ideas in American politics. In a study entitled *American Ideologies*, Kenneth Dolbeare and Patricia Dolbeare conspicuously declare that ideology is 'alive and well' in the United States and that 'ideologies are a major force active in the contemporary American political dynamic'.[8] They feel constrained to encourage their readers 'to take contemporary American ideologies seriously as important political forces in their own right and to cease viewing them as symptoms of psychological maladjustment, emotional immaturity or anti-technological romanticism'.[9] So convinced are they of their discovery that the Dolbeares insist that a thorough knowledge of available ideologies should no longer be seen as a form of subversive behaviour, but as a basic requirement of a civic education.

The claims of an American reawakening to ideology are not confined to academic interpretations of history and politics. More significantly, they extend to the way the American public thinks and acts politically. In particular, it is asserted that the 1960s and 1970s provided an ideologically enriched political environment in which candidates competing for electoral office appealed to voters on the basis of distinct ideological positions. According to the various studies on the 'new' American voter, the message was not only sent, it was received in the spirit in which it was given. The citizenry was seen as being responsive to ideological cues, and it is claimed that an increase occurred in the ideological reactions given to political campaigns during these years.[10] The changed situation is succinctly conveyed by Lewis Lipsitz.

> Between 1964 and 1972, ideology, which seemed to have disappeared as a significant political factor in the 1950s, came back with a vengeance. As issue-orientated politics re-emerged in the United States, the tendency of the 1950s electorate to embrace unstructured jumbles

of beliefs gave way to a trend toward ideological political thinking. People who held liberal views on one issue, such as Vietnam, were more likely to be liberal on other issues – and the same was true with conservatives.[11]

The combination of new issues, new voters, new types of candidate, declining party allegiance and the onset of media campaigning had allegedly produced a more issue-orientated and ideologically integrated form of politics which had in turn prompted a profound change in the attitude structure and voting behaviour of the American public.

The *third* response to America's experience with political ideas is one of genuine ambivalence stretching at times into utter confusion. According to this perspective, the case for America's close dependence on and usage of ideas is neither proved nor disproved. In some ways, the United States can seem to be intensely concerned and even preoccupied with ideas about the nature of rights, power and justice. It can even be said that political theory and philosophy have undergone a renaissance in the United States over the past twenty years. The publication of John Rawls's *A Theory of Justice* (1974)[12] and of Robert Nozick's *Anarchy, State and Utopia* (1974)[13] encouraged a whole genre of studies on the ethical basis and justifying principles of the modern state. In this light, the ideological intensity of the 1960s was significant only in revealing an American attachment to political ideas which had always been part of its culture. The decade led Daniel Bell to remark that: 'Politics in the United States has not been non-ideological. As many shades of ideology have been present in the United States as there are colors in the spectrum.'[14] The 1980s seemed to affirm this judgement when President Reagan launched his ideological assault on the positive state in what became known as the 'conservative revolution'.

In other respects, however, the United States can still seem to be exceptionally free from ideological constraints and conflicts. Even the loosely defined liberal–conservative dichotomy is hardly a dichotomy in fact. It is a diffuse and often nebulous sense of differentiation which appears to be getting weaker rather than stronger over time. New issues (e.g. consumer protection, the size of government, budget deficit, abortion, the justice and effectiveness of state benefits) have disrupted the lines of ideological definition even more. And President Reagan's 'conservative revolution' demonstrated that the potential for an ideologically motivated crusade against established bureaucracies, budgets and programmes was in the end very limited in scale. It was found that only a small proportion of the voters who elected President Reagan did so because he was a conservative, or because he had a conservative programme.[15] What had been hailed in the 1970s as an ideologically motivated electorate had apparently either melted away in the disaggregation of modern American politics, or had been a figment of a faulty methodology all along.[16] Whatever the reason, electoral analysts like Russell Neuman writing in 1986, and with the benefit of hindsight, could disclose soberly that even if the public could be shown to make slightly more use of political abstractions when it is given a great deal of encouragement to do so, 'the behaviour of the public changes only in degree, not in character'. Despite the 'most lenient definition of [the] conceptual yardsticks and the maximal opportunity for their use, only one in four members of the mass population make explicit or implicit use of the notion of liberalism or conservatism to organize their thinking and opinions'.[17] The mass of the American public seems to remain highly resistant to organising their thinking and opinions according to a structure of ideological principles.

In these respects, the United States can still appear to be as deficient in ideological thinking as it was reputed to be in the 1950s. In that era, David Riesmen was prompted to describe the predominant form of thinking in American society as an 'historic, unideological conservatism'.[18] America conserved itself by conserving its own lack of ideology. This attribute brought problems in its wake, not the least of them being the basic inability of individuals to see how their freedom was being conditioned and narrowed by a compulsive anxiety to conform to an unthinking mass culture.

The situation today can seem very similar to that described by Riesman. According to Robert Bellah and his associates, for example, American culture is still geared so much to individual well-being as to undermine the society's very capacity to engage in collective acts and communal purposes. American society does not even equip its citizens with the conceptual categories required to comprehend the existence of mutual relationships and experiences.[19] To Bellah,

Americans are not given the basic facility of thinking and speaking about the great issues of society, and therefore they cannot conceive of the need for, or the possibility of, a popular ideological mobilisation towards communal objectives. Whether or not this is an overstatement, it does highlight the concern that many Americans feel for the social stagnation and economic decline of their country. Americans are challenged by serious new issues (e.g. environmental degradation, resource limitation, nuclear dangers, drug abuse, terrorism, control of technology) and by the realisation that political choices can no longer be avoided by continuous economic expansion. The lack of response in the face of such a powerful stimulus is said to bear eloquent testimony to America's congenital inability to engage in any serious attempts at a theoretical re-examination, or an ideological reorientation, of its society.

The aim of this study has been to show that all three of these perspectives on the place of political ideas in America are flawed and misleading. Each one only conveys a part of the whole. The first outlook of 'no ideology' is not only an overstatement of American conformity, but it fails, for example, to take account of the egalitarian movement for black civil rights which rose to prominence during the 1950s. The second outlook of ideological spasms is also misleading because it gives the impression that ideological speculation in the United States is confined to short, sharp and exaggerated bursts of unsustainable activity. The third outlook of a 'problematic mix' is flawed not only because it tends to make each of the first two perspectives into caricatures of one another, but because it seeks to reconcile these two perspectives purely in terms of a chronological alternation of ideological inactivity (e.g. the 1950s) followed by periods of ideological activity (e.g. the 1960s).

None of these perspectives succeed in conveying what is the normal status and effect of ideas in American politics. They fail to give proper weight to the continuous presence and motivating force of ideas. They overlook the many and varied relationships that different ideas have had with one another in the American tradition. Furthermore, they underestimate the interaction between America's ideological impulses and its political history and social development. As the several chapters in this book have sought to demonstrate, the

United States does possess a political environment which has been, and continues to be, highly charged with potent political ideas. These ideas are grounded in America's past experience and in its current traditions. They may not be strictly comparable to the integrated ideological systems that are commonly associated with European politics. But what they lack in systematisation, they more than make up for in their susceptibility to being selectively employed in a prodigious variety of different combinations for a profusion of different purposes.

This unique American matrix of ideas resembles what geologists call a breccia. A breccia is a particular type of conglomerate rock. A conglomerate is essentially rock made up of pieces of other rock, held in a common base. Breccias are conglomerates in which the fragments are not rounded stones, but are coarse, angular and sharp pieces of crystal. America's ideological breccia contains a large number of jagged components which appear to be arbitrarily arranged with no pattern or logical relationship to one another. They retain their form and separate identities but are nevertheless held together in unison – albeit an unstable and imprecise unison.

Given that these crystalline values include principles that are not, under any circumstances, consistent with one another; and given that America has the reputation of possessing these values in such an immediate and unrefined form that they are said to instil a fear of individualism, of democracy, of liberty and of equality[20] – the question arises as to how these several ideas coexist with one another in a single political culture. It would appear that there is a clear potential for deep and irreconcilable tensions amongst America's basic ideals. But this has to be squared with the fact that these contradictions rarely become apparent. The impulse for following the individual components to their logical conclusions and to their respective priorities seems continually to be inhibited by the American tradition of regarding such principles as mutually assimilable in the context of the United States.

An explanation of the coexistence of these several controlling, yet divergent, ideals have continually taxed historians and social theorists. Numerous devices have been employed in an effort to provide an understanding of the relationship that exists amongst America's political ideals. One answer has been to try and reduce

American values into types. By reviewing the conclusions arrived at by prominent writers on American principles, it is possible to make a case for the existence of a set of core values distinguishable from other secondary values.[21] The chief problem associated with this solution is that these core values are themselves often highly unstable compounds of several values merged artificially into single entities. In a study produced by Robert Devine, for example, 'equality' embraced equality of opportunity, egalitarianism and conformity. 'Liberty' included individualism and freedom from government, while free enterprise, progress and the Protestant ethic were covered by 'property'.[22] Even if these classifications were to be immune from dispute, the problem would still arise as to how the limited number of core values actually coexist with one another in American society. Reducing the range of American values into permutations of freedom, individualism, achievement, equality, democracy, property, tolerance, progress, competition and so on does not necessarily clarify the relationship between America's operating ideals. In many respects, they confuse the issue even more by throwing into stark relief the dichotomies that exist amongst American principles.

It is possible, of course, to try and cram every American value into one overriding rubric. This was the tactic employed by Louis Hartz in *The Liberal Tradition in America*. Hartz sought to reduce all American history and every American principle to a universal liberal ethos.[23] The problem with Hartz's liberalism was that it needed to be so capacious in nature that it effectively undermined any definition that could be consistently assigned to it. At times, it risked becoming simply a ubiquitous representation of anything American. In reducing all ideologies in the United States to one amorphous idea of liberalism, Hartz succeeded simply in dismissing the puzzle of America's ethical pluralism instead of trying to explain it.

Defenders of the Hartzian consensus do claim that many values in America are essentially definable in the light of society's liberal norm. It is asserted, for example, that equality in America is not dependent upon any objective existence of equal conditions. Under the influence of the liberal orthodoxy, equality is reformulated into an equality of opportunity, or the freedom of individuals to compete equally for unequal rewards, possessions and status. It is quite true

222

Conclusion

that equality of opportunity is a recognised American ideal and that in opinion polls Americans can be shown to favour freedom over equality by a ratio of over three-and-a-half to one.[24] But it is also true that equality remains a potent political ideal in the United States. It has an established place in American history and in America's social and intellectual development. 'Equality, no matter how abused or disused, has always been the prevailing American norm.'[25] As a result, it is thought that Americans take the concern for equality more seriously than Europeans do[26] and because of this concern the issue of equality 'lies at the heart of policy making and political struggle' in contemporary America.[27] As a consequence, it cannot always be dismissed as simply an adjunct to liberalism. On the contrary, the sheer presence of the egalitarian principle acts as an inspirational and occasionally disruptive force in American society. It can excite and mobilise public energies in the cause of an improvement in the state of social equality, or of an enhancement in the equality of the rights of citizenship – even if this should be at the cost of increased government intervention and decreased personal liberty.

With the possibility of this sort of dichotomy in mind, another strategy for explaining America's multiple ideas centres upon the assertion that they can only be accounted for by reference to pairs of core ideals. This sort of explanation not only favours the reduction of American values into group formation, but seeks to account for their collective existence through the presence of a single division and a central and easily conceived tension. The composition of these dualities vary in name and nature. Allusions are made to the principled divisions between the 'individual' and 'the community', between 'the private interest' and the 'public purpose', between 'reformism' and 'conservatism', between 'liberty' and 'equality', between 'affirmative government' and 'anti-statism', and between 'capitalism' and 'democracy'.

Reducing American values into two generic forms, however, still raises more problems than it resolves. First, it does not avoid the persistent difficulty of determining which values rightfully belong to which camp, or which values, or value divisions, have priority over others in the reductive process towards two overall principles. In *The American Ethos*, for example, Herbert McClosky and John Zaller state at the outset that 'two major traditions of belief, capitalism and democracy, have dominated the life of the American nation from its inception'. They go on to point out that

despite their central importance in American life, the values of the ethos are often in conflict. Some of the conflicts arise within the same strand of the ethos – for example, the conflict between the democratic values of majority rule and minority rights. Most, however, occur between the two major strands of the ethos between the values of capitalism on the one side and democracy on the other. In our view, the tension that exists between capitalist and democratic values is a definitive feature of American life that has helped to shape the ideological divisions of the nation's politics.[28]

This might well be so, but there is considerable room for dispute over what is included in McClosky and Zaller's 'capitalism' and 'democracy'. In their scheme of analysis, liberty and equality, for example, are grouped together under democracy, while individual achievement and independence are located in the capitalism category.

The second problem in these sorts of dualities is more important. It is that in having reduced the field to pairs of monolithic principles, the question of their relationship to one another is overlooked. The chief difficulty here is that in classifying and even dramatising the existence of a cultural duality of this depth, such studies tend to exacerbate, rather than to explain away, the problem of the evident coexistence of American values. In reformulating American beliefs to two coalitions of principles centring, for example, upon liberty and equality, the position acquired is tantamount to a recognition of the formal irreducibility of liberty and equality to a single principle. In the words of Isaiah Berlin, 'everything is what it is: liberty is liberty, not equality or fairness or justice or culture, or human happiness or a quiet conscience'. If some liberty is sacrificed in order to gain an increase in equality, it must be remembered that 'an absolute loss of liberty occurs ... It is a confusion of values to say that although my "liberal", individual freedom may go by the board, some other kind of freedom -"social" or "economic" – is increased.'[29] These comments are particularly pertinent in the current context for they help to draw attention to the difficulty of embracing liberty and equality simultaneously. In this respect, it is noticeable that when Allan Bloom characterises American political culture as 'the majestic and triumphant march of two principles, the principles of freedom and equality, which give meaning to all that we have done or are doing',[30] he is prompted to add the following addendum. 'Everything that happens among us is a consequence of one or both of our principles – a triumph over some opposition to them, a discovery of a fresh meaning in them, a *dispute about which of the two has primacy*, and so forth.'[31]

The difficulty of ethical priority and cultural primacy has prompted a number of analysts to adopt a third strategy to explain America's multiple allegiance to cross-cutting ideas and values. Instead of having to determine which side of any duality takes precedence over the other, this strategy simply abandons the assessment in favour of a cycle of periodic supremacy, in which each side in turn alternates with the other for predominance.[32] In this instance, time is the answer to the relationship between, for example, individual achievement and equality. Rather than individualism following a linear form of progressive development, the assumption with this sort of cyclical device is that once the attachment to individualism has acquired a pre-eminent position, it stimulates a counter-reaction until the egalitarian impulse achieves a comparable predominance. Arthur Schlesinger's cyclical model is probably the best known example of this strategy.[33] He explains the recurrent pattern of American history by reference to the public's rhythmic swings between a concern for the rights of the few and a concern for the wrongs of the many. The latter had produced movements to increase 'democracy' (i.e. 'public purpose') while the former had generated demands to contain it (i.e. 'private interests').

But perhaps the most notable recent attempt to portray American history and social movement in recurrent terms comes in Samuel P. Huntington's *American Politics: The Promise of Disharmony*.[34] Huntington asserts that America has a potent political creed of liberty, equality, individualism, democracy and the rule of law. For the most part they co-exist together in a loose package of distant ideals, but there always remains a discrepancy between these ideals and the reality of political conduct. This gap produces a series of responses (i.e. cynicism – complacency – hypocrisy – moralism), each one of which leads on from its predecessor. It is the moralistic reaction to hypocrisy that produces convulsive surges of reform to close the gap between America's ideals and its attainments. According to Huntington, this cycle has produced four such outbursts of supercharged devotion to America's political creed (i.e. 'creedal passion') – namely the American Revolution, the Jacksonian era, the Progressive age and the *angst* of the 1960s and early 1970s.[35] They were all motivated by the desire to resolve the dichotomy between promise and practice in American politics. Inevitably they all ended in a reversion to complacency, cynicism and hypocrisy, mostly because it is not possible for any American government fully to live up to the ideals of the American creed.

Political cycles come in a variety of shapes and sizes. According to Charles Forcey, for example, 'each wave of reform has run its course at intervals of twenty years or so since the founding of the republic'.[36] Arthur Schlesinger's cycles bring reform around in a thirty-year time scale, mostly because 'each new generation, when it attains power, tends to repudiate the work of the generation it has displaced and to re-enact the ideals of its own formative days thirty years before'.[37] Samuel Huntington's recurrent pattern of responses, however, is longer, and therefore reform activity is confined to periods of maximum psychic disorder which occur only once in every sixty to seventy years. But the chief weakness of all these cyclical patterns is not that they fail to coincide with one another, but that when ideas are used to imprint a pattern on American history, the ideas themselves ultimately become reduced to mere functions of the historical cycle. In other words, the normal coexistence of American values and their everyday relationship to one another become obscured, if not obliterated, by the overlay of historical epochs, which simply divide the ideas off from each other in separate time frames.

Whatever strategies are employed to give some precise order or framework to America's diverse political beliefs, the end result is one of failure. The various explanatory devices discussed above ultimately break-down because, in the final analysis, America's amalgam of values defies systematisation and confounds attempts to give them an ordered arrangement. Logically and analytically the constituent values of the United States do not fit together into an integrated whole. Nevertheless, as has been intimated all through this book, different American values do exist alongside one another without occasioning implacable animosity.

American politics is routinely conducted in a language littered with political ideals and high moral purposes. And yet it is very rare for attachments to these profound principles to become reduced to stark and chronic polarities. In the practical sphere of political engagement and discourse, Americans seem to retain an idiosyncratic capacity to mix values together in a quite uninhibited and unselfconscious manner. To outsiders and to those American observers who turn their minds towards it, this attribute of using ideologies or parts of ideologies to produce a diversity of aggregated outlooks is wholly baffling.

Sometimes the issue is simply avoided by dismissing Americans as not being ideologically minded and by derogating American ideologies to the status of 'semi' or 'sub' ideologies. But this is begging the question for, as Allan Bloom reminds us: 'Contrary to the popular prejudice that America is a nation of unintellectual and anti-intellectual people, where ideas are at best means to ends, this country is actually nothing but a great stage on which theories have been played out as tragedy and comedy.'[38] Americans live and breathe amongst a profusion of ideological traditions and impulses. They retain a deep and instinctive fascination for questions concerning the role and justification of the modern state, even in an era when the state is normally seen as an indispensable feature of contemporary society. They revere the themes of liberty and democracy, but also make repeated demands for the provision of government-guaranteed rights, which invariably curtail some freedoms and delimit some of the government's capacity to engage in collective and purposive schemes of social improvement. Americans also press assiduously for greater participation in government, while at the same time adhering to anti-statist dogmas seeking to limit the sphere of government. They support the principles of free enterprise, but engage in populist assaults against the special interests and concentrated powers of successful capitalist organisations. They take the claims of civic obligation and local self-government seriously while simultaneously deferring to a highly individualistic political culture. And they hold strong beliefs on equality in a manifestly inegalitarian society.

Eclecticism on this scale is confounding in the scale of its licentiousness and extravagance. It is difficult to determine the means by which it is sustained. One explanation, advanced by Hadley Cantril and Lloyd Free, postulates that American political attitudes are split between the general and the practical.[39] According to their survey of public attitudes, Americans do not differentiate between liberalism and conservatism by means of a single evaluative criterion. At the abstract ideological level, a majority of respondents emerged as possessing conservative beliefs in favour of a minimal state. However, when enquiries were shifted to the level of tangible and immediate government programmes, then the study elicited just as strong a support for a practical liberalism. What Cantril and Free concluded was the existence of two simultaneous dimensions of meaning and attachment based upon ideological and operational frames of reference. This division between abstract values and their tangible repercussions is evident in opinion polls, where strong support is given, for example, to the principles of free enterprise while low prestige is afforded to those individuals like corporate executives and corporate board members who actually embody these principles in physical form.[40] This duality can sometimes lead to charges of double standards, and even of hypocrisy, especially by non-Americans. In his classic text on the position of blacks in the new world suggestively entitled *An American Dilemma: The Negro Problem and Democracy*,[41] the Swedish sociologist Gunnar Myrdal suggested that most Americans understood themselves as believers in the American principle of equality, irrespective of their actual treatment of the black minority. He argued that black equality would only ever be secured when whites became conscious of the discrepancy between their ideals and their actions. Implicit in Myrdal's analysis, however, was the understanding that the value of equality and the conditions of inequality were both authentically American characteristics.

In the end, the only way that America's manifold ideological characteristics and anomalies can be explained is by reference to the centrality of history and tradition in American political culture. American history and tradition do not act as a substitute for ideas, so much as constitute a process applied to ideas. What keeps Americans together in the diversity of their ideas is their belief in, and usage of, a largely unexamined amalgam of values authenticated by American experience. This provision of an accessible and amenable American experience promotes a peculiarly American approach to ideas, in which choices between conflicting values are evaded in favour conflicting constructions of an absorbent American past. In this way, theoretically opposed values are not reconciled, so much as passed over in practice as being mutually inclusive by virtue of being drawn from a common core of American ingredients.

The history of traditions and experiences, through which different values and beliefs can be given a form of mutual accommodation, is made constantly available to Americans. Whether it is the veneration given to the Constitution and the Founding Fathers, or the eternal nature of the natural rights which are thought to inform the Constitution, or the mechanistic timelessness of the Constitution's checks and balances,[42] the net effect is for the issues of modern American politics to be refracted through the lens of American history. For a country with supposedly little history and even less historical consciousness, the content and vocabulary of modern American politics is continually and habitually informed by an ever-present past – whether it be a debate between Alexander Hamilton and James Madison cited in support of one position or another in the making of modern American foreign policy, or a dispute over the nature of the American revolution converted into arguments for and against radical politics in the 1960s.

The British historian Peter Laslett brings out the full significance of the accessibility of American history in the following observation:

> What strikes me about Americans is that the events, the outcomes of the past are part and parcel of their citizenship in their country, of *being* Americans. It appears to matter enormously to every voter, every person, in the whole of the USA, that Abraham Lincoln and the North won the Civil War. It is the same with the events in which the Founding Fathers were caught up, and the beliefs and attitudes which they shared and handed down. But nothing in British history weighs like this, at least on me.[43]

American history is valuable to Americans not only because it provides a frame of reference which allows for a variety of possible courses of contemporary action, but also because it offers a source of legitimacy for all these widely-varying responses. It is important, therefore, that history, and with it America's political and ideological traditions, should be seen to be relevant and continually applicable to American life. This is one of the reasons why the ultimate stasis of historical cycles is so appealing to Americans, and why the United States has developed a 'cultural constitutionalism' in which the Constitution provides a popular sense of national history and tradition – very often irrespective of the public's actual knowledge of the document's precise content.[44] The most tangible and most immediately recognisable elements of the Constitution are the institutions of government. Their dynamics evoke potent images of balance and assimilation in American political practice. Indeed, the operational behaviour of such institutions are strongly suggestive of the ways in which political values can coexist in society. Aaron Wildavsky, for example, is convinced that 'the heart of American exceptionalism lies in the belief that liberty and equality are (or can be made to be) compatible' through the juxtaposition and interaction of different doctrinal groupings in government.[45]

In looking at the United States, it is important to distinguish between what may look like evaluative choices between political ideals and principles, and what in reality approximates far more to a gravitational movement from the world of abstract ideas and towards a transcendent dimension of compulsive connotations surrounding the properties of American history and society. Given the American predilection to the latter – and given that in the United States 'the theory that all liberal values are in harmony is powerfully reinforced by the belief ... that the conditions of American society are themselves the conditions of successful democracy'[46] – it is not general practice for conflicting ideas to be placed in direct confrontation with one another, nor openly compromised with one another in any deliberative sense. Instead they are normally treated as a composite set of differing, yet commonly rooted, ideas open to various historical and political interpretations and, therefore, open to competing constructions of legitimacy.

The United States might appear to possess a political culture that is fixed in conformity, in which diverse ideas are merely tolerated at the margins out of a sense of indifference. In reality, America's political culture harbours and encourages an ingenious use of a common pool of political principles and traditions. Leaders and movements of every persuasion select, sift and combine these ideas into a constantly changing array of differing permutations, in an effort to lend authority to their positions and purposes. Even if it is true that America has a creed which changes very little in content and has no settled theory that can order or resolve the value conflicts inherent within it, political leaders can and do address these tensions and seek to reorder the priorities of American beliefs. 'American statesmen have in fact given new meaning to the creed when they have interpreted and ordered its values.'[47] This competitive reordering, reformulating and regrouping of traditional values can produce quite arbitrary and capricious combinations of ideas. But it can also generate an equally surprising range of inventive, imaginative and innovative reactions to problems.[48] Now that the 'stultifying conflict between state communism and liberal capitalism', which 'paralysed politics and political thought'[49] for so long, show signs of abating, America's ideological licence may be recognised as being positively advantageous. The likelihood is that it will allow the United States to respond, in a more adaptive and appropriate manner, to the complex issues which will affect the post-cold war world.

With this background, Americans have cultivated an extraordinary facility with ideas and a pronounced expertise in dealing with their problems and consequences. Americans are encouraged to explore the ramifications of such principles of liberty, equality, individualism and democracy in a modern social context. They have an acute awareness of the potential for possible and actual clashes between such values. And they are sensitive to the contingencies and dangers of conflicting principles of political action. As a consequence, the problematic nature of political ideas is always on America's public agenda. While it is true that Americans still have the reputation of being ill-disposed towards ideologies and disciplined ideological thought in general, they are at the very least deeply ideological in practice. Furthermore, it can be said that their ideological preoccupations have been formed, not in spite of their American heritage, but very much because of it. In short, it is possible for Americans to be ideologically attentive and even speculative simply by exploiting the versatility of their country's own myriad political traditions.

Notes

Introduction

1 Leslie C. Berlowitz, 'Introduction', in Leslie Berlowitz, Denis Donoghue and Louis Menand (eds.), *America In Theory* (New York: Oxford University Press, 1988), p. ix.
2 Daniel Bell, *The End of Ideology* (New York: Collier-Macmillan, 1965); Seymour M. Lipset, *Political Man* (London: Heinemann, 1960), pp. 403-17.
3 Bernard Crick, 'The strange death of the theory of consensus', *The Political Quarterly*, 43, no. 1 (January–March 1972), p. 53.
4 Gregor McLennan, *Marxism, Pluralism and Beyond: Classic Debates and New Departures* (Oxford: Polity, 1989), p. 48.
5 *Ibid.*, p. 48
6 Quoted in Bernard Nossiter, 'Intellectuals agree: 'There are no answers any more', *The Washington Post* supplement published in the *Guardian Weekly*, 27 May 1979.

Chapter 1

1 Alexis de Tocqueville, *Democracy in America*, trans. by Henry Reeve, intro. by Henry S. Commager (London: Oxford University Press, 1946), p. 370.
2 Arthur M. Schlesinger, Jr., *The Politics of Hope* (London: Eyre and Spottiswoode, 1964), p. 63.
3 Thomas Jefferson, 'A summary view of the rights of British America', in Merrill D. Peterson (ed.), *The Portable Thomas Jefferson* (Harmondsworth, Middx: Penguin, 1977), p. 21.
4 Taken from the Preamble to the US Constitution.
5 Peter Gay, *The Enlightenment: An Interpretation, Volume II – The Science of Freedom* (London: Weidenfeld and Nicolson, 1970), p. 557.
6 Thomas Paine, *Common Sense*, ed. and intro. by Isaac Kramnick (Harmondsworth, Middx: Penguin, 1976), p. 100.
7 Leo Marx, *The Machine in the Garden: Technology and the Pastoral Ideal in America* (London: Oxford University Press, 1964).
8 Quoted in Richard Hofstadter, *The American Political Tradition and the Men Who Made It* (London: Jonathan Cape, 1967), p. 27. See also Albert K. Weinberg, *Manifest Destiny: A Study of Nationalist Expansion in American History* (Chicago: Quadrangle, 1963), p. 39.
9 Thomas Jefferson, 'First inaugural address', in Peterson (ed.), *The Portable Thomas Jefferson*, p. 292.
10 Henry N. Smith, *Virgin Land: The American West as Symbol and Myth* (New York: Vintage, 1950).
11 Perry Miller, *The New England Mind: The Seventeenth Century* (New York: Macmillan, 1939).

12 See Robert S. Fogarty, 'American Communes, 1865-1914', *Journal of American Studies*, 9, no. 2 (1976), pp. 145-62.
13 Quoted in J. W. Anderson, 'The idea of success', *Washington Post* supplement published in the *Guardian Weekly*, 29 August 1976.
14 See Oscar Handlin, *The Uprooted*, 2nd edn (Boston: Little, Brown, 1973); Oscar Handlin (ed.), *Immigration as a Factor in American History* (Englewood Cliffs, NJ: Prentice-Hall, 1959).
15 Quoted in Maldwyn Jones, *Destination America* (London: Fontana,1977), p. 15.
16 Quoted in Jones, *Destination America*, pp. 9-10.
17 Weinberg, *Manifest Destiny*, chs. 11-15.
18 'President Kennedy's inaugural address (January 20, 1961)', in Edmund S. Ions (ed.), *The Politics of John F. Kennedy* (London: Routledge and Kegan Paul, 1967), p. 50.
19 Clinton Rossiter, *Conservatism in America: The Thankless Persuasion*, 2nd edn, rev. (New York: Vintage, 1962), p. 72.
20 Max Lerner, *America as a Civilization: Life and Thought in America Today* (London: Jonathan Cape, 1958), p. 452.
21 Quoted in Alan P. Grimes, *American Political Thought* (New York: Holt, Rinehart and Winston, 1967), p. 157.
22 Henry S. Commager, *The Empire of Reason: How Europe Imagined and America Realized the Enlightenment* (London: Weidenfeld and Nicolson, 1978), p. 64.
23 Quoted in Hugh Honour, *The New Golden Land: European Images of America from the Discoveries to the Present Time* (London: Allen Lane, 1976), p. 248.
24 Wilfred E. Binkley, *President and Congress*, 3rd edn, rev. (New York: Vintage, 1962), p. 6.
25 Quoted in Jennifer Tucker and Martin Tucker, *The American West* (Oxford: Basil Blackwell, 1986), p. 19.
26 De Tocqueville, *Democracy in America*, p. 36.
27 *Ibid.*, p. 38
28 *Ibid.*, p. 66.
29 Frederick J. Turner, *The Frontier in American History* (Huntington, New York: R. E. Krieger, 1975), p. 38.
30 *Ibid.*, pp. 23, 38.
31 Daniel J. Boorstin, *The Genius of American Politics* (Chicago: University of Chicago Press, 1953), p. 9.
32 *Ibid.*, p. 9.
33 Richard M. Gummere, 'The classical ancestry of the United States Constitution', *The American Quarterly*, 14 (Spring 1962), pp. 3-18; Gilbert Chinard, 'Polybius and the American Constitution', *Journal of History of Ideas*, 1, no. 1 (January 1940), pp. 38-58.
34 Clinton Rossiter, *Seedtime of the Republic: The Origin of the American Tradition of Political Liberty* (New York: Harcourt, Brace and Co., 1953), p. 143.
35 See Michael Lienesch, 'In defense of the Anti-Federalists,' *History of Political Thought*, 4, no. 1 (Spring 1983), pp. 65-88; Herbert J. Storing, *What the Anti-Federalists Were For: The Political Thought of the Opponents of the Constitution* (Chicago: University of Chicago, 1981).
36 See Caroline Robbins, *The Eighteenth Century Commonwealthman: Studies in the Transmission, Development and Circumstance of English Liberal Thought from the*

Restoration of Charles II until the War with the Thirteen Colonies (Cambridge, Mass.: Harvard University Press, 1959).

37 See Bernard Bailyn, *The Ideological Origins of the American Revolution* (Cambridge, Mass.: Belknap, 1967); Gordon S. Wood, *The Creation of the American Republic, 1776-1787* (Chapel Hill, NC: University of North Carolina Press, 1969); Robert E. Shalhope, 'Toward a republican synthesis: the emergence of an understanding of republicanism in American historiography', *William and Mary Quarterly*, 29, no. 1 (January 1972), pp. 49-80.

38 Garry Wills, *Inventing America: Jefferson's Declaration of Independence* (Garden City, NY: Doubleday, 1978), p. xv.

39 Gay, *The Enlightenment: An Interpretation, Volume II*, pp. 555-67.

40 Austin Ranney, '"The Divine Science": Political Engineering in American Culture', *American Political Science Review*, 70, no. 1 (March 1976), p. 140.

41 Gay, *The Enlightenment: An Interpretation, Volume II*, p. 558.

42 Commager, *The Empire of Reason*, p. ix.

43 J. R. Pole, *Paths to the American Past* (New York: Oxford University Press, 1979), pp. xiii-xxiii.

44 Hannah Arendt, *On Revolution* (New York: Viking, 1963).

45 Alexander Hamilton, 'Federalist Paper No. 1', in Alexander Hamilton, James Madison and John Jay, *The Federalist Papers*, intro. Clinton Rossiter (New York: Mentor, 1961), p. 35.

46 James Madison, 'Federalist Paper No. 37', in Hamilton, Madison and Jay, *The Federalist Papers*, p. 226.

47 Irving Howe quoted in Godfrey Hodgson, 'States of gloom: the fading of an American dream', *Sunday Times*, 21 December 1975.

48 'Woodrow Wilson, speech for the declaration of war against Germany (April 2, 1917)', in Richard Hofstadter (ed.), *Great Issues in American History: From Reconstruction to the Present Day, 1864-1969* (New York: Vintage, 1969), p. 216.

49 Lerner, *America as a Civilization*, p. 883.

50 'Inaugural address of President Jimmy Carter (January 20, 1977)', in *Public Papers of Presidents of the United States: Jimmy Carter 1977*, Book 1 – January 20 to June 24 1977 (Washington, DC: United States Government Printing Office, 1977), p. 1.

51 'President Reagan's 2nd inaugural address (January 21, 1985)', in *Congressional Quarterly Almanac, 99th Congress 1st Session 1985, Volume XLI* (Washington, DC: Congressional Quarterly, 1986), p. 4D.

Chapter 2

1 E. M. Adams, 'Introduction: the idea of America', in E. M. Adams (ed.), *The Idea of America: A Reassessment of the American Experiment* (Cambridge, Mass.: Ballinger, 1977), p. 5.

2 See Sacvan Bercovitch, *The Puritan Origins of the American Self* (New Haven, Conn.: Yale University Press, 1976).

3 Quoted in Henry N. Smith, *Virgin Land: The American West as Symbol and Myth* (New York: Vintage, 1950), pp. 143-4.

4 Ira Katznelson and Mark Kesselman, *The Politics of Power: A Critical Introduction to American Government* (New York: Harcourt Brace Jovanovich, 1975), p. 72.

5   T. B. Bottomore, *Classes in Modern Society* (London: George Allen and Unwin, 1965), p. 41.
6   See Chapter 3, note 17.
7   Max Savelle, *Seeds of American Liberty: The Genesis of the American Mind* (Seattle, Wash.: University of Washington Press, 1948), p. 280.
8   Max J. Skidmore, *American Political Thought* (New York: St Martin's, 1978), p. 46.
9   Ernest Barker, 'Natural law and the American revolution', in Ernest Barker, *Traditions in Civility: Eight Essays* (Cambridge: Cambridge University Press, 1948), p. 328.
10 The preamble to the US Constitution asserts that 'we the people of the United States, in order to form a more perfect union ... and secure the blessings of liberty to ourselves and our posterity, do ordain and establish this Constitution.'
11 D. W. Minar, *Ideas and Politics: The American Experience* (Homewood, Ill.: Dorsey, 1964), p. 47.
12 Herbert McCloskey and John Zaller, *The American Ethos: Public Attitudes toward Capitalism and Democracy* (Cambridge, Mass.: Harvard University Press, 1984), p. 114. On the significance of 'individual achievement' on the origins and development of American society, see Seymour M. Lipset, *The First New Nation: The United States in Historical and Comparative Perspective* (New York: Norton, 1979).
13 Smith, *Virgin Land*, p. 36.
14 F. O. Matthiessen, *American Renaissance: Art and Expression in the Age of Emerson and Whitman* (London: Oxford University Press, 1941), p. 7.
15 Ian Todd and Michael Wheeler, *Utopia* (London: Orbis, 1978), p. 86.
16 Frederick J. Turner, *The Frontier in American History* (Huntington, NY: R. E. Krieger, 1975), p. 37.
17 Daniel Bell, 'The end of American exceptionalism', in Nathan Glazer and Irving Howe (eds.), *The American Commonwealth – 1976* (New York: Basic, 1976), p. 209.
18 Alexis de Tocqueville, *Democracy in America*, trans. by Henry Reeve, intro. by Henry S. Commager (London: Oxford University Press, 1946), p. 366.
19 *Ibid.*, p. 374.
20 *Ibid.*, pp. 366, 368.
21 Richard Hofstadter, *Social Darwinism in American Thought*, rev. edn (Boston: Beacon, 1955), chs. 1, 2.
22 Quoted in Matthew Josephson, *The Robber Barons: The Great American Capitalists, 1861-1901* (London: Eyre and Spottiswoode, 1962), p. 326.
23 See Robert G. McCloskey, *American Conservatism in the Age of Enterprise, 1865-1910: A Study of William Graham Sumner, Stephen J. Field and Andrew Carnegie* (New York: Harper and Row, 1964); Louis Auchincloss, *The Vanderbilt Era: Profiles of a Gilded Age* (New York: Scribner's, 1989).
24 Herbert Spencer, 'The coming slavery', in Alan Bullock and Maurice Shock (eds.), *The Liberal Tradition* (Oxford: Clarendon, 1967), p. 185.
25 Quoted in Harold J. Livesay, *Andrew Carnegie and the Rise of Big Business* (Boston: Little, Brown, 1975), pp. 74-5.
26 Quoted in McCloskey, *American Conservatism in the Age of Enterprise, 1865-1910*, p. 26.

27 Quoted in Herbert Schneider, *A History of American Philosophy* (New York: Liberal Arts Press, 1957), p. 212.
28 McCloskey, *American Conservatism in the Age of Enterprise, 1865-1910*, p. 67.
29 See Hofstadter, *Social Darwinism in American Thought*, chs. 2, 3; Joseph F. Wall, *Andrew Carnegie* (New York: Oxford University Press, 1970), ch. 12; Raymond Williams, 'Social Darwinism', *The Listener*, 23 November 1972.
30 *Lochner v. New York* 198 US 45 (1905).
31 *Lochner v. New York* 198 US 45 (1905).
32 *Lochner v. New York* 198 US 75 (1905).
33 Upton Sinclair, *The Jungle* (Harmondsworth, Middx: Penguin, 1965), p. 118.
34 *Ibid.*, pp. 119-20.
35 Quoted in Josephson, *The Robber Barons*, p. 441. See also Andrew Sinclair, *Corsair: The Life of J. Pierpoint Morgan* (Boston: Little, Brown, 1980).
36 See Charles Forcey, *The Crossroads of Liberalism: Croly, Weyl and the Progressive Era, 1900-1925* (New York: Oxford University Press, 1961), pp. 3–51; David W. Noble, 'Herbert Croly and American progressive thought', in John P. Roche (ed.), *American Political Thought: From Jefferson to Progressivism* (New York: Harper and Row, 1967), pp. 259-83.
37 Lester F. Ward, *Psychic Factors of Civilization* (New York: Ginn, 1892); Henry S. Commager, *The American Mind: An Interpretation of American Thought and Character Since the 1880s* (New York: Bantam, 1970), ch. 10; Peter J. Bowler, *Evolution: The History of an Idea* (Berkeley: University California Press, 1984), ch. 10.
38 Skidmore, *American Political Thought*, p. 167.
39 See Richard J. Barber, *The American Corporation: Its Power, Its Money, Its Politics* (London: MacGibbon and Kee, 1970); Arthur S. Miller, *The Modern Corporate State: Private Governments and the American Constitution* (Westport, Conn.: Greenwood, 1976); Paul A. Baran and Paul M. Sweezy, *Monopoly Capital: An Essay on the American Economic and Social Order* (Harmondsworth, Middx: Penguin, 1968).
40 See Lewis H. Lapham, *Money and Class in America: Notes and Observations on Our Civil Religion* (London: Weidenfeld and Nicolson, 1988); Paul Fussell, *Caste Marks: Style and Status in the USA* (London: Heinemann, 1984).
41 The ethical and moral standing of the small independent proprietor is still second to none in comparison to other occupational groups, see Seymour M. Lipset and William Schneider, 'The confidence gap during the Reagan years, 1981-1987', *Political Science Quarterly* 102, no. 1 (Spring 1987), p. 18.
42 See Theodore H. White, *The Making of the President, 1964* (London: Jonathan Cape, 1965).
43 Garry Wills, *Reagan's America: Innocents at Home* (London: Heinemann, 1988), pp. 146, 352-6, 380-2; Lance Morrow, 'Smile when you say that', *Time*, 28 October 1985.
44 See James D. Barber, *The Presidential Character: Predicting Performance in the White House* (Englewood Cliffs, NJ: Prentice-Hall, 1972).
45 See Michael Foley, 'From mighty oaks to little acorns: the problems of the presidential timber business', *Journal of American Studies*, 24, no. 1 (1990), pp. 85-92.
46 Lee Iacocca, *Iacocca: An Autobiography* (London: Sidgwick and Jackson, 1985),

pp. 340-1. For a similarly robust defence of individual achievement, see Joseph Epstein, *Ambition: The Secret Passion* (New York: E. P. Dutton, 1981).

47 Christopher Lasch, *The Culture of Narcissism: American Life in an Age of Diminishing Expectations* (New York: Norton, 1979).

48 Lasch, 'The narcissist society', *New York Review of Books*, 20 September 1976, p. 5.

49 Hugh Heclo, 'The American welfare state: the costs of American self-sufficiency', in Richard Rose (ed.), *Lessons From America: An Exploration* (London: Macmillan, 1974), p. 253.

50 James Fallows, *More Like Us: Making America Great Again* (Boston: Houghton Mifflin, 1989).

51 Stanley Feldman, 'Economic individualism and American public opinion', *American Politics Quarterly* 11, no 1 (January 1983), p. 12.

52 'The role of individual responsibility', *Public Opinion*, March/April 1987, p. 28.

53 *Ibid.*, p. 12. See also James R. Kluegel and Eliot R. Smith, *Beliefs About Inequality: Americans' Views of What Is and What Ought to Be* (New York: Aldine De Gruyler, 1986).

Chapter 3

1 Robert G. McCloskey, *American Conservatism in the Age of Enterprise, 1865-1910: A Study of William Graham Sumner, Stephen J. Field and Andrew Carnegie* (New York: Harper and Row, 1964), pp. 9, 8, 12.

2 David M. Potter, *People of Plenty: Economic Abundance and the American Character* (Chicago: University of Chicago Press, 1958); Louis M. Hacker, *The Triumph of Capitalism: The Development of Forces in American History to the End of the Nineteenth Century* (New York: Simon and Schuster, 1940), pp. 322-73, 401-24; Hacker, *The Course of American Economic Growth and Development* (New York: Wiley, 1970), pp. 172-243.

3 Kenneth M. Dolbeare and Patricia Dolbeare, *American Ideologies: The Competing Beliefs of the 1970s* (Chicago: Markham, 1971), p. 22.

4 F. A. Hayek, *The Road to Serfdom* (London: Routledge and Kegan Paul, 1976), pp. 36-7.

5 Adam Smith, *An Inquiry into the Nature and Causes of the Wealth of Nations, Volume 1*, textual editor W. B. Todd (Oxford: Clarendon, 1976), p. 454.

6 *Ibid.*, p. 456.

7 Peter Drucker, *The End of Economic Man: A Study of the New Totalitarianism* (London: Basic Books/Heinemann, 1940), p. 35.

8 *Ibid.*, p. 35.

9 *Ibid.*, p. 36.

10 Arthur M. Schlesinger, Jr., *The Vital Center: The Politics of Freedom* (Cambridge, Mass.: Riverside, 1962), p. 28.

11 Eric Bentley (ed.), *Thirty Years of Treason: Excerpts from Hearings before the House Committee on Un-American Activities, 1938-1968* (London: Thames and Hudson, 1972), p. 935.

12 *Ibid.*, pp. 934-5.

13 George C. Lodge, *The New American Ideology* (New York: Alfred A Knopf, 1976), p. 11.

14 Quoted in Arthur M. Schlesinger, *The American as Reformer*, preface by Arthur M. Schlesinger, Jr., (Cambridge, Mass.: Harvard University Press, 1968), p. 49.
15 Peter J. Berger, *The Capitalist Revolution: Fifty Propositions About Prosperity, Equality and Liberty* (New York: Basic, 1986).
16 According to Locke, the right to appropriate property is governed by the need to leave enough for the sustenance of others; by the amount that an individual can consume or exploit before the produce deteriorates; and by the extent of the property that a man can engage with his own labour.
17 John Locke, *Two Treatises of Government*, intro. by Peter J. Laslett (Cambridge: Cambridge University Press, 1967), p. 305.
18 See C. B. Macpherson, *The Political Theory of Possessive Individualism: Hobbes to Locke* (Oxford: Clarendon, 1962).
19 Carl Becker, *The Declaration of Independence: A Study in the History of Political Ideas* (New York: Peter Smith, 1933), p. 27.
20 William A. Williams, *The Contours of American History* (New York: Norton, 1988), pp. 29-30.
21 James Madison, 'Federalist Paper No. 54', in Alexander Hamilton, James Madison and Jon Jay, *The Federalist Papers*, intro by Clinton Rossiter (New York: Mentor, 1961), p. 339.
22 Louis Hartz, *The Liberal Tradition in America: An Interpretation of American Political Thought Since the Revolution* (New York: Harcourt Brace Jovanovich, 1955), p. 6.
23 *Ibid.*, p. 206
24 *Ibid.*, p. 6.
25 *Ibid.*, p. 122.
26 *Ibid.*, p. 211.
27 *Ibid.*, p. 62.
28 *Ibid.*, p. 219.
29 *Ibid.*, p. 219.
30 John P. Diggins, *The American Left in the Twentieth Century* (New York: Harcourt Brace Jovanovich, 1973), p. 147. See also Diggins, 'Knowledge and sorrow: Louis Hartz's quarrel with American history', *Political Theory*, 16, no. 3 (August 1988), pp. 355-76.
31 Hartz, *The Liberal Tradition in America*, p. 285.
32 The question was originally posed and popularised in Werner Sombart's *Why Is There No Socialism in the United States?*, intro. by C. T. Husbands (White Plains, NY: M. E. Sharpe, 1976). the question relates to a *general* absence of socialism in the United States. It should not be forgotten that pockets of socialist politics existed in immigrant communities. Socialist newspapers were often the most popular periodicals in immigrant neighbourhoods and socialist activists were notable local politicians. See Paul Buhle, *Marxism in the United States: Remapping the History of the American Left* (London: Verso, 1987). But the appeal of radical class politics and socialist movements was particularly prominent in areas of America's farmland. See Lowell K. Dyson, *Red Harvest: The Communist Party and American Farmers* (Lincoln, Neb.: University of Nebraska Press, 1982); James R. Green, *Grass-Roots Socialism: Radical Movements in the Southwest, 1895-1943* (Baton Rouge, La.: Louisiana State University Press, 1978).
33 Quoted in Hans Kohn, *American Nationalism: An Interpretive Essay* (New York: Macmillan, 1957), p. 18.

34 In America 'all socialist utopias came to nothing on roast beef and apple pie'
    (Sombart, *Why Is There No Socialism in the United States?*, p. 106). For a full
    exposition of Sombart's *embourgeoisement* thesis, see Sombart, *ibid.*, pp. 61-106.
    See also Loren Bariz, *The Good Life: The Meaning of Success for the American Middle
    Class* (New York: Alfred A. Knopf, 1989).
35 See Mike Davis, 'Why the US working class is different', *New Left Review*, No. 123
    (September–October 1980), pp. 3-46.
36 See Seymour M. Lipset, 'Socialism in America', *Dialogue*, 10, no. 4 (1977), pp.
    3-12.
37 Theodore J. Lowi, 'Why is there no socialism in the United States?: a federal
    analysis', *International Political Science Review*, 5, no. 4 (1984), p. 377.
38 Robert J. Goldstein, *Political Repression in Modern America from 1870 to the
    Present* (Cambridge, Mass.: Schenkman, 1978), chs. 5, 9.
39 See John H. M. Laslett and Seymour M. Lipset (eds.), *Failure of a Dream?: Essays
    in the History of American Socialism* (Garden City, NY: Anchor, 1974); Jerome
    Karabel, 'The failure of American socialism reconsidered', in Ralph and John
    Saville (eds.), *The Socialist Register, 1979* (London: Merlin, 1979), pp 204-28.
40 See C. T. Husbands' introductory essay in Sombart, *Why Is There No Socialism in
    the United States?*, pp. xxiii–xxvii.
41 Rowland Evans and Robert Novak, *Nixon in the White House: The Frustration of
    Power in the White House* (New York: Vintage, 1972), p. 372.
42 Gabriel Kolko, *The Triumph of Conservatism: A Reinterpretation of American
    History, 1900-1916* (New York: Free Press, 1963).
43 Hamish McRae, 'The real costs of "Big government"', *Guardian Weekly*, 29
    January 1978.
44 Charles Lindblom, *Politics and Markets* (New York: Basic, 1977).
45 Jacques S. Gansler, *Affording Defense* (Cambridge, Mass.: Massachusetts Institute
    of Technology Press, 1989), pp. 79-94.
46 Lee Iacocca, *Iacocca: An Autobiography* (London: Sidgwick and Jackson, 1985),
    p. 199.
47 See Seymour M. Lipset, 'American "Exceptionalism" in North American
    perspective: why the United States has withstood the worldwide socialist
    movement', in E. M. Adams (ed.), *The Idea of America: A Reassessment of the
    American Experiment* (Cambridge, Mass.: Ballinger, 1977), pp. 130-5.
48 Lodge, *The New American Ideology*, pp. 20, 19.
49 Michael Harrington, *Socialism* (New York: E. P. Dutton, 1972), pp. 111-18.
50 Peter d'A. Jones, *The Consumer Society: A History of American Capitalism*
    (Harmondsworth, Middx: Penguin, 1965), p. 259.
51 Michael Harrington, *The Twilight of Capitalism* (New York: Simon and Schuster,
    1976); Daniel Bell, *The Cultural Contradictions of Capitalism* (New York: Basic,
    1976); Robert Heilbroner, *Business Civilization in Decline* (New York: Norton,
    1976).
52 David G. Green, *The New Right: The Counter-Revolution in Political, Economic and
    Social Thought* (New York: Harvester 1987); Nick Bosanquet, *After the New Right*
    (London: Heinemann, 1983).
53 Robert E. Muller, *Revitalizing America: Politics for Prosperity* (New York: Simon
    and Schuster, 1981); Robert Reich, *The Next American Frontier* (New York:
    Times Books, 1983); Lester Thurow, *The Zero-sum Society* (New York: Basic,

1980); Ira Magaziner and Robert Reich, *Minding America's Business* (New York: Vintage, 1982).

54 'President Reagan's inaugural address (January 20, 1981)', in *Congressional Quarterly Almanac, 97th Congress 1st Session 1981, Volume XXXVII* (Washington, DC: Congressional Quarterly, 1982, p. 12E.

55 Ian C. Macmillan, 'The politics of new venture management', *Harvard Business Review*, November–December 1983, pp. 8-16; Peter F. Drucker, 'Our entrepreneurial economy', *Harvard Business Review*, January – February 1984, pp. 58-64; Leslie Wayne, 'The new entrepreneurs', *Dialogue*, No. 67, 1/1985; Victor Kiam, *Going For It!: How to Succeed as an Entrepreneur* (New York: William Morrow, 1986).

56 Quoted in *New Statesman*, 17 July 1987.

57 'Avis's workers unite', *The Economist*, 22 July 1989.

58 Andrew Shonfield, *Modern Capitalism: The Changing Balance of Public and Private Power* (London: Oxford University Press, 1965), p. 298. See also David Vogel, 'Why businessmen distrust their state: the political consciousness of American corporate executives', *British Journal of Political Science*, 8, Part 1 (January 1978), pp. 45-78.

59 'Oath of office and second inaugural address (January 20, 1973)', in *Public Papers of Presidents of the United States: Richard Nixon 1973* (Washington, DC: United States Government Printing Office, 1975), p. 15.

60 'President Reagan's inaugural address (January 20, 1981)', p. 12E.

61 'President Reagan's 2nd inaugural address (January 21, 1985)', in *Congressional Quarterly Almanac, 99h Congress 1st Session 1985, Volume XLI* (Washington, DC: Congressional Quarterly, 1986), p. 3D.

62 'President Reagan's economic policy address (February 5, 1981)', in *Congressional Quarterly Almanac, 97th Congress 1st Session 1981, Volume XXXVII*, p. 15E.

63 Garry Wills, 'What happened?', *Time*, 9 March 1987.

Chapter 4

1 *The United States of America: A Government by the People* (Washington, DC: United States Information Service, 1966), p. 1.

2 F. W. Walbank, *Polybius* (Berkeley: University of California Press, 1972).

3 M. J. C. Vile, *Constitutionalism and the Separation of Powers* (London: Oxford University Press, 1967); W. B. Gwyn, *The Meaning of the Separation of Powers: An Analysis of the Doctrine from its Origins to the Adoption of the United States Constitution* (New Orleans, La.: Tulane University Press, 1965).

4 Vile, *Constitutionalism and the Separation of Powers*, ch. 5.

5 Quoted in Bernard Bailyn, *The Ideological Origins of the American Revolution* (Cambridge, Mass.: Belknap, 1967), p. 67.

6 Correa Walsh, *The Political Science of John Adams: A Study in the Theory of Mixed Government and the Bicameral System* (New York: Knickerbocker Press, 1915). pp. 37-59, 74-9.

7 Gordon S. Wood, *The Creation of the American Republic, 1776-1787* (Chapel Hill, NC: University of North Carolina Press, 1969), pp. 207-22.

8 Gordon S. Wood, 'Democracy and the Constitution', in Robert A. Goldwin and William A. Schambra (eds.), *How Democratic is the Constitution?* (Washington,

DC: American Enterprise Institute, 1980), p. 8.

9 Jon Roper, *Democracy and Its Critics: Anglo-American Democratic Thought in the Nineteenth Century* (London: Unwin Hyman, 1989), p. 35.

10 Wood, *The Creation of the American Republic*, p. 410.

11 Quoted in Richard Hofstadter, *The American Political Tradition: And the Men who Made It* (London: Jonathan Cape, 1967), p. 5.

12 James Madison, 'Federalist Paper No. 10', in Alexander Hamilton, James Madison and John Jay, *The Federalist Papers*, intro. Clinton Rossiter (New York: Mentor, 1961), p. 81.

13 *Ibid.*, p. 80.

14 James Madison, 'Federalist Paper No. 51', in Hamilton, Madison and Jay, *The Federalist Papers*, p. 322.

15 Wood, 'Democracy and the Constitution', in Goldwin and Schambra (eds.), *How Democratic is the Constitution?*, p. 16.

16 Cecilia M. Kenyon, 'Men of little faith: the Anti-federalists on the nature of representative government', in Jacke P. Greene (ed.), *The Reinterpretation of the American Revolution, 1763-1789* (New York: Harper and Row, 1968), pp. 291-320; Herbert Storing, *What the Anti-Federalists Were For* (Chicago: University of Chicago Press, 1981).

17 Michael Parenti, 'The Constitution as an elitist document', in Goldwin and Schambra (eds.), *How Democratic is the Constitution?*, pp. 39-58.

18 See Edward Pessen, *Jacksonian America: Society, Personality and Politics* (Homewood, Ill.: Dorsey, 1969), ch. 7; Robert V. Remini, *The Revolutionary Age of Andrew Jackson* (New York: Harper and Row, 1976), ch. 5.; James S. Chase, 'Jacksonian democracy and the rise of the nominating convention', in Frank O. Gattell (ed.), *Essays on Jacksonian America* (New York: Holt, Rinehart and Winston, 1970), pp. 85-97.

19 Alexis de Tocqueville, *Democracy in America*, trans. by Henry Reeve, intro. by Henry S. Commager (London: Oxford University Press, 1946), p. 53.

20 *Ibid.*, p. 54.

21 Quoted in Henry Raymont, 'Harsh indictment of America by Dickens', *The Times*, 31 March 1970.

22 *Ibid.*

23 Wood, *The Creation of the American Republic*, pp. 603-8.

24 Abraham Lincoln, 'The Gettysburgh Address, 1863', in Richard D. Heffner, *A Documentary History of the United States*, rev. edn (New York: Mentor, 1976), p. 157.

25 Woodrow Wilson, quoted in 'Speech for declaration of war against Germany', in Richard Hofstadter (ed.), *Great Issues in American History: From Reconstruction to the Present Day, 1864-1969* (New York: Vintage, 1969), p. 216.

26 Robert Dahl, *Who Governs?: Democracy and Power in an American City* (New Haven, Conn.: Yale University Press, 1961), pp. 316-17.

27 See Martin P. Wattenberg, *The Decline of American Political Parties, 1952-1980* (Cambridge, Mass.: Harvard University Press, 1984); William Crotty, *American Parties in Decline*, 2nd edn (Boston: Little, Brown, 1984); Benjamin Ginsberg and Martin Shefter, *Politics by Other Means: The Declining Importance of Elections in America* (New York: Basic, 1990).

28 See Donald L. Robinson (ed.), *Reforming American Government: The Bicentennial*

Papers of the Committee on the Constitutional System (Boulder, Colo.: Westview, 1985); James L. Sundquist, *Constitutional Reform and Effective Government* (Washington, DC: Brookings, 1986).

29 See Chapter 5.
30 Samuel P. Huntington, 'The democratic distemper', in Nathan Glazer and Irving Kristol (eds.), *The American Commonwealth – 1976* (New York: Basic, 1976), p. 11.
31 James M. Burns, *The Deadlock of Democracy: Four-Party Politics in America* (London: John Calder, 1963), pp. 205-6.
32 *Ibid.*, p. 324.
33 Alvin Toffler, *The Third Wave* (London: Pan Books, 1981) p. 402.
34 David S. Broder, 'The case for responsible party government', in Jeff Fishel (ed.), *Parties and Elections in an Anti-Party Age: American Politics and the Crisis of Confidence* (Bloomington, Ind.: Indiana University Press, 1978), p. 22.
35 Lloyd Cutler, 'To form a government', *Foreign Affairs*, 59, no. 1 (1980), p. 127.
36 'The crisis of confidence (July 15, 1979)', in *Congressional Quarterly Almanac, 96th Congress 1st Session 1979, Volume XXV* (Washington, DC: Congressional Quarterly, 1980), p. 46E.
37 Jane J. Mansbridge, *Beyond Adversary Democracy* (Chicago: University of Chicago Press, 1983).
38 Gregor Dallas, 'New York, 1865', *History Today*, December 1987, p. 22. See also Alexander B. Callow, *The Tweed Ring* (New York: Oxford University Press, 1966); *The City Boss in America: An Interpretive Reader*, ed. with commentary by Alexander B. Callow (New York: Oxford University Press, 1976).
39 See Michael Parenti, *Democracy for the Few*, 3rd edn (New York: St Martin's Press, 1980); E. E. Schattschneider, *The Semisovereign People: A Realist's View of Democracy in America* (Hinsdale, Ill: Dryden, 1975); Thomas R. Dye and L. Harmon Zeigler, *The Irony of Democracy: An Uncommon Introduction to American Politics*, 6th edn (New York: Brooks-Cole, 1983); Thomas R. Dye, *Who's Running America?: the Conservative Years*, 4th edn (Englewood Cliffs, NJ: Prentice-Hall, 1986); Bertram Gross, *Friendly Fascism: The New Face of Power in America* (New York: M. Evans, 1980).
40 Maurice Cranston, 'The destiny of democracy', *Times Literary Supplement*, 4 June 1976.
41 L. J. Sharpe, 'American democracy reconsidered: part II – conclusions', *British Journal of Political Science*, 3, Part 2 (April 1973), p. 132.
42 *Ibid.*, p. 134.
43 See Edmund S. Morgan, *Inventing the People: The Rise of Popular Sovereignty. in England and America* (New York: Norton, 1988).
44 Bert A. Rockman, *The Leadership Question: The Presidency and the American System* (New York: Praeger, 1984), p. 49.
45 *Ibid.*, p. 41.
46 Ralph Gabriel, *The Course of American Democratic Thought*, 2nd edn (New York: Ronald Press, 1956), p. 361.
47 J. Allen Smith, *The Spirit of American Government* (New York, 1905), p. 305.

Chapter 5

1 Walter D. Burnham, 'The turnout problem', in A. James Reichley (ed.), *Elections American Style* (Washington, DC: Brookings, 1987), p. 128.
2 Sidney Verba and Norman H. Nie, *Participation in America: Political Democracy and Social Equality* (Chicago: University of Chicago Press, 1972).
3 James W. Prothro and Charles M. Grigg, 'Fundamental principles of democracy: bases of agreement and disagreement', *Journal of Politics*, 22, no. 2 (May 1960), pp. 276-94.
4 Herbert McCloskey, 'Consensus and ideology in American politics', in Raymond E. Wolfinger (ed.), *Readings in American Political Behaviour*, 2nd edn (Englewood Cliffs, NJ: Prentice-Hall, 1970), p. 389.
5 See Michael Corbett, *Political Tolerance in America* (New York: Longman, 1982).
6 See Arthur F. Bentley, *The Process of Government* (Cambridge, Mass.: Belknap, 1908); David Truman, *The Governmental Process* (New York: Alfred A. Knopf, 1951); Robert A. Dahl, *Who Governs?* (New Haven, Conn.: Yale University Press, 1961); Nelson W. Polsby, *Community Power and Political Theory* (New Haven, Conn.: Yale University Press, 1963). For a commentary on the background and development of pluralism, see Gregor McLennan, *Marxism, Pluralism and Beyond: Classic Debates and New Departures* (Oxford: Polity, 1989), pp. 17-56; Grant Jordan, 'The pluralism of pluralism: an anti-theory?', *Political Studies*, 38, no. 2 (June 1990), pp. 286-301.
7 Larry Sabato, *PAC Power* (New York: Norton, 1985).
8 'The crisis of confidence (July 15, 1979)', in *Congressional Quarterly Almanac, 96th Congress 1st Session 1979, Volume XXXV* (Washington, DC: Congressional Quarterly, 1980), p. 46E.
9 See W. Russell Neuman, *The Paradox of Mass Politics: Knowledge and Opinion in the American Electorate* (Cambridge, Mass.: Harvard University Press, 1986), pp. 20-21.
10 Alexis de Tocqueville, *Democracy in America*, trans. by Henry Reeve, intro. by Henry S. Commager (London: Oxford University Press, 1946), p. 376.
11 Robert A. Dahl, *A Preface to Democratic Theory* (Chicago: University of Chicago Press , 1956), p. 150
12 *Ibid.*, p. 137.
13 This view is challenged by Brian Barry, in particular, who asserts the necessary existence of at least some interests which are common to all members of society, see Brian Barry, *Political Argument* (London: Routledge and Kegan Paul, 1965), chs. 11, 12.
14 See Jack Walker, 'A critique of the elitist theory of democracy', *American Political Science Review*, 60, no. 2 (June 1960), pp. 285-95; Peter Bachrach, *The Theory of Democratic Elitism: A Critique* (London: University of London, 1969).
15 James Madison, 'Federalist Paper No. 10', in Alexander Hamilton, James Madison and John Jay, *The Federalist Papers* intro by Clinton Rossiter (New York: Mentor, 1961), p. 79.
16 *Ibid.*, p. 79.
17 *Ibid.*, p. 83.
18 Kenneth M. Dolbeare and Murray J. Edelman, *American Politics: Policies, Power and Change*, 2nd edn (Lexington, Mass.: D. C. Heath, 1974), p. 257.

19 It has been pointed out that James Madison's comments about groups never amounted to a generalised and comprehensive theory about the character of American politics. In particular, it is claimed that the reputed 'father of American pluralism' never believed that the interplay of groups would lead to an automatic and benevolent state of equilibrium. On the contrary, it is thought that Madison believed and hoped that groups would neutralise one another and allow enlightened and rational statesmen to fill the breach of public leadership. See, for, example, Gordon S. Wood, 'Democracy and the Constitution', in Robert A. Goldwin and William A. Schambra (eds.), *How Democratic is the Constitution?* (Washington, DC: American Enterprise Institute, 1980), pp. 11-12.

20 See Walker, 'A critique of the elitist theory of democracy'.

21 Joseph Schumpeter, *Capitalism, Socialism and Democracy*, 3rd edn (New York: Harper and Row, 1942).

22 For example, see Geraint Parry, *Political Elites* (London: George Allen and Unwin, 1969), p. 125.

23 C. Wright Mills, *The Power Elite* (London: Oxford University Press, 1956).

24 *Ibid.*, pp. 4, 9.

25 *Ibid.*, p. 20.

26 In *The End of the American Era* (New York: Atheneum, 1980), Andrew Hacker concurs with this interpretation of American pluralism being 'essentially a characterization of the old middle class' (p. 33). But under the influence of recent social changes, even the middle classes no longer correspond to the pluralist model. 'Does it actually matter that we can be Methodists or Lutherans, that we hail from Ohio or Oregon, that our grandparents were Germans or Swedes? These plural features may add color to the national landscape, but their influence on attitudes and behaviour is more apparent than real at a time when much of America is becoming a single homogeneous nation' (pp. 33-34).

27 Mills, *The Power Elite*, p. 244.

28 See Leonard Silk and Mark Silk, *The American Establishment* (New York: Basic, 1980); G. William Domhoff, *Who Rules Now? A View from the 1980s* (Englewood Cliffs, NJ: Prentice Hall, 1983); Thomas R. Dye, *Who's Running America?: The Conservative Years*, 4th edn (Englewood Cliff, NJ: Prentice-Hall, 1986).

29 See E. E. Schattschneider, *The Semisovereign People: A Realist's View of Democracy in America* (Hinsdale, Ill.: Dryden 1972); Theodore Lowi, *The End of Liberalism: Ideology, Policy and the Crisis of Public Authority* (New York: Norton, 1969); Peter Bachrach and Morton S. Baratz, 'Two faces of power', *American Political Science Review*, 56, no. 4 (December 1962), pp. 947-52; W. A. Kelso, *American Democratic Theory* (Westport, Conn.: Greenwood, 1978); Charles Lindblom, *Politics and Markets* (New York: Basic, 1977).

30 See Bachrach, *The Theory of Democratic Elitism*; and Robert A. Dahl, *Polyarchy* (New Haven, Conn.: Yale University Press, 1971).

31 For the differences in attitudes and principles between elites and masses, and the consequent dependence of liberal values upon the moderation, tolerance and attentiveness of elites, see Herbert McCloskey, 'Consensus and ideology in American politics', pp. 383-410; Herbert McCloskey and Alida Brill, *Dimensions of Tolerance: What Americans Believe About Civil Liberties* (New York: Sage, 1983); Herbert McCloskey and John Zaller, *The American Ethos, Public Attitudes Toward Capitalism and Democracy* (Cambridge, Mass.: Harvard University Press, 1984);

Neuman, *The Paradox of Mass Politics*; Verba and Nie, *Participation in America*.

32 Bachrach, *The Theory of Democratic Elitism*, pp. 8-9.

33 *Ibid.*, pp. 32, 94. For a sustained denial that apathy is both inherent and neces-
    sary to a stable democratic order, see Carole Pateman, *Participation and Demo-
    cratic Theory* (Cambridge: Cambridge University Press, 1970).

34 Robert A. Dahl and Charles E. Lindblom, *Politics, Economics and Welfare*, 2nd edn
    with a new preface (Chicago: University of Chicago Press, 1976); Dahl, 'Plural-
    ism revisited', *Comparative Politics*, 10, no. 2 (January 1980), pp. 191-203; Dahl,
    Dilemmas of Pluralist Democracy (New Haven, Conn.: Yale University Press,
    1982); Dahl, *A Preface to Economic Democracy* (New Haven, Conn.: Yale Univer-
    sity Press, 1985).

35 See, for example, McLennan, *Marxism, Pluralism and Beyond*, pp. 17-56; and
    Michael Margolis, 'Democracy: American style', in Graeme Duncan (ed.),
    Democratic Theory and Practice (Cambridge: Cambridge University Press, 1983),
    pp. 115-32.

36 David Held, *Political Theory and the Modern State: Essays on State, Power and
    Democracy* (Oxford: Polity, 1989), p. 44.

37 See Alan Crawford, *Thunder on the Right: The 'New Right' and the Politics of
    Resentment* (New York: Pantheon, 1980); Sylvia Tesh, 'In support of "Single
    Issue" politics', *Political Science Quarterly* 99, no. 1 (Spring 1984), pp. 27-44.

38 It is in the nature of pluralism that for every argument supporting its presence,
    there is one denying it. Single-issue groups, for example, are highly prominent
    organisations, but they are also notorious for basing their appeal upon non-
    negotiable differences. 'They hold their own single cause to be a moral absolute.
    They do not aim at gaining majority support or even at attracting majority
    following. Otherwise they might have to compromise.' (Peter F. Drucker, *The
    New Realities* (London: Heinemann, 1989), pp. 96-7.) Likewise the public
    interest movement can be seen as vindicating pluralism, but it can just as easily
    be construed as repudiating it. It is claimed to be state-oriented, elitist and not
    concerned with negotiation and partnership, so much as with wanting to
    'dominate the policy making process just as business had traditionally done'
    (David Vogler, 'The public interest movement and the American reform
    tradition', *Political Science Quarterly*, 95, no. 4 (Winter 1980-1), pp. 607-27).

39 John F. Manley, *American Government and Public Policy* (New York: Macmillan,
    1976), pp. 24-5.

Chapter 6

1 Richard Hofstadter, *The Age of Reform: From Bryan to FDR* (London: Jonathan
   Cape, 1962), p. 61.

2 John D. Hicks, *The Populist Revolt: A History of the Farmers' Alliance and the
   People's Party* (Minneapolis, Minn.: University of Minnesota Press, 1931); C.
   Vann Woodward, *Origins of the New South, 1877-1913* (Baton Rouge, La.:
   Louisiana State University Press, 1951); Margaret Canovan, *Populism* (London:
   Junction Books, 1971).

3 'The Populist platform, 1892', in Richard D. Heffner, *A Documentary History of
   the United States*, rev. edn (New York: Mentor, 1976), pp. 197-8.

4 *Ibid.*, p. 200.

5 Walter D. Burnham, *Critical Elections and the Mainsprings of American Politics*

(New York: Norton, 1970), *passim*.

6 For the importance of rural isolation as a motivating force in the Populist movement, see James Turner, 'Understanding the Populists', *The Journal of American History*, 67, no. 2 (September 1980), pp. 354-73.

7 Hofstadter, *The Age of Reform*, pp. 70-84.

8 'The Populist party platform, 1892', in Heffner, *A Documentary History of the United States*, p. 201.

9 Christopher Lasch, *The Agony of the American Left* (Harmondsworth, Middx: Penguin, 1973), p. 18.

10 *Ibid.*, p. 20.

11 Hofstadter, *The Age of Reform*, pp. 58-9.

12 Everett Walters, 'Populism and its significance in American history', in Frank O. Gattell and Allen Weinstein (eds.), *American Themes: Essays in Historiography* (New York: Oxford University Press, 1968), pp. 325-37.

13 Lewis L. Gould (ed.), *The Progressive Era* (Syracuse, NY: Syracuse University Press, 1974); Arthur A. Ekirch, Jr., *Progressivism in America: A Study of the Era from Theodore Roosevelt to Woodrow Wilson* (New York: New Viewpoints, 1974); Samuel P. Hays, *The Response to Industrialism, 1885-1914* (Chicago: University of Chicago Press, 1957).

14 Richard Hofstadter, *The Progressive Historians: Turner, Beard, Parrington* (London: Jonathan Cape, 1969).

15 A. J. Beitzinger, *A History of American Political Thought* (New York: Dodd, Mead, 1972), pp. 482-508; Henry S. Commager, *The American Mind: An Interpretation of American Thought and Character Since the 1880s* (New York: Bantam, 1970), pp. 317-43.

16 Charles B. Forcey, *The Crossroads of Liberalism: Croly, Weyl, Lippmann and the Progressive Era, 1900-1925* (New York: Oxford University Press, 1961); Melvin I. Urofsky, *Louis D. Brandeis and the Progressive Tradition*, ed. by Oscar Handlin (Boston, Little, Brown, 1981); David E. Price, 'Community and control: Critical democratic theory in the progressive period', *American Political Science Review*, 68, no. 4 (December 1974), pp. 1663-78.

17 See J. A. Thompson *Progressivism*, British Association of American Studies Pamphlet No. 2 (British Association of American Studies, 1979); Ekirch, *Progressivism in America*, ch. 7. The urge to remedy social and political ills by an infusion of democracy is a theme in American liberalism which continues to find expression. See Austin Ranney, 'The political parties: reform and decline', in Anthony King (ed.), *The New American Political System* (Washington, DC: American Enterprise Institute, 1978), pp. 213-47; Benjamin Barber, *Strong Democracy: Participatory Politics for a New Age* (Berkeley, Calif.: University of California Press, 1984).

18 Hofstadter, *The Age of Reform*, p. 213.

19 Hays, *The Response to Industrialism, 1885-1914*, p. 89.

20 Herbert Croly, *The Promise of American Life* (New York: Capricorn Books, 1964).

21 David W. Noble, 'Herbert Croly and American progressive thought', in John P. Roche (ed.), *American Political Thought: From Jefferson to Progressivism* (New York: Harper and Row, 1967), pp. 259-83.

22 George E. Mowry, *Theodore Roosevelt and the Progressive Movement* (New York: Hill and Wang, 1960), pp. 131-82.

23 Arthur S. Link, *Woodrow Wilson and the Progressive Era, 1910-1917* (New York: Harper and Row, 1954), pp. 1-80.

24 Woodrow Wilson, *The New Freedom: A Call for the Emancipation of the Generous Energies of a People*, intro. and notes by William E. Leuchtenberg (Englewood Cliffs, NJ: Prentice-Hall, 1961), p. 125.

25 Richard Hofstadter, *The American Political Tradition: And the Men Who Made It* (London: Jonathan Cape, 1967), pp. 251-7.

26 Arthur M. Schlesinger, Jr., *The Age of Roosevelt: The Crisis of the Old Order* (London: Heinemann, 1957).

27 Arthur M. Schlesinger, Jr., *The Age of Roosevelt: The Coming of the New Deal* (London: Heinemann, 1960); William E. Leuchtenberg, *Franklin D. Roosevelt and the New Deal, 1932-1940* (New York: Harper and Row, 1963).

28 Hubert H. Humphrey, *The Political Philosophy of the New Deal* (Baton Rouge, La.; Louisiana State University Press, 1970), p. x.

29 See Howard Zinn (ed.), *New Deal Thought* (Indianapolis, Ind.: Bobbs-Merrill, 1966).

30 Joseph P. Lash, *Dealers and Dreamers: A New Look at the New Deal* (Garden City, NY: Doubleday, 1988).

31 See Hofstadter, *The Age of Reform*, ch. 7; Paul K. Conkin, *The New Deal* (London: Routledge and Kegan Paul, 1968); James M. Burns,. *The Lion and the Fox* (London: Secker and Warburg, 1956); Eric Goldman, *Rendezvous With Destiny* (New York: Alfred A. Knopf, 1972), pp. 328-73.

32 Hofstadter, *The American Political Tradition*, pp. 324-38.

33 Barton J. Bernstein, 'The New Deal: the conservative achievements of liberal reform', in Barton J. Bernstein and Allen J. Matusow (eds.), *Twentieth Century America: Recent Interpretations*, 2nd edn (New York: Harcourt Brace Jovanovich, 1972), p. 246.

34 Ira Katznelson and Mark Kesselman, *The Politics of Power: A Critical Introduction to American Government* (New York: Harcourt Brace Jovanovich, 1975), p. 485.

35 For example, see the history of the poverty programme after President Johnson's flamboyant declaration of 'a war on poverty' in 1964 – Allen J. Matusow, *The Unravelling of America: A History of Liberalism in the 1960s* (New York: Harper and Row, 1984), pp. 217-71.

36 See Alonzo L. Hamby, *Liberalism and Its Challengers: FDR to Reagan* (New York: Oxford University Press, 1985); James L. Sundquist, *Politics and Policy: The Eisenhower, Kennedy and Johnson Years* (Washington, DC: Brookings, 1968); Stephen W. Rousseaus, 'The Great Society: an old New Deal', *The Nation*, 10 May 1965.

37 Max J. Skidmore, *American Political Thought* (New York: St Martin's Press, 1978), p. 226.

38 Leuchtenberg, *Franklin Roosevelt and the New Deal, 1932-1940*, p. 35.

39 *Ibid.*, pp. 89, 88.

40 Samuel Lubell quoted in David S. Broder, 'Consensus politics: end of an experiment', *Atlantic Monthly*, October 1966.

41 Theodore Lowi, *The End of Liberalism: Ideology, Policy and the Crisis of Public Authority* (New York: Norton, 1969).

42 Matusow, *The Unravelling of America*, passim; Milton Viorst, *Fire in the Streets: America in the 1960s* (New York: Simon and Schuster, 1980); Arthur M.

Schlesinger, Jr., *Crisis of Confidence: Ideas, Power and Violence in America* (London: Andre Deutsch, 1969).

43 M. Stanton Evans, *Clear and Present Dangers: A Conservative View of America's Government* (New York: Harcourt Brace Jovanovich, 1975).

44 Philip E. Converse, Warren E. Miller, Jerrold G. Rusk and Arthur C. Wolfe, 'Continuity and change in American politics: politics and issues in the 1968 election', *American Political Science Review*, 63, no. 4 (December 1969), p. 1088.

45 See Hamby, *Liberalism and Its Challengers*, pp. 256-81; Marvin E. Gettleman and David Mermelstein (eds.), *The Great Society Reader: The Failure of American Liberalism* (New York: Vintage, 1967); George E. Reedy, *The Twilight of the Presidency* (New York: New American Library, 1970); Herbert Y. Schandler, *The Unmaking of a President: Lyndon Johnson and Vietnam* (Princeton, N.J: Princeton University Press, 1977); Godfrey Hodgson, *In Our Time: America from World War II to Nixon* (London: Macmillan, 1976); Steve Fraser and Gary Gerstle (eds.), *The Rise and Fall of the New Deal Order, 1930-1980* (Princeton, NJ: Princeton University Press, 1989).

46 See Peter Steinfels, *The Neoconservatives: The Men Who Are Changing America* (New York: Simon and Schuster, 1979); Irving Kristol, *Reflections of a Neoconservative: Looking Back, Looking Ahead* (New York: Basic, 1984).

47 Paul Tsongas, *The Road From Here: Liberalism and Realities in the 1980s* (New York: Alfred A. Knopf, 1981).

48 For the divergences in the liberal ranks, see James H. Duffy, *Domestic Affairs: American Programmes and Priorities* (New York: Simon and Schuster, 1978) and Randall Rothenberg, *The Neoliberals: Creating the New American Politics* (New York: Simon and Schuster, 1984).

49 Alexander Cockburn, 'The L-word in crisis', *New Statesman and Society*, 4 November 1988.

50 Arthur M. Schlesinger, Jr., 'Reaganism is dead: long live liberalism', *Washington Post* supplement published in *Guardian Weekly*, 8 May 1988; Michael Kinsley, 'Hypocrisy and the L-word', *Time*, 1 August 1988; J. K. Galbraith, 'The death of liberalism', *The Observer*, 26 March 1989.

51 See Lloyd A. Free and Hadley Cantril, *The Political Beliefs of Americans: A Study of Public Opinion* (New Brunswick, NJ: Rutgers University Press, 1967).

52 See Michael Foley, 'Presidential leadership and the presidency', in Joseph Hogan (ed.), *The Reagan Years: The Record in Presidential Leadership* (Manchester: Manchester University Press, 1990), pp. 46-9; Everett C. Ladd, 'Politics in the '80s: an electorate at odds with itself', *Public Opinion* (December/January 1983).

53 Nicholas Lemann, 'The unfinished war', *Atlantic Monthly*, December 1988.

54 Matusow, *The Unravelling of America*, p. 11.

Chapter 7

1 Aaron Wildavsky, 'The Goldwater phenomenon: purists, politicians and the two-party system', *Review of Politics*, 27, no. 3 (July 1965), pp. 386-413.

2 Quoted in Theodore H. White, *The Making of the President, 1964* (London: Jonathan Cape, 1965), p. 216.

3 *Ibid.*, p. 216.

4 *Ibid.*, p. 217.

5 'President Reagan's inaugural address (January 20, 1981)', in *Congressional*

Quarterly Almanac, 97th Congress 1st Session 1981, Volume XXXVII (Washington, DC: Congressional Quarterly, 1982), p. 11E.

6 William Schneider, 'The November 4 vote for president: what did it mean?', Austin Ranney (ed.), *The American Election of 1980* (Washington, DC: American Enterprise Institute, 1981), pp. 240-8.

7 See Alan Crawford, *Thunder on the Right: The 'New Right' and the Politics of Resentment* (New York: Pantheon, 1980).

8 Louis Hartz, *The Liberal Tradition in America: An Interpretation of American Political Thought Since the Revolution* (New York: Harcourt Brace Jovanovich, 1955), p. 151.

9 *Ibid.*, pp. 145-58.

10 Russell Kirk, 'Prescription, Authority and Ordered Freedom', in Frank S. Meyer (ed.), *What is Conservatism?* (New York: Holt, Rinehart and Winston, 1963), p. 24.

11 *Ibid.*, p. 36.

12 Kirk, 'The problem of the new order', in William F. Buckley, Jr. (ed.), *American Conservative Thought in the Twentieth Century* (Indianapolis, Ind.: Bobbs-Merrill, 1970), p. 367.

13 Clinton Rossiter, *Conservatism in America: The Thankless Persuasion*, 2nd edn (New York: Vintage, 1962), p. 22.

14 Peter Viereck, 'The philosophical "New Conservatism" (1962)', in Daniel Bell (ed.), *The Radical Right* (Garden City, NY: Anchor, 1963), p. 188.

15 Rossiter, *Conservatism in America*, p. 73.

16 *Ibid.*, p. 74.

17 *Ibid.*, pp. 74, 75.

18 Viereck, 'The philosophical "New Conservatism" (1962)', in Daniel Bell (ed.), *The Radical Right*, p. 188.

19 *Ibid.*, p. 198.

20 F. A. Hayek, *The Constitution of Liberty* (London: Routledge and Kegan Paul, 1960), pp. 20-1.

21 Quoted in Milton Friedman and Rose Friedman, *Free To Choose* (London: Secker and Warburg, 1980), pp. 28-9.

22 Milton Friedman, *Capitalism and Freedom* (Chicago: University of Chicago Press, 1962).

23 Barry Goldwater, *The Conscience of a Conservative* (Shepardsville, Ky.: Victor, 1960), p. 13.

24 *Ibid.*, p. 71.

25 *Ibid.*, p. 73.

26 Goldwater, *The Conscience of a Majority* (New York: Pocket Books, 1971), p. 19.

27 *Ibid.*, p. 9. See also M. Stanton Evans, *Clear and Present Dangers: A Conservative View of America's Government* (New York: Harcourt Brace Jovanovich, 1975).

28 Robert Nozick, *Anarchy, State and Utopia* (Oxford: Blackwell, 1974).

29 Brian Barry, review of *Anarchy, State and Utopia* by Robert Nozick, *Political Theory*, 3, no. 3 (August 1975), p. 331.

30 Viereck, 'The philosophical "New Conservatism" (1962)', in Bell (ed.), *The Radical Right*, pp. 185-207.

31 Richard Hofstadter, *The Paranoid Style in American Politics and Other Essays* (New York: Vintage, 1967), chs. 2-4.

32 Frank S. Meyer, 'The recrudescent American conservatism', in William F. Buckley (ed.), *American Conservative Thought in the Twentieth Century* (Indianapolis, Ind.: Bobbs-Merrill, 1970), pp. 75-92.
33 Margaret Canovan, *Populism* (London: Junction Books, 1971), *passim*.
34 John Higham, *Strangers in the Land: Patterns of American Nativism, 1860-1925* (New York: Atheneum, 1968).
35 Wyn C. Wade, *The Fiery Cross: The Ku Klux Klan in America* (New York: Simon and Schuster, 1988).
36 David Caute, *The Great Fear: The Anti-Communist Purge Under Truman and Eisenhower* (London: Secker and Warburg, 1978); Seymour M. Lipset and Earl Raub, *The Politics of Unreason: Right Wing Extremism in America, 1790-1970* (London: Heinemann, 1971), ch. 6.
37 Quoted in John H. Bunzel, *Anti-Politics in America: Reflections on the Anti-Political Temper and the Distortions of the Democratic Process* (New York: Vintage, 1970), p. 36.
38 Christopher Lasch, *The Agony of the American Left* (Harmondsworth, Midd., Penguin, 1973), p. 192.
39 Lipset and Raub, *The Politics of Unreason*, p. 345.
40 Jody Carlson, *George C. Wallace and the Politics of Powerlessness: The Wallace Campaigns for the Presidency 1964-1976* (New Brunswick, NJ: Transaction, 1981).
41 Lipset and Raub, *The Politics of Unreason*, chs. 6-10.
42 Crawford, *Thunder on the Right*; Kevin P. Phillips, *Post-Conservative America: People, Politics and Ideology in a Time of Crisis* (New York: Random House, 1982).
43 Aaron Wildavsky, 'Government and the people', in Ronald E. Pynn (ed.), *Watergate and the American Political Process* (New York: Praeger, 1975), p. 38.
44 A. James Reichley, 'Religion and the future of American politics', *Political Science Quarterly*, 101, no. 1 (Spring 1986), pp. 23-46; Robert C. Liebman and Robert Wuthnow (eds.), *The New Christian Right* (Hawthorne, NY: Aldine, 1983).
45 Daniel C. Maguire, *The New Subversive: Anti-Americanism of the Religious Right* (New York: Continuum Publishing, 1982).
46 Richard A. Viguerie, with an introduction by Jerry Falwall, *The New Right: We're Ready To Lead* (Naperville, Ill.: Caroline House, 1981).

Chapter 8

1 Bernard Bailyn, *The Ideological Origins of the American Revolution* (Cambridge, Mass.: Belknap, 1967), p. 307.
2 *Ibid.*, p. 308.
3 Straughton Lynd, *Intellectual Origins of the American Radicalism* (London: Faber and Faber, 1969), p. 4.
4 J. R. Pole, *The Pursuit of Equality in American History* (Berkeley: University of California Press, 1978), p. 3.
5 J. R. Pole, 'Equality: an American dilemma', in Leslie C. Berlowitz, Denis Donoghue and Louis Menand (eds.), *America In Theory* (New York: Oxford University Press, 1988), p. 70.
6 Ronald Dworkin, 'A nation in search of equality', *The Observer*, 25 June 1978. See also Edmund S. Morgan, *Inventing the People: The Rise of Popular Sovereignty in England and America* (New York: Norton, 1988).

7 Henry S. Commager, *The Empire of Reason: How Europe Imagined and America Realized the Enlightenment* (London: Weidenfeld and Nicolson, 1978), p. 102.

8 Daniel Bell, 'The end of American exceptionalism', in Nathan Glazer and Irving Kristol, (eds.), *The American Commonwealth – 1976* (New York: Basic, 1976), p. 209.

9 See Hugh Brogan, *Tocqueville* (London: Fontana, 1973), pp. 28-34.

10 Abraham Lincoln, 'The Gettysburg Address', in Richard D. Heffner, *A Documentary History of the United States*, rev. edn (New York: Mentor, 1976), p. 157.

11 W. H. Riker, *Democracy in the United States*, 2nd edn (New York: Macmillan, 1965), p. 20.

12 Alexis de Tocqueville, *Democracy in America*, trans. by Henry Reeve, intro. by Henry S. Commager (London: Oxford University Press, 1946), p. 363.

13 *Ibid.*, pp. 197, 192.

14 Gordon S. Wood, *The Creation of the American Republic, 1776-1787* (Chapel Hill, NC: University of North Carolina Press, 1969), p. 71.

15 *Ibid.*, p. 73.

16 See Tocqueville, *Democracy in America*, p. 137.

17 Pole, *The Pursuit of Equality in American History*, p. 13.

18 Martin Diamond, 'The Declaration of Independence and the Constitution: liberty, democracy and the Founders', in Glazer and Kristol (eds.), *The American Commonwealth – 1976*, pp. 48-9.

19 Pole, *The Pursuit of Equality in American History*, p. 2.

20 *Ibid.*, p. 176.

21 *Ibid.*, p. 2.

22 *Ibid.*, p. 292.

23 *Ibid.*, p. 3.

24 Dumas Malone, *Jefferson and His Time, Volume 6: The Sage of Monticello* (Boston: Little, Brown, 1981), pp. 341-2.

25 See John H. Franklin, *Reconstruction: After the Civil War* (Chicago: University of Chicago Press, 1961), chs. 6-8.

26 In the *Civil Rights Cases* 109 US 3 (1883), the Supreme Court established a narrow construction of the Fourteenth Amendment. 'No state ... shall deny to any person ... the equal protection of the laws' was taken to mean that only states, in the form of state officials acting under state law, were subject to the prohibitory clauses of the Amendment. Private discriminatory practices, therefore, were outside the scope of the Amendment and, as such, the United States Congress had no power in these circumstances to enforce the provisions of the Amendment.

27 *Plessy* v. *Ferguson* 163 US 537 (1896).

28 C. Vann Woodward, *The Origins of the New South, 1877-1913* (Baton Rouge: Louisiana State University Press, 1951), chs. 13, 14; Woodward, *The Strange Career of Jim Crow*, 3rd edn. rev. (New York: Oxford University Press, 1974), pp. 67-109.

29 Manning Marable, *Race, Reform and Rebellion: The Second Reconstruction in Black America, 1945-1982* (London: Macmillan, 1984), pp. 8, 10.

30 Gunnar Myrdal, *An American Dilemma: The Negro Problem and American Democracy* (New York: Harper, 1944).

31 *Brown v Board of Education of Topeka* 347 US 483 (1954).
32 *Brown v. Board of Education of Topeka* 347 US 495.
33 John White, *Black Leadership in America, 1895-1968* (London: Longman, 1985), ch. 7; David J. Garrow, *Bearing the Cross: Martin Luther King, Jr. and the Southern Christian Leadership Conference* (London: Jonathan Cape, 1988).
34 Martin L. King, Jr., 'The dream of freedom', in Armin Rappaport and Richard P. Trinia (eds.), *Present in the Past: Source Problems in American History* (New York: Macmillan, 1972), pp. 476-7.
35 President John F. Kennedy, 'We face a moral crisis', in Henry S. Commager (ed.), *The Struggle for Racial Equality: A Documentary Record* (New York: Harper and Row, 1967), pp. 164-6.
36 Herbert S. Parmet, *JFK: The Presidency of John F. Kennedy* (Harmondsworth, Middx: Penguin, 1984), p. 267; Theodore C. Sorensen, *Kennedy* (London: Pan, 1965), p. 549.
37 King, 'The last plea of Martin Luther King', *The Sunday Times*, 7 April 1968.
38 The Civil Rights Act of 1964 (i) reduced the restrictions on voting registration and on literacy tests in particular; (ii) it outlawed a set of employment practices whenever they were based on race, colour, religion, national origin or sex; (iii) it improved the ability of the federal government to hasten the desegregation of public schools; and (iv) it barred discrimination in public accommodations when such discrimination and segregation was supported by state laws or official action, when interstate travellers were being served, or when a substantial portion of the goods sold or entertainment provided had moved in interstate commerce.

    The Voting Rights Act of 1965 intensified the drive against discriminatory voting practices in the South by providing for the federal registration of voters and for the federal supervision of elections in seven southern states.

    The Civil Rights Act of 1968 introduced measures to prevent racial discrimination in the sale and rental of housing.
39 George D. Jackson, *Blood In My Eye* (New York: Random House, 1972).
40 See Malcom X, *The Autobiography of Malcom X* (New York: Grove, 1965); Stokeley Carmichael and Charles V. Hamilton, *Black Power: The Politics of Liberation in America* (New York: Vintage, 1967); Eldridge Cleaver, *Soul on Ice* (New York: Dell, 1968); Bobby G. Seale, *Seize the Time* (New York: Random House, 1970).
41 US Bureau of the Census, *Statistical Abstract of the United States, 1988* (Washington, DC: United States Government Printing Office, 1987), pp. 247, 436, 435. See also Michael White, 'US whites 12 times richer than blacks', *Guardian Weekly*, 3 August 1986; 'Black Americans: still trailing behind', *The Economist*, 3 March 1990.
42 Martin Shapiro, 'The Supreme Court: from Warren to Burger', in Anthony King (ed.), *The New American Political System* (Washington, DC: American Enterprise Institute, 1978), p. 200.
43 *Ibid.*, p. 201.
44 George F. Will, 'Reverse discrimination', *Newsweek*, 10 July 1978.
45 *Bakke v Regents of the University of California* 553 P.2d 1152 (1976).
46 Pole, *The Pursuit of Equality in American History*, p. 292.
47 Sidney Verba and Gary R. Orren, *Equality in America: The View from the Top*

(Cambridge, Mass.: Harvard University Press, 1985).

48 Sidney Verba and Gary R. Orren, 'The meaning of equality in America', *Political Science Quarterly*, 100, no. 3 (Fall 1985), p. 376.

49 *Ibid.*, p. 376.

50 For example, see Herbert McClosky and John Zaller, *The American Ethos: Public Attitudes towards Capitalism and Democracy* (Cambridge, Mass.: Harvard University Press, 1984), pp. 266-77: James L. Sundquist, 'Has America lost its social conscience – and how will it get it back?', *Political Science Quarterly*, 101, no. 4 (Winter 1986-87), pp. 513-33.

51 Nathan Glazer, *The Limits of Social Policy* (Cambridge, Mass.: Harvard University Press, 1988); Charles Murray, *Losing Ground* (New York: Basic Books, 1984); Lawrence Mead, *Beyond Entitlement* (New York: Free Press, 1986).

52 Mead, *Beyond Entitlement*, p. 10.

53 McClosky and Zaller, *The American Ethos*, pp. 86-94; James R. Kluegel and Eliot R. Smith, *Beliefs About Inequality: Americans' Views About What Is and What Ought To Be* (New York: Aldine De Gruyter, 1986).

54 Seymour M. Lipset and William Schneider, 'Racial equality in America', *New Society*, 20 April 1978, p. 130. See also Seymour M. Lipset and William Schneider, 'The Bakke case: how would it be decided at the bar of public opinion', *Public Opinion* (March–April 1978), pp. 38-44; Paul Sniderman and Michael G. Hagen, *Race and Inequality: A Study in American Values* (Chatham, NJ: Chatham House, 1985).

55 McClosky and Zaller, *The American Ethos*, p. 93.

56 *Ibid.*, p. 94.

57 Lipset and Schneider, 'Racial equality in America', p. 130.

58 *Ibid.*, p. 130.

59 *Ibid.*, p. 130.

60 *Ibid.*, pp. 130, 131.

61 Pole, 'Equality: an American dilemma', in Berlowitz *et al.* (eds.), *America In Theory*, p. 76.

62 Verba and Orren, 'The meaning of equality in America', p. 397.

Chapter 9

1 President Bush continued this theme in office. From 1989 to 1990 he championed a constitutional amendment to prohibit any defacement of the American flag.

2 See Lawrence Feinberg, 'Accentuating the positive', *Guardian Weekly*, 29 March 1987.

3 Quoted in Paul D. Erikson, *Reagan Speaks: The Making of an American Myth* (New York: New York University Press, 1985), p. 108.

4 See Elie Kedourie, *Nationalism*, 3rd edn (London: Hutchinson, 1966); Frederick Hertz, *Nationality in History and Politics* (London: International Library of Sociology and Social Reconstruction, 1950); Eugene Kamenka (ed.), *Nationalism: The Nature and Evolution of an Idea* (Canberra: Australian National University Press, 1973).

5 Hans Kohn, 'Nationalism', in *International Encyclopaedia of the Social Sciences, Volume 11* (New York: Macmillan/Free Press, 1968), p. 66.

6 Kohn, *Nationalism: An Interpretive Essay* (New York: Macmillan, 1957), p. 3.

7 Marcus Cunliffe, 'Formative events from Columbus to World War I: Part 1', in Michael P. Hamilton (ed.), *American Character and Foreign Policy* (Grand Rapids, Mich.: William B. Eerdmans, 1986), p. 7.

8 Ernest R. May, *Imperial Democracy: The Emergence of America as a Great Power* (New York: Harcourt, Brace and World, 1961); William A. Williams, *The Contours of American History* (New York: Norton, 1988), pp. 343-70.

9 'Woodrow Wilson, speech for the declaration of war against Germany (April 2, 1917)', in Richard Hofstadter (ed.), *Great Issues in American History: From Reconstruction to the Present Day, 1864-1969* (New York: Vintage, 1969), p. 218.

10 'President Kennedy's inaugural address (January 20, 1961)', in Edmund S. Ions (ed.), *The Politics of John F. Kennedy* (London: Routledge and Kegan Paul, 1967), p. 52.

11 *Ibid.*, p. 50.

12 'President Reagan's inaugural address (January 20. 1981)', in *Congressional Quarterly Almanac, 97th Congress 1st Session 1981, Volume XXXVII* (Washington, DC: Congressional Quarterly, 1982), p. 11E.

13 Poll quoted in James Q. Wilson, *American Government: Institutions and Policies*, 3rd edn (Lexington, Mass.: D. C. Heath, 1986), p. 82.

14 Herbert Croly, *The Promise of American Life* (New York: Capricorn Books, 1964).

15 Frederick J. Turner, *The Frontier in American History* (Huntington, NY: R. E. Krieger, 1975).

16 Kohn, *American Nationalism*, ch. 3; Ralph H. Gabriel, *The Course of American Democratic Thought*, 2nd edn (New York: Ronald Press, 1956), ch. 10.

17 Quoted in A. J. Beitzinger, *A History of American Political Thought* (New York: Dodd, Mead, 1972), p. 279.

18 Ernest L. Tuveson, *Redeemer Nation: The Idea of America's Millenial Role* (Chicago: University of Chicago Press, 1968).

19 A. K. Weinberg, *Manifest Destiny: A Study of Nationalist Expansion in American History* (Chicago: Quadrangle, 1963).

20 Arthur A. Ekirch, Jr., *Ideas, Ideals and American Diplomacy: A History of Their Growth and Interaction* (New York: Appleton–Century–Crofts, 1966), chs. 2, 3; Richard Hofstadter, 'Cuba, the Philippines, and manifest destiny', in Richard Hofstadter, *The Paranoid Style of American Politics and Other Essays* (New York: Vintage, 1967), pp. 145-87; Richard Leopold, 'The roots of imperialism', in Allen Weinstein (ed.), *Origins of Modern America, 1860-1900* (New York: Random House, 1970), pp. 205-16.

21 Quoted in Kohn, *American Nationalism*, p. 183.

22 John L. O'Sullivan, 'Manifest destiny', in Hans Kohn (ed.), *Nationalism: Its Meaning and History*, rev. edn (Princeton, NJ: D. Van Nostrand, 1965), p. 142.

23 Quoted in Henry N. Smith, *Virgin Lands: The American West as Symbol and Myth* (New York: Vintage, 1950), p. 40.

24 Ekirch, *Ideas, Ideals and American Diplomacy*, pp. 43-4.

25 Foster R. Dulles, *America's Rise to World Power, 1989-1954* (New York: Harper and Row, 1963), chs. 1-4; May, *Imperial Democracy, passim*.

26 After the Spanish–American War of 1898, Cuba was never formally annexed to the United States, The war had been fought ostensibly to provide for Cuban autonomy. Although Cuba was granted self-rule in a treaty of settlement, the United States, nevertheless, claimed the right to intervene in the island's affairs

to 'protect life, property and individual liberty'.
27 Robert E. Osgood, *Ideals and Self-Interest in America's Foreign Relations: The Great Transformation of the Twentieth Century* (Chicago: University of Chicago Press, 1953).
28 Quoted in James O. Robertson, *American Myth, American Reality* (New York: Hill and Wang, 1980), p. 272.
29 Quoted in Charles W. Kegley, Jr. and Eugene R. Wittkopf, *American Foreign Policy: Pattern and Process*, 3rd edn (London: Macmillan, 1987), p. 40.
30 Quoted in Michael H. Hunt, *Ideology and United States Foreign Policy* (New Haven, Conn.: Yale University Press, 1987), p. 183.
31 'Excerpts from Bush address', *Guardian Weekly*, August 19 1990. Such declarations of professed principle never managed to extinguish the old debate over American ideals and self-interest. The response below was typical of the ensuing dispute. 'United States foreign policy in the Gulf can be summed up in one word: petrol. But it has failed to acknowledge the simplicity of this objective. The United States talks of standards, civilisation, morality and international law' (Sabiha Knight, 'Washington prepares its jihad', *Independent*, 24 August 1990).
32 James Chace, 'Dreams of perfectability; American exceptionalism and the search for a moral foreign policy', in Leslie C. Berlowitz, Denis Donoghue and Louis Menand (eds.), *America in Theory* (New York: Oxford University Press, 1988), p. 250.
33 Robert D. Schulzinger, *American Diplomacy in the Twentieth Century* (New York: Oxford University Press, 1984), p. 5.
34 Quoted in Robertson, *American Myth, American Reality*, p. 272.
35 The term 'realism' here refers to the need to recognise that international affairs is a struggle for power and that the United States needs to concern itself with self-protection and self-promotion in pursuit of its own national interest (see Kegley and Wittkopf, *American Foreign Policy*, pp. 73-6).
36 Robert A. Pastor, *Condemned to Repetition: The United States and Nicaragua* (Princeton, NJ: Princeton University Press, 1987); Walter La Feber, *Inevitable Revolution: The United States in Central America* (New York: Norton, 1983); Jenny Pearce, *Under the Eagle: United States's Intervention in Central America and the Caribbean* (London: Latin America Bureau, 1981).
37 John P. Diggins, 'Knowledge and sorrow: Louis Hartz's quarrel with American history', *Political Theory*, 16, no. 3 (August 1988), p. 373.
38 Louis Hartz, *The Liberal Tradition in America: An Interpretation of American Political Thought Since the Revolution* (New York: Harcourt Brace Jovanovich, 1955), p. 286.
39 In October 1983, President Reagan authorised an American invasion of the Caribbean island of Grenada. Although it was a British Commonwealth country, Reagan failed to involve or even to consult the Thatcher government in his invasion plans. At the US–USSR summit meeting at Reykjavik in October 1986, President Reagan at one stage suggested the complete elimination of both countries' nuclear forces over ten years. Even though this was not agreed to, the proposal demonstrated that an American President was prepared to remove the United States's nuclear umbrella over Western Europe without even consulting his NATO partners.
40 See Richard N. Rosencrance (ed.), *America as an Ordinary Country: United States Foreign Policy and the Future* (Ithaca, NY: Cornell University Press, 1976).

41 'Inaugural address of President Jimmy Carter (January 20, 1977)', in *Public Papers of Presidents of the United States: Jimmy Carter 1977, Book 1 – January 20 to June 24 1977* (Washington, DC: United States Government Printing Office, 1977), p. 2. See also Gaddis Smith, *Morality, Reason and Power: American Diplomacy in the Carter Years* (New York: Hill and Wang, 1986).

42 Joshua Muravchik, *The Uncertain Crusade: Jimmy Carter and the Dilemmas of Human Rights Policy* (Lanham, Md.: Hamilton, 1986), p. 227.

43 George E. Reedy, *The Twilight of the President* (New York: Mentor, 1970), p. 28.

44 Robert S. Hirschfield, 'The power of the contemporary presidency', in Robert S. Hirschfield (ed.), *The Power of the Presidency: Concepts and Controversy* (New York: Atherton, 1968), p. 245.

45 John E. Mueller, *War, Presidents and Public Opinion* (New York: Wiley, 1973); Jong R. Lee, 'Rallying around the flag: foreign policy events and presidential popularity', *Presidential Studies Quarterly*, 7, no. 3 (Fall 1977), pp. 252-6.

46 Alton Frye, 'The American character and the formation of United States foreign policy – Part 2', in Hamilton (ed.) *American Character and Foreign Policy*, p. 150.

47 It should be acknowledged that there is an alternative construction of the political vulnerability of the American state. This view sees the fragmentation and incoherence of the political system as a consequence of an underdeveloped national identity, rather than as a result of a robust national identity (for example see M. J. C. Vile, *Constitutionalism and the Separation of Powers* (Oxford: Clarendon, 1967), p. 335; Bert A. Rockman, *The Leadership Question: The Presidency and the American System* (New York: Praeger, 1984), pp. 62, 72). This view tends to confine American nationalism to the formal structure of political authority, rather than to its *de facto* expression on occasions of heightened and immediate national concern (see note 44). It also ignores the libertarian ethos of American nationalism that is often expressed through the values of a limited and fragmented state.

48 Hans Kohn, 'Nationalism', in Hans Kohn (ed.), *Nationalism: Its Meaning and History*, 2nd edn (Princeton, NJ: D. Van Nostrand, 1965), p. 20. See also Henry S. Commager, *The Empire of Reason: How Europe Imagined and America Realized the Enlightenment* (London: Weidenfeld and Nocolson, 1978), pp. 171-5.

49 Kohn, 'Nationalism', in *International Encyclopaedia of the Social Sciences, volume 11*, p. 66.

50 Michael Howard, *War and the Liberal Conscience* (Oxford: Oxford University Press, 1981), p. 116.

51 Bernard Crick, review of *The Great Fear* by David Caute, *Guardian Weekly* 10 September 1978. See also Antonio Gramsci, 'State and civil society', in Antonio Gramsci, *Selections from the Prison Notebooks* (New York: International Publishers, 1971), pp. 272-305.

Chapter 10

1 Lewis Lipsitz, *American Democracy* (New York: St Martin's Press, 1986), p. 73.

2 Louis Hartz, *The Liberal Tradition in America: An Interpretation of American Political Thought Since the Revolution* (New York: Harcourt Brace Jovanovich, 1955), p. 9.

3 Clinton Rossiter, *Conservatism in America: The Thankless Persuasion*, 2nd edn, rev. (New York: Vintage, 1962), pp. 140-1.

4 Lance Morrow, 'The ark of America', *Time*, 6 July 1987.

5 Hans Kohn, *Nationalism: An Interpretive Essay* (New York: Macmillan, 1957), p. 8.

6 Alexander Bickel, *The Least Dangerous Branch: The Supreme Court at the Bar of Politics* (Indianapolis, Ind.: Bobbs-Merrill, 1962), p. 31.

7 Kohn, *Nationalism*, pp. 8-9.

8 Quoted in Everett C. Ladd, 'The Constitution as ideology', *Dialogue*, No. 79 1/1989.

9 Donald J. Devine, *The Political Culture of the United States: The Influence of Member Values on Regime Maintenance* (Boston: Little, Brown, 1972), p. 88.

10 Ladd, 'The Constitution as ideology'.

11 *Ibid.*

12 Daniel J. Boorstin, *The Genius of American Politics* (Chicago: University of Chicago Press, 1953), p. 13.

13 *Ibid.*, p. 12.

14 *Ibid.*, p. 18.

15 Quoted in Christopher Hitchens, 'Bob Bork bounces back to 1787', *New Statesman*, 25 September 1987.

16 For example, see Charles M. Hardin, *Presidential Power and Accountability: Towards a New Constitution* (Chicago: University of Chicago Press, 1974); Lloyd N. Cutler, 'To form a government', *Foreign Affairs*, 59, no. 1 (Fall 1980), pp. 126-43.

17 Gary Wasserman, *The Basics of American Politics*, 3rd edn (Boston: Little, Brown, 1982), p. 8.

18 James Madison, 'Federalist Paper No. 51', in Alexander Hamilton, James Madison and John Jay, *The Federalist Papers*, intro by Clinton Rossiter (New York: Mentor, 1961), p. 323.

19 *Ibid.*, p. 323.

20 M. J. C. Vile, *Constitutionalism and the Separation of Powers* (Oxford: Clarendon Press, 1967), pp. 1, 8.

21 Ernest Barker, 'Natural law and the American revolution', in Ernest Barker, *Traditions in Civility: Eight Essays* (Cambridge: Cambridge University Press, 1948), pp. 312-13.

22 Ralph H. Gabriel, *The Course of American Democratic Thought*, 2nd edn (New York: Ronald Press, 1956), p. 14.

23 Edward S. Corwin, *Presidential Power and the Constitution: Essays by Edward S. Corwin*, ed. and intro. by Richard Loss (Ithaca, NY: Cornell University Press, 1976), p. 21.

24 Alexis de Tocqueville, *Democracy in America*, trans. by Henry Reeve, intro. by Henry S. Commager (London: Oxford University Press, 1946), p. 207.

25 Bertrand Russell, *Power: A New Social Analysis* (London: Basic, 1940), p. 73.

26 Arthur S. Miller, 'The politics of the American judiciary', *Political Quarterly*, 49, no. 2 (April–June, 1978), p. 200.

27 Kohn, *American Nationalism*, p. 67.

28 Philip Allott, 'Making sense of the law: lawyers and legal philosophy', *The Cambridge Review*, 108, no. 2297 (1987), p. 66.

29 *Ibid.*, p. 66.

30 *Ibid.*, p. 66.

31 Ronald Dworkin, *Law's Empire* (London: Fontana, 1986), p. 407.

32 See Herbert Weschler, 'Towards neutral principles of constitutional law', *Harvard Law Review*, 73, no. 1 (1959), pp. 1-35; William H. Rehnquist, 'The notion of a living constitution', *Texas Law Review*, 54 (1976), pp. 693-707.
33 See Arthur S. Miller, *Towards Increased Judicial Activism: The Political Role of the Supreme Court* (Westport, Conn.: Greenwood, 1982); Richard Neely, *How the Courts Govern America* (New Haven, Conn.: Yale University Press, 1981).
34 Morton Keller, 'Power and rights: two centuries of American constitutionalism', *Journal of American History*, 74, no. 3 (December 1987), p. 675.
35 See Max Lerner, 'The Supreme Court and American capitalism', in Robert G. McCloskey (ed.), *Essays in Constitutional Law* (New York: Alfred A. Knopf, 1957), pp. 107-50; Arthur S. Miller, *The Supreme Court and American Capitalism* (New York: Free Press/Collier Macmillan, 1968), pp. 50-71.
36 *Lochner v. New York* 198 US 48 (1905).
37 *Lochner v. New York* 198 US 53 (1905).
38 *West Coast Hotel Co. v. Parrish* 300 US 391 (1937).
39 *Schenck v. United States* 249 US 52 (1919).
40 *New York Times Co. v. United States* 403 US 713 (1971).
41 *New York Times Co. v. United States* 403 US 725 (1971).
42 *Roe v. Wade* 410 US 113 (1973).
43 *Roe v. Wade* 410 US 116 (1973).
44 *Roe v. Wade* 410 US 159 (1973).
45 *Roe v. Wade* 410 US 164, 165 (1973).
46 Another constitutional controversy which the Court failed to resolve was the point at which life was formed in the womb. The Court refused to enter into this discussion and so left the question of the personal rights of the unborn wholly unaddressed. It thereby hoped to avoid the thorny problem of whether abortion might be challenged on the same Fourteenth Amendment grounds as the Court had just used to validate a woman's right to choose an abortion.
47 Richard C. Cortner, *The Supreme Court and the Second Bill of Rights: The Fourteenth Amendment and the Nationalization of Civil Liberties* (Madison: University of Wisconsin, 1981).
48 Taken from Justice Oliver Wendell Holmes's dissenting opinion in *Lochner v. New York* 198 US 76.
49 A. E. Dick Howard, 'The Supreme Court and the Constitution', *Dialogue*, no. 67 1/1985.

Conclusion

1 Daniel J. Boorstin, *The Genius of American Politics* (Chicago: University of Chicago Press, 1953), p. 8.
2 Philip E. Converse, 'The nature of belief systems in mass publics', in David E. Apter (ed.), *Ideology and Discontent* (New York: Free Press, 1964), pp. 206-61.
3 'Constraint' is the Philip Converse's term for attitude structure.
4 Angus Campbell, Philip E. Converse, Warren E. Miller and Donald L. Stokes, *The American Voter* (New York: Wiley, 1960), p. 543.
5 Herbert Marcuse, *One-Dimensional Man: Studies in the Ideology of Advanced Industrial Society* (Boston: Beacon, 1964). See also Christopher Brookeman, *American Culture and Society since the 1930s* (London: Macmillan, 1984), chs. 8, 9.

6 Michael Hunt, *Ideology and Foreign Policy* (New Haven, Conn.: Yale University Press, 1987).
7 David Caute, *The Great Fear: The Anti-Communist Purge under Truman and Eisenhower* (London: Secker and Warburg, 1978), p. 21.
8 Kenneth M. Dolbeare and Patricia Dolbeare, *American Ideologies: The Competing Beliefs of the 1970s* (Chicago: Markham, 1971), p. 2.
9 *Ibid.*, p. 13.
10 See Norman H. Nie and Kristi Anderson, 'Mass belief systems revisited: political change and attitude structure,' *Journal of Politics*, 36, no. 3 (August 1974), pp. 540-91; Norman H. Nie, Sidney Verba and John Petrocik, *The Changing American Voter* (Cambridge, Mass.: Harvard University Press, 1976); Gerald M. Pomper, 'From confusion to clarity: issues and American voters, 1956-1968', *American Political Science Review*, 66, no. 2 (June 1972), p. 415-28; Warren E. Miller and Teresa E. Levitan, *Leadership and Change* (Cambridge, Mass.: Winthrop, 1976).
11 Lewis Lipsitz, *American Democracy* (New York: St Martin's Press, 1986), p. 195.
12 John Rawls, *A Theory of Justice* (Oxford: Oxford University Press, 1972).
13 Robert Nozick, *Anarchy, State and Utopia* (Oxford: Basil Blackwell, 1974).
14 Daniel Bell, 'The end of American exceptionalism', in Nathan Glazer and Irving Kristol (eds.), *The American Commonwealth – 1976* (New York: Basic, 1976), p. 215.
15 See Chapter 7, note 6.
16 See George F. Bishop, Alfred A. Tuchfarber and Robert W. Oldendick, 'Change in the structure of American political attitudes: the nagging question of question wording', *American Journal of Political Science*, 22, no. 2 (May 1978), pp. 250-69; John L. Sullivan, James E. Pierson and George E. Marcus, 'Ideological constraint in the mass public: a methodological critique and some new findings', *American Journal of Political Science*, 22, no. 2 (May 1978), pp. 233-49; Michael Margolis, 'From confusion to confusion: issues and the American voter, 1956-1972', *American Political Science Review*, 71, no. 1 (March 1977), pp. 31-43.
17 W. Russell Neuman, *The Paradox of Mass Politics: Knowledge and Opinion in the American Electorate* (Cambridge, Mass.: Harvard University Press, 1986), p. 20.
18 David Riesman, *The Lonely Crowd: A Study of the Changing American Character*, rev. edn (New Haven, Conn.: Yale University Press, 1970), p. xii.
19 Robert Bellah, Richard Madsen, William M. Sullivan, Ann Swidler and Steven M. Tipton, *Habits of the Heart: Americans in Search of Themselves* (New York: Harper and Row, 1985).
20 See Alexis de Tocqueville, *Democracy in America*, trans. by Henry Reeve, intro. by Henry S. Commager (London: Oxford University Press, 1946), chs. 14, 20; Riesman, *The Lonely Crowd, passim*; Robert Lane, *Political Ideology: Why the American Common Man Believes What He Does* (New York: Free Press, 1962), pp. 57-81.
21 For a representative sample of core values, see the analysis provided by Max Lerner, *America As a Civilization: Life and Thought in the United States Today* (London: Jonathan Cape, 1958), pp. 64-7.
22 Donald J. Devine, *The Political Culture of the United States: The Influence of Member Values on Regime Maintenance* (Boston: Little, Brown, 1972), p. 185.
23 Louis Hartz, *The Liberal Tradition in America: An Interpretation of American Political Thought Since the Revolution* (New York: Harcourt Brace Jovanovich, 1955).

24 See the Gallup survey of six European nations and the United States on attitudes to liberty and equality in Lipsitz, *American Democracy*, pp. 176-7.
25 Aaron Wildavsky, 'Government and the people', in Ronald E. Pynn (ed.), *Watergate and the American Political Process* (New York: Praeger, 1975, p. 38.
26 Seymour M. Lipset, 'American "exceptionalism" in North American perspective: why the United States has withstood the worldwide socialist movement', in E. M. Adams (ed.), *The Idea of America: A Reassessment of the American Experiment* (Cambridge, Mass.: Ballinger, 1977), p. 143.
27 Sidney Verba and Gary R. Orren, *Equality in America: The View from the Top* (Cambridge, Mass.: Harvard University Press, 1985), p. vii.
28 Herbert McClosky and John Zaller, *The American Ethos: Public Attitudes towards Capitalism and Democracy* (Cambridge, Mass.: Harvard University Press, 1984), p. 1.
29 Isaiah Berlin, *Four Essays on Liberty* (London: Oxford University Press, 1969), pp. 125-6.
30 Allan Bloom, 'Liberty, equality and sexuality', *Commentary*, April 1987.
31 *Ibid.*, my italics.
32 See Everett C. Ladd and Seymour M. Lipset, 'Public opinion and public policy', in Peter Duignan and Alvin Rubushka (eds.), *The United States in the 1980s* (Stanford, Calif.: Hoover Institution, 1980), pp. 49-84; W. L. Bennett, *Public Opinion on American Politics* (New York: Harcourt Brace Jovanovich, 1980).
33 Arthur M. Schlesinger, *Paths to the Present* (New York: Macmillan, 1949).
34 Samuel P. Huntington, *American Politics: The Promise of Disharmony* (Cambridge, Mass.: Belknap. 1981).
35 *Ibid.*, ch. 5.
36 Charles B. Forcey, *The Crossroads of Liberalism: Croly, Weyl, Lippmann and the Progressive Era, 1900-1925* (New York: Oxford University Press, 1961), pp. xv-xvi.
37 Arthur M. Schlesinger, Jr., 'The cycles of American politics', in Arthur M. Schlesinger, Jr., *The Cycles of American History* (Harmondsworth, Middx: Penguin, 1989), p. 30.
38 Bloom, 'Liberty, equality and sexuality.'
39 Lloyd A. Free and Hadley Cantril, *The Political Beliefs of Americans: A Study of Public Opinion* (New Brunswick, NJ: Rutgers University Press, 1967).
40 For more on the mix of strong support for the principle of free enterprise and the profit motive, and for the personal distrust of those who run large businesses and the need for government regulation in the area of competition and consumer protection, see Robert Y. Shapiro and John M. Gilroy, 'The polls: regulation – part I', *Public Opinion Quarterly*, 48, no. 2 (Summer 1984), pp. 531-42; Robert Y. Shapiro and John M. Gilroy, 'The polls: regulation – part II', *Public Opinion Quarterly*, 43, no. 3 (Fall 1984), pp. 666-77; Seymour M. Lipset and William Schneider, 'The confidence gap during the Reagan years, 1981-1987', *Political Science Quarterly*, 102, no. 1 (Spring 1987), pp. 11-19; 'The joy of business', *The Economist*, 15 June 1985.
41 Gunnar Myrdal, *An American Dilemma: The Negro Problem and Democracy* (New York: Harper, 1944).
42 Michael Foley, *Laws, Men and Machines: Modern American Government and the Appeal of Newtonian Mechanics* (London: Routledge, 1990).

43 Peter Laslett, review of *The Past is a Foreign Country* by David Lowenthal, *Guardian Weekly*, 10 August 1986.

44 Michael Kammen, *A Machine That Would Go of Itself: The Constitution in American Culture* (New York: Alfred A. Knopf, 1986).

45 Aaron Wildavsky, 'President Reagan as a political strategist', in Charles O. Jones (ed.), *The Reagan Legacy: Promise and Performance* (Chatham, NJ: Chatham House, 1988), p. 298. See also Aaron Wildavsky, 'The party of government, the party of opposition, and the party of balance: an American view of the consequences of the 1980 election', in Austin Ranney (ed.), *The American Elections of 1980* (Washington, DC: American Enterprise Institute, 1981), pp. 329-50; Aaron Wildavsky, 'A world of difference – the pubic philosophies and political behaviours of rival American cultures', in Anthony King (ed.), *The New American Political System, Second Version* (Washington, DC: American Enterprise Institute, 1990), pp. 263-86.

46 L. J. Sharpe, 'American democracy reconsidered: part II and conclusions', *British Journal of Political Science*, 3, Part 2 (April 1973), p. 159.

47 Mary P. Nichols, review of *American Politics: The Promise of Disharmony* by Samuel P. Huntington, *The Review of Politics*, 45, no. 1 (January 1983), pp. 150-1.

48 For a dramatic and convincing demonstration of the force of changing ideas in Washington politics, see Martha Derthick and Paul J. Quirk, *The Politics of Deregulation* (Washington, DC: Brookings, 1985).

49 John E. Trent, 'Thoughts on political thought: an introduction', *International Political Science Review*, 11, no. 1 (January 1990), p. 13.

Index